Hill's Ups and Downs

Sorrow and Smiles
1000 Miles to the Shetland Isles

By

Tony Hill

The right of Tony Hill to be identified as the author of this work has been asserted by him in accordance with the Copyright, Designs and Patents Act, 1988

Copyright ©2016 Tony Hill

ISBN 978-0-9934886-8-9

All rights reserved. No part of this publication may be reproduced, stored in retrieval system or transmitted in any form or by any means electronic, mechanical, photocopying, recording or otherwise, without the prior permission of the publisher, except in the case of brief quotations embodied in critical articles and reviews.

Published by
Llyfrau Cambria Books, Wales, United Kingdom.
*Cambria Books is a division of
The Cambria Publishing Co-operative Ltd.*

Cover Artwork by John Francis Studio.
Cover design by Carolyn Michel.

For:

Morgan-Rhys
Hafina
Nicole
Rina
Richard

CHAPTERS

Prologue 1
Merthyr to Ross 7
Ross to Evesham 33
Evesham to Brinklow 51
Brinklow to Stamford 65
Stamford to Northlands 79
Northlands to Wrawby 97
Wrawby to Scarborough 113
Rest Day 129
Scarborough to Guisborough 145
Guisborough to South Shields 157
South Shields to Powburn 169
Powburn to Lauder 189
Lauder to Inverkeithing 217
Rest Day 237
Inverkeithing to Inver 245
Inver to Newtonmore 259
Newtonmore to Inverness 285
Inverness to Dornoch 307
Dornoch to Helmsdale 327
Helmsdale to Kirkwall 347
Rest Day 367
Kirkwall to Lerwick 377
Lerwick to Hermaness 391
North Camp, Hermaness to Lerwick 407

Back to Merthyr 423
Epilogue 425

Prologue

Immediately after Cherie's death, I had not had the house to myself. Then, suddenly, the house became silent, except for the sounds caused by the machines and me. A little singing or whistling, the sharpness of cutlery and crockery being transferred from dishwasher to cupboards, the muted sounds of BBC News 24, the rumble of the tumble drier and the occasional shock to the system brought about by the phone ringing. There was a strange realisation that this silence of a sort was now a permanent feature of this household.

So, I busied myself with preparations for my cycling trip from Merthyr to the Shetland Isles. When Cherie had first started to get ill, after a bowel cancer diagnosis 19 months before, I had attempted to purge my worries by taking to the local hills on my mountain bike. In between frequent hospital visits, I would cycle for miles, getting some relief for my torn emotions through the physical exertion of pedalling up long inclines through pine-scented forests. The magnificent views from the crests and ridges caressed my soul and set my tired body to sleep at night in a way that might have eluded me had I tried a more sedentary solution. I had not kept as fit as I would have liked over the past nineteen months or so, but I had continued cycling to work, a round trip of eight miles a day, interspersed with random trips to the gym, occasional runs and the long therapeutic mountain bike jaunts. I used physical exercise as a way of helping to exorcise tension.

On a whim one day, I said to Cherie, 'When you're gone, I think I'll cycle to the Shetland Islands.'

Cherie thought it was a good idea and it became cemented in my mind. The 'Land's End to John O'Groats' trek didn't appeal to me; I didn't like the idea of being carted by someone all the way down to Cornwall for me to then start pedalling back the same way I had just come. It wasn't the way I wanted to begin my sojourn – I wanted to cycle from our house and just keep going, Forest Gump fashion, as far as possible.

The time had come.

I changed the tyres on my mountain bike from the knobbly rough-terrain type, to smooth road tyres – I needed all the help I could get and a mountain bike was not really the kit I should have been using for such a trip - too heavy and not designed to reduce wind drag. I didn't bother with any proper luggage carrying panniers for the bike; I already had a back rack and I hoped that my medium sized rucksack would fit on to it secured by bungee cords. I bought a good quality sleeping bag that I trusted would keep me warm; an expensive, but very light weight, all weather, one man tent; and, a semi-inflatable sleeping mat that I expected to be a comfortable base for my weary body after a day in the saddle and a probable night in the pub.

The only thing left to do was visit my doctor. After a night in the hospital, trying to sleep on the uncomfortable chair by Cherie's side, I felt the daunting presence of what I later discovered to be my first case of piles. The closest I had come to piles before was as a spotty teenager. For a whole week I had used Father's piles cream on my face, mistaking it for my acne treatment. With all my attention focused on Cherie and then her funeral, it was several weeks after the appearance of the haemorrhoid that I finally got around to making an appointment to see the doctor. I had delayed the visit to the doctors' surgery until the last possible day.

'What time's your flight tomorrow?' asked the doctor. His jaw dropped, his eyebrows rose and his eyes widened with momentary shock as I told him I was cycling and not flying. When I further pointed out to him that I was cycling to Scotland and beyond, he cocked his head to one side and asked me to repeat what I presume he couldn't believe he heard right first time.

'Scotland,' I said. 'The Shetland Islands, in fact.'

At this point he uttered the words which inspired the poem I later wrote*: 'I wouldn't recommend it.'

But, it wasn't an unequivocal rebuttal, so I didn't have to face up to the prospect of failing before I'd got to pedal my first revolution. I was still worried though. I hadn't even taken the trouble to get on my bike and try pedalling down the road to see what the haemorrhoid felt like when bisected by a positively non-gelatinous saddle. The prospect of cycling with piles was daunting. My bum got uncomfortable just sitting on the settee so I suppose I was applying the ostrich strategy – burying my head in the sand. It wasn't so much that I thought it would be ok - it was more the case that I didn't want to think about it. I seemed to remember someone telling me that piles could be dangerous if they burst – lots of blood. If one thing was going to burst a haemorrhoid short of stabbing the little bastard with a pin, it was cycling eight hundred miles to the Shetlands.

'Head back in the sand, Laddie,' I thought to myself.

By seven o'clock that evening, everything was sorted and packed and my checklist had all been crossed off, save for the toiletries and a few other things I needed in the morning. I had my usual 10 – 20 minute catnap then got ready to go to the pub with Yogi and Ken. The company and banter of my friends was mixed pleasantly with five or six pints of Guinness and a few cigars, before I headed for home, earlier than usual. It occurred to me that it would probably be some time before I would see anyone I knew again, and a sensation of loneliness melded with my feelings of anticipation, trepidation and excitement, at the prospect of what was to come in the weeks ahead.

Cycling to the Shetland Islands. I had told many of the people I knew, of my plans, including friends, relatives and colleagues. I was determined to succeed, even though I had resigned myself to the fact that I might have to take the train if the physical exertion became too much.

'How far will I get?' I wondered, as I fell asleep in my lonely bed, in my empty house.

*A steroid for my haemorrhoid in the cream, I do believe,
Is what the doctor gave the day before I was to leave.
Emergency appointment - he didn't seem to mind:
'As long as you're prepared to wait, and wait, and stay behind.'

I said, 'I'm off tomorrow and in need of some relief.'
'What time d'you fly?' he asked and then gaped in disbelief,
As I said I was to cycle up to the Shetland Isles
'I wouldn't recommend it, not with that case of piles.'

But he said to me, 'You go, if you feel that go you must.'
He didn't make it clear if the thing would grow or bust.
Not that I have seen it mind, just felt it with my thumb,
Bit like a dangleberry, hanging from my bum

'Put the cream on twice a day but do not rub it in,
'An applicator is supplied for you to go within.
'If it's still there in seven days, don't use it any more,
Just hope the damn thing doesn't grow and drag along the floor.'

Merthyr to Ross

Tuesday, July 3rd

I woke with the alarm at 8 o'clock and resisted the temptation to doze. I sorted out my usual black coffee with a couple of slices of toast and settled down to watch the BBC breakfast news. Then I had a second cup of coffee, a shower, a shave and cleaned my teeth before getting into my cycling garb.

I've possessed a pair of those snazzy Lycra cycling shorts for a while. They're supposed to help reduce soreness with the help of an inner leather gusset and they have done the trick on local rides of twelve to twenty miles. Would it work on this mammoth trip though? I'd have to wait and see. I donned one of two tops I'd picked up in a Gloucester outdoor shop the previous Saturday. I'd bought them at the same time as my tent and camping pillow. I was told that this particular type of tee shirt is designed to 'wick' sweat away from your body – 'hmmm, that might well be useful.' I had chosen a white and a yellow one - bright colours that drivers would hopefully see before knocking me off, or worse still, running me over. From the jungle of shoes under my bed, I selected a pair of my oldest training shoes surmising that these would be the most comfortable. They looked pretty disgusting. The old decrepit trainers had long been relegated to walks through the countryside or used for scuffling along my unpaved, puddle strewn back lane to put the rubbish out. More recently, they were the first choice for building the walls and a patio in our garden. The concrete was still on the shoes to prove it; I did my best to chip it off but failed.

It took ages to pack. I tried numerous combinations and was never really satisfied. The rucksack was too small to carry what I needed but still too big to go on the bike. Eventually I strapped the sleeping bag, tent, waterproofs and flask to the outside of the rucksack to create a cumbersome bundle that could only be picked up with the effort usually reserved for a session in the gym on a day when I felt like a good workout. Kitted up, it just remained for me to get the dead weight securely on to the bike.

I wheeled the machine through my terraced house from the back kitchen, through the living room, along the hall and out of the front door, and parked it on the pavement, propped up against the wall. Back in the hall, I strained to pick up the rucksack. Crikey, even after discarding several items like a Stanley knife, spanners and other possible essentials, it still weighed a ton. Not only that, but the load with its sundries clumsily hanging off it, was cumbersome and getting the bundle on to the bike was a crocodile fight. The bungees, stretched to their full extent, were just as dangerous as any reptile as I tried time and again, to secure the load without toppling the whole lot. The bike just would not stay. I struggled to attach the rucksack but it slid away from me. Then the handle bar lost its tenuous attachment to the wall, and the front wheel left the ground so the bike reared up depositing everything on to the pavement. I was in danger of losing my eye to an escaped bungee hook as I continued to wrestle in vain.

'What the hell do I do now?' Worried, I pondered the bike and the bundle on the floor for a minute, understanding that my gaze alone could not solve the problem. Maybe the rest did me good or perhaps it was luck, but as I turned back into the struggle, the next round was mine.

I locked the front door, put the key safely into my bum bag and pulled the laden bike from the wall. Awkwardly I cocked my leg over, making sure to clear, not only the familiar saddle, but also the baggage, piled high and strapped behind it. It was like learning to ride a bike all over again it was so top heavy. I wobbled down the road taking a short cut. As I pulled out on to the main Brecon Road, I didn't even think about my piles, which was just as well given the lack of serious attention that I had given to my problem. Perhaps, it also had something to do with the one hundred percent concentration I needed to keep my balance, as I seriously started to doubt how far I was going to get on my precarious two wheeled contraption.

Merthyr Tydfil is a bit like a funnel. You can go south (downwards if you were a liquid) towards Cardiff quite easily. However, if you want to go in any other direction you have to climb steep hills. My route would take me east towards Abergavenny along the infamous 'Heads of the Valleys' road, the A465. ('Deads of the Valleys' would be more appropriate given the number of fatalities that had occurred on this terrible three lane highway.) There was no way that I could avoid some serious climbs but there was a lot of internal debate going on in my head as to which climb would be the least painful. The most direct route was straight up to Dowlais passing the OP chocolate works, but it was ladder-steep. I decided to take the route north, which made a fair detour, but one with a gradient I hoped I would be able to pedal. As I teetered through Cefn Coed, I passed Ken's house and noticed Yogi's car was parked outside.

'Shall I drop in for a coffee?' I had been with Ken and Yogi the night before. Was there anything new to say? I had only pedalled a mile. Now was not the time to stop, so I passed by, feeling the pressure on my legs as the embryonic gradient made its presence felt.

'Hell, this is hard work,' I thought, as I approached the Heads of the Valleys. Now, suddenly, I had traffic to contend with. Not just lots of cars but heavy lorries too. As I ploughed on up the hill I became aware of the passage of time. This was taking an age. Soon the hill became too steep to cycle and I dismounted in inelegant fashion. Now, pushing my top heavy overloaded mount, there were frequent heart-stopping moments as exhaling trucks thundered inches from me. As they rumbled away, leaving me in a wake of dust, I realised that the traffic calmed bumps of the ladder to Dowlais would have been the better option after all.

'Too late now,' I thought, as heat from my exertion and the strengthening sun caused the sweat to flow and my sunglasses to creep irritatingly down my nose. Eventually, I reached Dowlais top. Only two and a half miles from home, this was the first milestone. The sun was really blazing by now and I called in to a 'Happy Diner' to get a canned drink. The drink didn't last long and I was off again – burping along the Heads of the Valleys road, so called because it chops off the tops of many of the former mining valleys: the Taf, the Rhymney, the Sirhowey (of Kinnock fame) the Ebbw. The ride was now a long haul, slow motion roller coaster. My progress faltered as I dismounted to shove the bike up the sides of each young valley, but picked up as gradients flattened and I could pedal towards the tops of the watersheds. Then, best of all, came the freewheel down into the next valley.

There is something special about coasting downhill on a pushbike. For me, it's got something to do with the free ride – no petrol, no diesel, no engine noise and the opportunity afforded to feel the rush of fresh air with unimpeded panoramas. No fly-stained windscreen, no rear view mirror, bright red shiny roof pillar viewed from inside the car cockpit. No radio or booming bass CD and even in the rain, no squeaky wipers. No smell of Halford's lemon air freshener, just the scents of the outside world – that place that exists beyond the inside that we so naturally gravitate towards for the bulk of our lifespan. It's the same feeling of freedom gained from sailing, windsurfing or walking. I find a special pleasure in getting there under my own steam. That's not to say that in the past I haven't been rather pleased with engine power. And, Cherie always preferred it.

Once we had gone sailing in our little twenty-three foot yacht on Milford Haven. The name of the boat was 'Halcyon' and it was indeed a halcyon day, as we navigated, under sail, between the buoys that picked out the main shipping channel – red cans for port and green cones for starboard. The river itself fills a valley that once was land and perhaps the word 'river' is misleading, because even five miles from the sea itself, when the tide was in the water stretched a distance of quarter of a mile from bank to bank. There was plenty of space for all manner of craft - big yachts, small yachts, gas-guzzling motor cruisers – even the Pembroke Dock to Rosslaire ferry. And just a quarter of mile downstream, leviathan oil tankers from all over the world tied up on jetties the size of Brighton Pier. Yes, there was plenty of space out there.

Cherie sat opposite me, 'Want anything to eat?'

'Dunno, what have we got?'

'Cheese, biscuits, sandwich. I'm not cooking while you're sailing.'

Cherie didn't like sailing. She asked, 'Do we have to use the sails?'

'Yes, we do!'

'I don't like it when it tips over.'

'It's not tipping – it's *supposed* to lean over.'

'Well I don't like it ... and what's the point anyway?

'What's the point in having a sailing boat if you don't use the bloody sails?' I retorted gruffly.

She carried on, 'We'd get there a damn sight quicker if you just switched the engine on. Why do we have to zigzag all over the place? Why can't we just go in a straight line?'

'But it's not the same,' I insisted for the ... goodness knows how many times I had tried to explain. 'And I can't hear the radio if anyone wants to call us up ... and anyway, that's what's sailing's all about!' I was exasperated. We'd had this discussion so many times before.

Cherie was unconvinced, 'I don't see the point.'

But this day I was having my way and the engine was off.

Dark blue, the river reflected the sky and was hardly ruffled by a gentle breeze that was powerful enough to fill the sails and drive us, tacking across the waterway towards the sea and the village of Dale, some four miles to the west. I didn't know the river that well but I was aware that if we were to helm the boat out of the navigation channel, there could be problems. I explained.

'We don't want to go outside these buoys, Cherie. It looks OK but we could get stuck on a mud bank. And, there's all sorts of wreckage under the surface once you're out of the channel.'

There followed a pensive silence from Cherie. We hadn't owned the boat for long, and I had never received any formal training. Consequently, I hadn't completely mastered the art of tacking (turning the boat into the wind). Nevertheless, I pulled the manoeuvre off most of the time and therefore saw no need to get out of the shipping channel when Cherie alerted me with a startled cry,

'Tony! It's the ferry!' There was real concern in her voice but I was used to her getting nervous on the water and I blotted out her pleas and refused to turn the engine on.

'Don't worry – no problem,' was my captain-like answer. Our boat was headed out of the channel and away from the ferry -- and it was miles away in any case. I was more afraid of running aground or hitting something underwater as we headed for the shallows. We needed to tack back into the waterway.

'Ready About!' I pushed the tiller away from me.

'Tony! Tony!' Cherie's voice punctuated each part of the manoeuvre. 'Lee Ho!' I called, swapping sitting positions with a reluctant Cherie as we criss-crossed to sit on opposite sides in the cockpit. The boat steered obediently back towards the centre of the river.

'Tony - what the hell are you doing ...' Cherie's head craned forwards, her eyes bright like a startled animal ... 'the ferry, Tony ... THE FERRY!'

'Cherie!' my voice was raised and assertively crisp. 'Don't panic. I'm going to tack again now.' It was just a case of tacking to port to bring us back towards the green cones and out of the shipping channel.

'Ready about ... Lee Ho!' Confident Captain Hill shouted the time-honoured commands once more. Push the tiller away, neatly swap sides again and pull in the sheets – easy-peasy. The boat obeyed and swung to port, now facing directly down the Haven. Still turning a little more, we headed out of the channel to relative safety. I glanced coolly over my shoulder and noticed how close the ferry now was. Cherie was silent but her face was set in inquisition, 'Why don't you just stick the engine on and save all this hassle.'

'Blimey, that thing must be moving ...' I kept my thoughts to myself, not wanting to acknowledge that Cherie's alert might have had some worth after all ... 'that ferry was a good half a mile away just now.' Suddenly, my secret relief was interrupted. The foresail filled with wind on the wrong side and our little boat turned back towards the ferry.

'Tony, you're heading straight for it,' Cherie's voice surprisingly now quieter and resigned.

'Quick, turn the engine on!' I relented at last. I was shocked. I couldn't believe how fast the ferry had moved. It was upon us. We both jumped as a loud horn boomed across the water. Who said power gives way to sail? Cherie pushed the starter and the engine turned over ... and over ... but nothing happened.

'Keep going!' I yelled.

Cherie kept her thumb on the starter screaming at me, 'I am, I am!'

The horn boomed again. This time it didn't stop as it droned ominously louder. Now, I was scared. 'Throttle, I need more throttle.' I'd forgotten to push the throttle lever forward in my fluster. The ship bore down on us like a slowly moving block of council flats. The swoosh of the ship's bow wave now mingled with the siren horn and the sound of my name as Cherie desperately screamed it. A wall of white paint blotted out the familiar riparian colours of the far bank, and I could see hundreds of rivets neatly lined up on the ship's hull.

Suddenly, we felt a shudder as our engine spluttered into life, the clanking for once muted. At last, we reclaimed control of the steering from the wind. Pulling ungracefully away from disaster, the sails flapping uselessly and the boom confused, I cowered and averted my gaze from the onlookers aboard the ferry. Cringing as the Captain and crew swore inaudibly at me from the bridge, I could feel their eyes boring into me.

'I told you to use the engine, Tony.' There was no getting away from it. Cherie was right. With the crisis over, we turned the boat into mid channel once more and I chanced a look at the ferry, now small again as it started its turn towards the terminal. The sheets now in their cleats and the sails set, I cut the engine.

'Why don't you leave the engine on now, Dear?' Cherie's familiar request repeated for the umpteenth time.

I meekly resumed my anti-motor argument, 'Look, the ferry's gone and we've got the river to ourselves again.'

Cherie didn't answer. She disappeared below and called out through the companionway, 'What did you say you wanted to eat?'

'Cheese and biscuits,' I said, 'and what about some wine?'

'Good idea - not while we're sailing though.' With this, she won the debate.

I reluctantly started the engine and spent the next five minutes de-rigging the sails. Motoring down the river in the sunshine, we sipped our wine as the engine thudded on beneath us, and talked about the pig roast and the friends that awaited us on the floating pontoon just off Dale. I was aware of how frightened Cherie must have been as I incompetently aimed our boat on a collision course for the ferry.

But as far as Cherie was concerned, it was already in the past. She knew I had learned a lesson and made no more of it. She used her magic switch and the whole trauma was gone in an instant. Did I ever tell her how much I loved that about her?

It was only after Cherie died that Isobel, her sister, told me just how much she had disliked sailing. Yes, she liked tiddling along and enjoying the scenery, or sunbathing in the nude out at sea, far from prying eyes. And she loved to stop off for a bar snack at one of the many pubs along the river, or beach the boat for the night at some remote inlet. But the rest of it – the real sailing – she only went along with it for my sake and she rarely complained. And never even reminded me again of that day, the day that wonderful fifteen horsepower boat engine prevented certain disaster.

As I shot down towards Ebbw Vale, the folly of not wearing a helmet struck me. But then I never had. I had always taken the risk of incurring head injuries for the pleasure of a 'Wheee', the affectionate term I coined for freewheeling. On my way to work there are six 'whees'. I mused what the opposite of a 'wheee' might be. 'Wheeze' was the obvious choice! And I was in line for a wheeze as I began to climb to the highest point on the Heads of the Valleys - 1350 feet. It wasn't long before I had to dismount. Progress halted to a trickle again, time stood still and my mind wandered to the awesome task ahead of me.

'Anything is possible.' How many times had I heard that before? It was just a case of being absolutely determined, focussed and single minded, with a heavy dose of working really, really hard – then anything *was* possible. As I climbed onwards, these thoughts gave me inspiration and filled me with confidence. Of course I could get to the Shetlands on my bike! Then I argued with myself: For all the famous success stories, do we ever get to hear about all the lowly unsung failures? Never mind the monumental ones like the inability of Titanic to complete its maiden voyage, or the Charge of the Light Brigade. Or, one of my own personal failures: being a member of the world's worst football team, as a teenager, Cornelly United under 15's. We lost most games, the worst one being a 24-0 drubbing.

As I reached the slow brow, I realised that a big 'wheee' was coming up, probably the best part of four miles down the Black Rock Gorge towards Abergavenny, and I had become aware of a wobble in my front wheel. This was nothing to do with the general instability of the bike but something technical that could undo me. I reached a burger van just past the signposted 'highest point' and pulled in to buy another can and investigate the fault. It occurred to me that the tyre might not be sitting correctly on the wheel, probably the result of me changing it the day before. I had an unhappy knack of doing jobs that resulted in making things worse. I decided to deflate the tyre, squiggle it about a bit, then pump it back up. This was pretty close to the limit of my technical expertise and I went about the task with enthusiastic pessimism.

When it didn't work, I knew I'd have to find a bike shop in Abergavenny and hope they would help me on the spot. If they couldn't, I might be held up for some time.

'Damn it,' I thought. 'I've only gone eighteen miles.' But, surprisingly, my simple ploy worked and I hazarded downward glances at the front wheel to confirm the fact as I dangerously picked up speed down the long hill to Abergavenny.

The market town was busy and it wasn't clear from signposts where I was supposed to go. I stopped and asked some passers-by who gave complicated instructions that I half managed to memorise and follow. After some confusion, I ended up where I wanted to be - on the back road from Abergavenny to Ross via Skenfrith.

The B4521 quickly turned into a real stinker, at least for cycling. Most of the time, I was forced to walk as the road rose and fell steeply like the trace of a cardiograph and sweat beaded down my cheeks and along my arms to drip off my elbows. I was beginning to realise that cycling with such a heavy load for so many miles was totally different to anything I had experienced before. Usually, I don't have to get off to walk. The gearing on a mountain bike is so low that it's almost possible to go up a wall. Skinny kids with bare, bony torsos trying to cover their spots with a suntan, demonstrate this in the parks and back streets all the time – pedalling up impossible inclines and pulling wheelies like circus clowns on unicycles. Dropping down to these super low gears does, of course, mean that you have to pedal much faster to keep up any speed.

Probably because they have never experienced anything more extreme than a Sturmy Archer three speed system, lots of 'born again' middle-aged cyclists fail to understand the gearing. Their brains get used to going at a reasonable lick on the flats and down the hills. When they encounter an uphill, they drop down the gears but compensate for their lack of speed over the ground by subconscientiously pedalling like bill-ee-o. This has the effect of instantly wearing them out so the next time they get on a bike, it's to demonstrate the quick release saddle adjustment to a prospective buyer at a car boot sale.

I generally just accept the fact that I'm going to go a lot slower up hills and I keep my pedalling rate constant. But now with my burden, it dawned on me, 'What's the point?' The bike computer told me I was covering three miles an hour. I could walk at that speed, give my backside relief from the saddle, and rest my pedalling muscles as I employed my walking ones.

Under normal conditions, another option would be to select a higher gear then come off the saddle to bear down with my full body weight on the pedals, but with the heavy load I was carrying and its high centre of gravity, the natural sideways movement of the bike when ridden this way would have had me off in seconds. I also had to consider how far I had to go. I couldn't afford to 'go for it' as I normally would. I had to conserve my energy and be kind to my sinews and muscles. On this road, there were numerous hills but they didn't last for long, so I continuously alternated between freewheeling and walking. It didn't bother me that progress was slow. I had so far to go there was absolutely no point in rushing. In fact, there were a few sharp reminders from Cherie. I was hit by a strong feeling that she was following me, as she so often did when we went out riding on our bikes.

'Hey ... you! Slow down, it's not a race!'

I couldn't resist stopping and looking over my shoulder. And there she was, her hair auburn, long and wavy and wearing a pink tee shirt with a neat little pair of powder blue shorts that capped her toned brown legs. She was as I remembered her in the early days and she was pushing a crock of a bike that my daughter had pulled out of a skip years before. At five foot four and what Dorothy Perkins would call petite, I was surprised how strong she could be. She hadn't ridden a bike for years when we decided to cross the Brecon Beacons for a picnic one summer's day.

No plan was made as to how far we were going, but we ended up eating sandwiches, drinking red wine and dipping our toes into the cool waters of the Talybont Reservoir, on the other side of the mountain range, nearly twenty miles from home. The ride back felt like sixty miles, but Cherie ground endlessly at the pedals and I felt guilty that I had allowed her to come so far on such a boneshaker. And, of course, when she called out to me, I did slow down - I always would. I never raced against her and there was no question of competition between us. We always worked together and we complimented each other in most everything we did. But, she was so physically capable that I sometimes failed to notice that I was forcing the pace beyond her comfortable limit.

By one o'clock the sun was reaching its zenith. I hoped there might be a pub where I could get a drink and something to eat, but this back road was quiet. There were a few houses dotted along the route but no real settlements. Occasionally a car passed by. As a geography teacher, I would tell my kids in school that in areas like this there were an insufficient number of people (or 'threshold population') to sustain local services like schools, shops and, most importantly, pubs. But, to my surprise, as I rounded yet another backwater bend, I saw a sign advertising afternoon teas.

I have seen these enterprises in remote spots before. When you're in the car looking for a pub, they fleetingly make you think you've found one. You see the sign, assume it's a pub, and it takes a second or two before you equate 'Afternoon Teas' with 'Unlicensed' and drive on. But this was a sellers' market, so I dismounted, wheeled the bike up the drive and manoeuvred it to awkwardly rest against the wall. The place was really just someone's house with a pretty garden and a country kitchen. I ambled back to sit at a small round table that wobbled on uneven paving slabs and spent ten minutes collecting my thoughts and relaxing amongst the summer fragrances of the garden. At last, my food arrived and I was impressed. Substantial cheese and plenty of tomato, on expensive bread, served with a thoughtfully arranged side salad, made even more impressive by the ridiculously small bill.

As I munched away, an elderly couple moved across my line of vision. The gentleman wore a brown sports jacket and, typically for his generation, a collar and tie. He was broad shouldered and tall and appeared to be in good shape. By comparison, his wife, in an old lady's checked cotton dress, was tiny and very frail with grey wavy hair and no weight in her face – should looked as if she would fall apart in a strong wind. She stooped as she walked and they both wandered aimlessly debating where to sit and whether the place was serving, given the apparent lack of staff. The sight of me eating must have kept them hanging around. I had finished my meal and I thought it only polite to address their quandary.

'They are open. Try looking in the kitchen.'

They both thanked me and went over to seek the chef. When they returned, we resumed our conversation. Incredibly, the man was in his ninetieth year and his wife was five years younger. He had been in the police force, but, after his retirement at the age of fifty-five, he had travelled the world as a judge in sheep-showing competitions. He had, in fact, been officially retired for thirty five years, and I marvelled at his good fortune. Then, three coincidences emerged.

'Where have you come from today?' I asked.

'We're on our way back from Southampton, where we've been to see a friend of ours coming in on one of the BT Global Challenge boats.' The friend had come in on the last boat, the 'Isle of Man', and, as a result, they had been kept waiting until the next morning for its arrival. The other boats had come in the night before.

I told them, 'My sister-in-law is Chey Blythe's personal assistant.'

They already knew that the BT Global Challenge was the brainchild of the famous 'Round the World yachtsman' and we chatted about the race for a while.

Then, a second coincidence:

'Where are you going?'

I sheepishly replied, 'The Shetland Islands.'

I didn't really feel confident that I was going to cycle that much of my journey and at this point on Day 1, it seemed an awful long way away. I felt embarrassed and a bit stupid but the gentleman boomed,

'That's absolutely marvellous! My word, you must be fit.'

I was heartened that they acknowledged the distance factor with some respect rather than derision, and they went on to tell me that they had only returned from the Orkneys (the Shetlands' nearest neighbours) themselves a few weeks ago.

They asked me, 'Are you going to Orkney as well as the Shetlands?'

'Yes.'

'What ferry are you taking?'

My planning had not been rigorous to say the least, and my ferry options had been weighed up from evidence provided by my 'AA Road Atlas of Great Britain, 1999', in which the ferry routes are shown as dotted lines. The only dotted line on the map was from Scrabster, a few miles north east of Thurso on the north coast of Scotland, to Stromness on Orkney, so that was my answer to the gentleman and his good lady.

After a short pause he said, 'Do you know there's a foot ferry from John O'Groats to the southern tip of the

Orkneys? It's not as far, it's cheaper and, what's more, they'll let you take your bike on?'

'That's very interesting, I didn't know about that,' I admitted. I thought to myself, 'This is incredible.'

I would have liked to have gone to John O'Groats, even though I hadn't wanted to do the Land's End to John O'Groats thing. Sticking to my original Scrabster plan, I would have taken the A9 to Thurso missing out John O'Groats, as I cut off the northeast corner of Scotland. Who would have thought, on a sleepy back road on Day One, that I would glean such useful intelligence?

The third coincidence came up when I asked them where they were headed.

'We live in Cheshire, but we decided to head back via the scenic route through Wales.'

The elderly lady spoke up, 'We don't come from Cheshire originally you know, we're from Liverpool.'

'Whereabouts?' I enquired.

'Aintree.'

'Wouldn't you know it?' I thought. 'Small world.' Aintree was just up the road from Cherie's parents, her birthplace, and the home she knew up until the age of seventeen. I kept my connections with Liverpool to myself and said goodbye to the couple leaving them to eat their sandwiches.

Feeling happy with the unexpected human contact, I hauled the bike off its staging post wall, mounted, and pedalled off in an easterly direction for Skenfrith. The road continued its serious spurts of ups and downs and I jumped on and off the bike getting ever more used to the routine. An hour later I was in trouble. The first twinges of cramp attacked the muscles in the back of my left leg just above the knee. I immediately dismounted. I knew all about cramp from years of playing football with short legs in grass that was too long. I knew that a minor seizure was a warning but if I carried on I would get a major attack. If that happened, the muscle tissue would be scarred and it would take weeks to heal – it would mean the end of my trip. But, this was an embryonic seizure and I hoped I had acted in time. As I walked the up-hills and the flat sections, I only risked the saddle to freewheel downhill.

I could see from my map that I still had a few miles to go before I reached Ross so I decided to rest, thinking my muscle would be able to recuperate. I pulled on to the right hand side of the road where an access road to a farm had created a rare piece of flat ground that broke the line of bank, ditch and hedge. Better still, it was grassed. Beyond the wire fence, a few horses were grazing in the sunshine and one started to head towards the fence but, I took no notice and purposefully avoided holding out anything that might have been construed as food or friendship. I leaned the bike against the fence and removed my waterproofs from the back rack to serve as a pillow.

In the deserted sunshine, on this green country road, I lay down to sleep. Just as I was dropping off, I was stirred from a semi slumber by an engine in very close proximity. A woman in a towering Range Rover passed alongside me – I think it was her lane. I smiled what I hoped would be a friendly smile that was thankfully returned. After that I couldn't drop off to sleep. Although I tried for quarter of an hour, it occurred to me that I had had more rest time than a cramp struck footballer in a cup final facing extra time ... and they always seem to manage to shake off their seizures. I'd probably taken half an hour all told. I would just take it easy for the rest of the trip to Ross.

I told myself, 'Don't put any pressure on the pedals and, if in doubt, get off and walk.' But as soon as I started back I knew that this was not cramp.

'No, no, no! ... I've done something here.' It now felt like a hamstring injury. I was devastated. I just couldn't believe it. I've had aches and pains from cycling before, but I have never injured myself. In my planning, I hadn't even considered the possibility of a muscle or ligament strain - tiredness and fatigue maybe, but not this, not on Day One! I sat astride the bike, cupped my face in my hands as I closed my eyes and took several deep breaths...

'What now?' After a minute or so, I got off the bike and dejectedly started to walk - I couldn't cycle any more.

'On Day One – unbelievable.' I repeated the words over and over. 'You're too old for this Billy Boy - face the facts.'

Cycling to the Shetlands sounds fine when you say it. It's as if you *are* going to do it, but it disguises the reality of how hard it really is. It's not even as if, like Ian Botham when he walked from John O 'Groats to Land's End, I had a support entourage. No posh hotels, hearty suppers, hot baths or foot massages from expert physiotherapists. Not even any companions.

'Argggggh...' I continued cursing as I shoved my bike along, my spirits sinking with each step. At last, the B road ended in a T junction as it hit the main A49 and I turned towards Ross, hoping to find a camp site soon.

Just a mile down the road, and two miles from Ross I came to a place that was not really a place, Peterstow and no more than a small collection of houses with a post office.

I bought some assorted snacks and a drink and asked, 'I wonder, are there any campsites around here?'

'Yes, just down the road.' My spirits were slightly raised and then given a further boost.

'You'll see the pub on the left, the Yew Tree.' A pub, eh? Things were looking up in a relative sort of way. I cruised down the hill towards Ross, and absent-mindedly sailed straight past the pub. After backtracking fifty yards, I wandered around the outside of the pub. It was now quarter to four and there was no sign of life except for the sound of a radio somewhere in the building. After about ten minutes of milling about, knocking knockers, ringing mute bells that may have worked out of ear shot, and politely shouting, I eventually found a thin man that looked as if he had just got out of bed, and struck a deal - £4.00 to camp for the night.

Wheeling the bike over to a portakabin toilet/shower block I pitched the tent close by, thinking that a guaranteed walk to the loo in the middle of the night would be a lot easier. It didn't look as if I would have to face the flip side of that coin: many other merry campers doing the same thing and keeping me awake. The camp site looked quite deserted. There were no other tents, and, although there were quite a few caravans, most seemed to be unoccupied.

Now was the time to put up the new one-man super-duper tent I had bought in the Gloucester outdoor shop the previous Saturday.

'What *exactly* are you looking for,' the helpful sales woman enquired.

'I'm after something extra light weight because I'm touring on a mountain bike.'

I continued proudly, 'But, it needs to be 100% waterproof; I'm headed for Scotland, you see.' She gave me a knowing smile and nodded her head repeatedly like a doctor when he recognises the symptoms you are describing.

'Terra Nova I would recommend, yes, Terra Nova - definitely. There's the two man version over there.' She pointed to a yellow and green tent that had been erected on the shop floor carpet. 'We've got the one-man version in stock too. Would you like to see it?'

'Yes, please.' She was very helpful and a model salesperson. Within minutes, she had put up the tent and given me a list of do's and don'ts. I was impressed.

'Great, how much is it?'

'They've used these all over the world, even on Mount Everest.' She appeared not to hear but went on to fill me in on the technical aspects of the poles.

'They're made of titanium. They look like ordinary tent poles but they're not. These won't break in a gale.'

I sensed an evasion strategy and guessed that this Mount Everest tent with poles stronger than bridge supports was going to cost me.

'How much is the tent?' I asked quietly.

The saleswoman had not finished with the poles: 'They're made in this country, not the Far East, they look the same but these are much better. These are the ones the mountaineers use. I wouldn't take the risk ...'

'Yes,' I interrupted to let her know I understood. But, she wasn't ready to answer the ultimate question yet.

'It's the same with all outdoor equipment, you get what you pay for...' Suddenly, her clichéd delivery had become blatantly text book.

I cocked my head, smiled and let my face repeat, 'The Price?' It was time to talk money.

'Two hundred and fifty pounds,' she said nonchalantly. I wasn't too surprised though and I made no objections. If I was going to get stuck in the middle of the Grampian Mountains in a hurricane, I wanted to be sure my home wasn't going to fly off into the North Sea. I just wished that I had thought the same way about my baggage and bought some decent panniers for my bike.

And the tent did go up 'in no time', just as the sales girl had demonstrated. I washed the day out of my breathable tee shirt and underwear and proudly rigged a line to dry them between my bike and the tent. It was now eight o'clock and I needed some food. I was still morbidly dejected about my leg injury but was slightly cheered by the fact that I couldn't feel any pain or even discomfort as I walked. Still, I thought it was a good idea to catch a bus into Ross and give my leg a chance to rest from cycling. It had been ages since I had caught a bus and I wondered how reliable they were these days. My reservations were confirmed as I waited over half an hour. I had arrived at the stop ten minutes early having gleaned the timetable at the campsite house beforehand. The driver must have known he was late as he wielded the heavy bus at high speed around the twists to Ross; so much so, that I couldn't relax and I was relieved to get out.

Ross is a pretty town, and I wandered its near deserted streets after shop closing time. I needed to find a bank to get out some drinking tokens. It didn't take too long, although my bank was the last one I happened upon. For some strange reason I don't even understand myself, I was determined to find *my* bank even though I knew I could get cash out of any of the others. I broke into the notes to buy post cards for Nicole, Cherie's eldest daughter and MR, her youngest child, Morgan-Rhys. I had promised Cherie's children that I would send a post card to one of them every day, so that was a mission I had successfully fulfilled on this first day.

The weather was still beautiful so I called into a pub, ordered a pint of Strongbow and a cigar, and went out the back to the beer garden I had seen advertised on a board at the front. It was really more of a yard and I settled at a table in an elevated and 'decked' area that was half completed.

Sitting there with the yard to myself, sadness came upon me, and I suddenly missed Cherie being with me. I thought of her as always, sitting, not opposite, but to my left forming a right angle so she could be on my 'good side'. I am completely deaf in my right ear and have been since the age of four when an undetected dose of mumps apparently put paid to my stereo perception for life – nerve deafness the doctor had told my mother. As a child of the fifties, it was a foregone conclusion that my tonsils and adenoids would be whipped out - everybody's were in those days when 'vestigial' meant useless. This was supposedly to stop the spread of any future infection to my other ear. Unfortunately, there is no cure for nerve deafness and no hearing aid that will work: you can't amplify nothing.

I loved the fact that Cherie had switched on to my disability very early in our courting days, and she always remembered where to stand and where to sit so I could best hear her. It was one of those things that showed she loved me and how she cared, not through an occasional act, but all the time, whenever we were together. I rarely caught her out and hardly ever had to remind her - when I did, she was usually under the influence of alcohol. Naturally, few other people are as aware of this as Cherie. It is usually up to me to manoeuvre myself into positions where I will be able to hear what's going on.

I used to be very embarrassed about my deafness, but these days I will usually own up straight away; indeed, I will take the initiative and ask, 'Do you mind if I sit here?

I'm a bit deaf you see and I won't be able to hear if I sit anywhere else.' Hardly anyone objects.

And, if I'm walking along the street with someone, I'll nimbly skip around to make sure they're on my 'right side'. It usually works, although I had a strange experience with a friend of my brother's in Tewksbury. Talking to Gerry I found him on my wrong side, so I skipped behind and around him. We chatted for a while, but soon he was on the wrong side again. I did the skipping manoeuvre again but within seconds, we were wrong once more. Patiently, I skipped around to Gerry's right hand side. Then, he did the same thing again.

'What the hell are you playing at?' I wondered in mock anger.

He replied in his Gloucester accent, 'I'm stone deaf in me right ear – what are *you* playing at?' Touché!

As I sipped my cider and puffed on my Hamlet cigar, I gazed over a vista that was not impressive – an angular landscape of roofs and house extensions met the sky while beer barrels and crates cluttered the foreground. Cherie's absence on this journey took me back to a trip we had taken together two years previously. The motorbike, a 1989 Honda VFR was not bad as a touring bike, but we had it loaded like a pack mule. We were biking from Merthyr to the Costa Dorada in Spain via the west coast of France then through the Pyrenees, later planning to meet up with friends at their hired villa near Gerona. The load was significantly increased because we were planning to camp. The back rack was piled high and held in place with the ever-trusty bungees. The back seat had throw-over panniers filled to capacity and I could feel Cherie, dressed like Darth Vader, clumsily trying to cock her leg over the saddle and the huge stack of luggage. All her weight pushed down on the left side foot peg and I struggled to hold the bike as my rather inadequate short legs barely reached the ground. To make matters worse, the lead from her intercom was plugged in and now tried to tangle around every possible projection like an unwanted Russian vine. But she carried on with grim determination and a few expletives. There were so many things I loved about her and, as I sat there on the decking, my tears tried in vain to fill the void.

There was no life in Ross; so, having taken a few photos earlier, I just needed to get some food before heading back to the campsite. I ambled into a quiet covered mall and sauntered into the supermarket to get a few items including wet wipes. I had been sweating profusely all day and I would have welcomed something to freshen me up a bit as I rode along. I then tracked down what was to be the first of many chip shops on my journey and sat under the covered roof off a thoroughfare to enjoy them soaked with curry sauce. It must have been good. One man passed, looked me over and soon appeared with a carbon copy meal that he tucked into on the next bench. I don't think he fancied me – it was my meal that got him going.

I caught the bus back to the campsite feeling relieved that my leg still seemed to be OK. In the tent, I phoned my mum who told me there had been horrendous and prolonged thunderstorms where she lived in Gwent, and indeed elsewhere including Devon and, nearer to me, Hereford, just ten miles up the road to the north. There was nothing here, so I had been lucky in some respects. It was now eight o'clock and time to get into the pub at the end of Day One. Tuesday night in a backwater, it was bound to be quiet, but I had a pleasant chat with the bar maid and an engaging conversation with a bloke who worked in the sewage farm business. It was very interesting talking to him, and I remember him telling me, that, most of the South Wales coast was now fairly well served with sewage treatment works and that many new plants had been built in recent years. I'm sure the 'Surfers against Sewage' would be pleased.

I turned in at about half past eleven and fell into sleep with a troubled mind. What would my leg be like when the morning came?

The Ride:

Merthyr to Ross

Distance: 41 miles.

Ross to Evesham

Wednesday, July 4th

The sound of light rain on the tent woke me from a good night's sleep. I dozed for a short while and by the time I got up it had stopped and the sun had come out. I boiled water on the Trangia stove and made my customary mug of strong, black unsweetened coffee. As I sat in the entrance to the tent, I thought about the day ahead and worried whether my leg would be up to the pedalling. The signs were promising. There wasn't the slightest twinge of discomfort on the walk to the loo, let alone pain, to remind me that I had suffered so badly the day before.

I packed everything away, but the result was a mess. I still ended up with a badly balanced load held in place by elastic bands. Then I started off and instantly, I was stabbed deep in the back of my left leg at every turn of the pedal, and I knew for certain that something was seriously wrong. There was no way that I was going to be able to cycle; from years of playing football, I knew how long a muscle pull in the leg would take to heal. If past form was anything to go by, I would be out of action for at least three weeks.

'Drat!'

But, I had mentally prepared myself the previous day. I had decided that as long as I could walk, then I should be able to cover the miles at a rate somewhere between walking and cycling as I could still cover ground downhill at speed in freewheeling mode. And, there was no way I was going to give up now. I thought about the purpose of the trip. To get away on my own was the main priority and if I ended up walking and catching trains and buses, so be it. There was still a journey to be made and much to think about on the way.

For a mile and a half I 'wheeed' down the hill towards Ross, following the route of the scary bus ride the evening before, until I reached the main roundabout at its junction with the A40. As soon as I came on to the mile section of dual carriageway that leads up to the start of the M50 and Ross Spur, I was forced to get off and push. There was a slight gradient that, even with the big load, would normally have caused me no problem, but now my leg was shot. As I walked up the hard shoulder, a continuous procession of traffic, including scores of heavy lorries, fanned me with their wind, and my snail-like progress deflated me. I had wanted to take my breakfast in Ledbury, some twelve miles away on the A449, but it now looked as if it would have to be skipped; by the time I reached Ledbury it would probably be lunchtime. Just as I approached the roundabout where the Ledbury road left the busy dual carriageway, an idea came to me. The pain I was getting only came when I was pedalling - walking presented no problem at all. Not only that, but it kicked in at the bottom of each revolution and disappeared once that point had been passed.

'Maybe, if I lower the saddle, my leg will be less extended and it might help.' I leaned over, freed the quick release mechanism on the saddle post and twisted the saddle down two inches. Cocking my leg over the load, I tapped the pedal back with my toe to give me some drive with my right leg and pushed off. Tally Ho! It worked. I couldn't believe it at first, and I cautiously monitored every turn of the pedal, waiting for the stab ... but it didn't come.

I yelled out, 'YES!'

As the hedgerows now jubilantly flashed past, I pondered the miracle. I must have had the saddle a bit high yesterday and suffered an over-extension injury of some kind. Perhaps a ligament or tendon had been overstretched rather like a weak spring, and of course, at my age, once it had gone, it was totally gone. But, now, lowering the saddle, the injured part was not being asked to work to its limit and it could function again ... FANTASTIC!

On the other hand, it did feel strange. I had often noticed others with their bikes set up incorrectly. Too low a saddle makes them look comical as they go along with their bent legs rising up towards the handlebars somewhere in the region of their ears. Too high a saddle looks painful, as the rider has to slew his or her bum alternately from side to side to reach the pedals. I sensed that my low saddle coupled with my short legs might make me look like Toulouse Lautrec on wheels. The miles disappeared behind me, and it looked as if I would have breakfast after all – just as well, I was getting hungry. As I reached the traffic lights in Ledbury, I turned left on to the High Street and started to look for somewhere to eat. I coasted down the main drag and noticed the tourist information office. I didn't really want to forestall breakfast any longer, but I thought I'd try to keep ahead of the game and find a campsite for the night *en route*. I needn't have bothered.

The tourist information lady explained, 'Where you're going is out of our area. You're going too far east - we've got no information at all. Sorry.'

I had more luck with my next question, 'Can you suggest somewhere I might get a good breakfast in Ledbury?'

'Just up the hill there on the left next door to the bakery.' Content with this information, I wheeled my bike up the hill. To be on the safe side, I decided to unload, and chained my bike to a parking sign pole, feeling like John Wayne tying up outside a saloon (but doubtless looking one thousand times less cool). I clumsily crossed the threshold of the cafe, wielding my rucksack with all its bits hanging off, and thankfully sat at a table to order a rather late breakfast. I was served a mighty portion and the lady acceded to my request to fill my thermos with tap water and ice. Still, I felt a little Dick Turpined when I saw the bill. Perhaps I had been spoiled by the numerous breakfasts that Cherie and I had 'stolen' from Messrs ASDA, Tesco, Safeway or Lord Sainsbury for the minimal price they charge, secure in the belief you will spend a fortune elsewhere in the store. We never bought anything else after the meal, and in so doing, felt we scored a minor victory against the giant corporations.

I left the café, again man-handling the weighty rucksack that forced me into an awkward and exaggerated gait. As I untied my aluminium horse, a lady came out from the shop across the pavement to apologise for rearranging my bike after it had fallen down around its parking pole prop. Still tethered by the U Lock it must have been quite a feat for her to get it upright again. We British really are so polite. Not only had the kind lady, who was not young by any means, taken the time and trouble to struggle and to pull my bike back to dignity, but she felt the need to come and say sorry, presumably in case I noticed that some tampering had been going on. Needless to say, as I humped my rucksack thankfully to the floor, it would have been the last thing I would have noticed.

Ledbury was by now quite busy, as I loaded up and set off through the town maintaining the heading on which I had arrived. At the end of the main street, there were no relevant sign posts to indicate my route. I stopped and pondered for a while before heading off left down a hill. Something didn't seem right, but I kept going until a roundabout forced me left again. By now it was clear I was on a bypass and I had lost my bearings. I took out the compass that I never really expected to use, and confirmed that I was going the wrong way. I turned the bike around and started to trundle back up the hill that only minutes before I had whizzed down. In a car, this would have been nothing, but I was not in a car and this was an energetic detour that I could have well done without, having only covered sixteen miles. Stoical, rather than annoyed, I vowed to take more care next time.

Why didn't I look at the compass before setting off? It would have told me straight away the general direction I should have been heading. Sometimes I just don't think. It is a failing of mine.

I turned right, once more into Ledbury's main street; and, as I headed uphill back towards the café and the traffic lights, I was confronted with a view I had seen before - it was like looking at a photo. Riding back from Bicester shopping village on our motorbike a few years before, Cherie and I had taken the scenic route through the Cotswolds taking in Hereford, Chipping Norton and Ledbury. Now, I was approaching the High Street from the same direction I had seen it that day. The sadness hit me like an adrenalin rush. Suddenly I was back with Cherie. My chest heaved and tears fell on my cheeks and I was totally overcome with grief. A few moments later, my despair was replaced with a warm glow that rippled through the whole of my body and I felt in it an overwhelming benevolence and closeness to the one I missed so much. I also saw the same pub she had spotted that warm late summer's afternoon.

Typically, Cherie was thinking food as her voice cut in through the intercom, 'Shall we call in, Tony?'

'What do you reckon, or would you rather keep going?' We still had quite a way to go. Did we really want to stop?

'May as well stop, I could do with something to eat.' So we parked the bike up on the road and explored a side alley that led into a secluded beer garden tastefully planted, with the scent of honeysuckle hanging in the air. Half a dozen trestle tables were taken but, ominously, no one was eating food.

'You've been riding all day. I'll go and see what's going on ...' Cherie took off her helmet and her hair fell about her shoulders. Flicking it nonchalantly into place, she placed her lid and gloves on the table and continued '... What do you want?'

'I don't mind – anything.' I often let Cherie choose my food. More often than not, when I picked from a menu, I would look across at Cherie and her meal would be far more appealing than my own. She would always take time to pore over the prospective delights and would regularly have trouble selecting from them. A popular solution was to pick two different meals for herself, give one to me then we would swap half way through.

'What do you want to drink?'

'Anything soft.' I never touched alcohol on the bike. Cherie left her helmet and gloves on the table and disappeared. Minutes later she returned with a scowl carrying two drinks and some crisp packets tucked under her armpits.

'No bloody food!' It bothered her more than it did me.

This memorable little interlude of no particular significance played out before me again. I carried on up the High Street to the traffic lights and realised that, had I turned left, instead of right after breakfast and my chat with the bike- righting lady from the shop, I would have been on the correct road in twenty seconds. I blamed the lady for distracting me, but thanked her the same time. I would never have had that flashback had I not approached Ledbury from the north, as Cherie and I had done on that balmy afternoon.

The temperature soared as the sun climbed in the sky; and, as I made my way towards Pershore, my leg ominously started to play up once more despite the lower saddle position. Cycling was now a real grind and I tried to ease what was discomfort, rather than real pain, by easing the pressure on the pedals and inevitably slowing down to little more than a crawling pace. I was demoralised, only half way into my second day, and I decided I would look for more salubrious accommodation that night. If I could get a room in a pub or a cheap hotel, I could have a bath and maybe the hot water would improve my leg.

A seemingly deserted pub called The Gay Dog showed signs of life as I passed by. I silently argued with myself whether or not I should go in for a drink. Catching sight of a definite light in one of the windows tipped the balance; I turned sharply to make the second entrance into the car park. Propping the bike out of sight around the back of the building, I walked from the brightness of the day into a dark spacious room with a heavily patterned carpet, to join the only other people in the pub - one couple and the bar man. I resisted the sensible option of a long soft drink, and ordered a pint of Strongbow. Chatting to my three new companions, and with my thirst sharpened from hours of pedalling in the hot sun, I was soon on to my second.

The male half of the couple was the chef at the pub and it turned out he used to work in Port Talbot (I chose not to ask him if he remembered a football team called Cornelly United). Coincidentally, the woman's mother came from Merthyr - Welsh people are everywhere, it seemed. I moaned to them about my leg and asked if they knew of any hotels or pubs I could stay in around the Pershore area. The bar man was very helpful. He looked up a place he knew in his Yellow Pages, and also phoned before handing me the receiver. I booked a room for the night; although I felt a little wimpy, I told myself that I deserved it, having battled through the day with my injury. Sorely tempted to get a third drink, I managed to resist, and said thanks and cheerio to the tiny gathering.

As I set off, my legs felt like I was wearing concrete wellies and my soul was equally weighed down. Within a matter of hundred yards, I passed over a major landmark – the M5 motorway. I got off the bike and spent a few minutes looking north as the route, busy as usual, disappeared towards the horizon. North was the direction I should have been going, were it not for the fact that I had decided to go up the east side of Britain. Still, the M5, a major north/south artery, was a milestone, marking my lateral progress across Britain and drawing a line between The West and The Midlands. As I leaned on the railing overlooking the stream of traffic, it reminded me of driving up to Liverpool to see Cherie's parents, before we abandoned the motorway in favour of the route through Wales. The flashback compounded my melancholy demeanour and filled me with a forlorn sadness. As the columns of cars and lorries filed like never ending trains under my feet, the sight of a lone motorbike took me back to a trip Cherie and I had made four years earlier when we had an old Kawasaki GT 750.

We had set off from Merthyr headed for West Wales to catch the ferry from Fishguard to Rosslaire. Then, we took the coast road north to Dublin, eventually meeting up with Gareth, a friend who had moved back to Bangor near Belfast. Like us, Gareth enjoyed a drink and we naturally gravitated towards the pubs as we were given a guided tour of Bangor. At our third alehouse, we settled at a bay window table overlooking a dark sea as alcohol accelerated the camaraderie.

Suddenly, Cherie interrupted the smooth flow of banter and laughter, 'What's that?'

We followed the line of her finger and could just make out a white smudge on the grey canvas of the sea.

'Is it a ship?' Gareth went for the most likely option.

'It can't be; it's the wrong shape.' I could see that the mystery object had no lines to define it and added speculatively '... I think it's a UFO!' We all laughed.

'Yes, it's got to be a UFO,' Cherie agreed, and we all went on to develop the theory to ridiculous extremes that we found immensely funny. The truth though, remained a total enigma. Despite the fact we were more taken by the fantasy than the fact, casual glances out to sea confirmed that the UFO was getting bigger. Eventually, the clear lines of a ship could be distinguished although the vessel itself only made up a fraction of the total - the bulk of what we could see was seemingly, a huge white cloud. Gareth's eyes narrowed and his face registered the retrieval of something from his subconscious.

'I think it could be one of those new ferries. They work on the same principle as a jet ski – they're twice as fast as normal ferries.'

Cherie had the best eyesight, 'Yes, it looks like a water jet coming out the back of the ship.'

The ship quickly drew closer and it was confirmed. As the afternoon wore on, we returned to the subject of the new style ferry. I was captivated by the idea of a ferry that worked like a jet ski and an idea occurred to me.

I put it to Cherie, 'Do you think we could change our tickets? Instead of going back the way we came, maybe we could take the jet-ski ferry across to Scotland and ride back to Wales that way.' It was appealing, not only because I wanted to have a go on the new ferry, but also because neither of us had been to Scotland before.

'I don't mind, Dear,' was Cherie's predictable answer. 'It's up to you.' We debated the possible pros and cons but decided that if, with little extra expense it could be organised, it would be more of an adventure than retracing our steps back through Ireland to Rosslaire.

It was a bad decision. For one thing, it meant we didn't start our journey until late afternoon because of the ferry times. It also meant we didn't make any progress south, something we would have done if we had set off at nine o'clock in the morning. And, this happened to be a time when there was a north/south split in the weather - the north getting battered with wind and rain while the south was bathed in glorious sunshine. Of course, we now got the former. We rode off the ferry at Stranraer in a deluge, to find there were no campsites as we continued to head east, passing not far from Lockerbie on the A75. The daylight had a right to be there but the weather stole it, as we passed not a single village. For some reason, every settlement had been engineered off the route with a bypass. Only signposts indicated with a large 'D' shape, places such as Creetown, Twynholm and Leaths that must have existed out of sight of the road. As the bike buzzed dependably between our legs through puddles, Cherie and I rode on in silence as the rain pummelled us.

We took a detour into Dumfries to get some cash from a machine, but had to slog onwards for another hour until, as night fell early somewhere between Gretna Green and Carlisle, we at last saw a sign for a campsite. Following occasional wigwam signposts along winding country lanes for an interminable five miles more, we eventually entered the grounds of a grand castle and paid a king's ransom for the privilege of taking up the space required for a motorbike and a two-man tent.

As this memory passed before me, Cherie took centre stage and I saw the two of us, together once more. My heart fell away as I remembered how she used to be. How many women have I met that would put up with things as Cherie did. It was completely my idea to come through Scotland and it had been lousy one. We discovered later that the weather had been fine further south. If we had stuck to our original plan and headed down through Ireland at the beginning of the day, we needn't have even got wet. But Cherie hadn't held it against me or once complained. There had been no groans when the night joined the rain and long hours in the saddle made our bums sore. Spludging in grass, that turned to mud in seconds, not a single grumble as we unrolled our instantly soaked tent. In our full leather biking gear, covered with one piece waterproofs, every movement was a challenge and we must have looked like Neil Armstrong and Buzz Aldrin in their moon suits as we struggled to put our tent together - but not a murmur of dissent. Ever pragmatic, Cherie had the ability to put her thoughts into actions. I wondered how she made keeping calm look so simple and I felt my love for her well up.

I stayed a minute longer on the bridge over the M5 and the sadness started to shrink. I took a photograph to remind me of the scene and the moment, then mounted and set off. After just a few minutes, I felt strangely rejuvenated and my pace picked up as I quickly covered the four miles to Pershore. I found my accommodation straight away, an old coaching inn in the centre of town. Once more hiding my bike around the back to avoid unloading, I went to book in. The reception area was lavishly furnished with an oak balustrade that curved impressively to the first floor. Suddenly, it struck me that I hadn't enquired about the price.

'Sixty pounds for a single, Mr Hill,' replied the young female receptionist.

'Sixty?' I echoed. 'That's too much for me, I'm afraid. Are you prepared to come down on that?' I was not quite the suited businessman with the executive briefcase, and I suspected that my custom was not really welcome.

'No sir, that's our price.'

'What are you, five star or something?'

'No sir, two star.'

I made my apologies and unbooked the room. The girl was kind enough to make a recommendation though. To her, I must have looked very trail weary, my face bearing the stains of sweat wiped repeatedly with a grubby forearm, and my white tee shirt a top contender for a whiter than white detergent advert. Add to that, the whiff of stale cider on my breath and she had enough evidence to surmise the sort of place that would best suit me. Following her directions, I found the pub and entered a small noisy room with a beer stained carpet and chipped Formica tables crammed with people of all ages. Half fighting my way to the bar, I managed, after several attempts to get myself heard by a large woman with Dickensian breasts.

'Have you got any rooms for tonight?'

'Full up, love,' she said apologetically.

'Damn.' I was cursing the bad luck rather than the lady. The place might have looked a bit rough, but it had a warm and friendly atmosphere and it was only sixteen quid for bed and breakfast. I also had a distinct feeling that there might have been a bit of what the Irish call 'the craic' there and I imagined an exciting night might be in store.

A youngish bloke, sitting with some friends, shouted across the bar, 'You can stay with me for a tenner!' He laughed with his mates.

'You serious?' Suddenly my hopes were revived. Was he joking?

After a short pause he went on, 'Yeah, why not?'

'OK, thanks, I'll take you up on that'. Funny how things fall into place sometimes, isn't it?

'Do you get up early in the morning?' he asked.

Getting up early was no problem for me, but I put it to him, 'How early?'

'Very early.'

'How early's very early?'

'Five o'clock.'

I was out of luck after all. I didn't mind getting up early, but that was ridiculous. And, I couldn't blame the bloke for wanting a total stranger, out of his place before he left for work. There was no solution - so close yet so far. I didn't bother with a drink, but I did get some information about a pub that did B & B just outside Evesham, about five miles away. I thanked my 'would be' landlord and said cheerio as I left.

Pedalling back through Pershore, I was impressed enough by the church to take a photograph, but back on the bike my leg was aching badly and it occurred to me that some medication might be a partial answer. I found a chemist and asked for advice, and ibuprofen was recommended. I can't remember if I took one there and then. Being a man, the sensible and immediate remedy for my aches and pains probably didn't occur to me. Either way I carried on, picked up the A44, and slogged off for Evesham. Half an hour later I found the pub I had been told about back in Pershore. It was now five o'clock but my luck wasn't improving. There was no one around and all the doors were locked. Leaning over a hedge, I managed to get the attention of a neighbour who was noisily cutting his hedge.

'Anyone around, do you know?' I had to repeat the question.

'They should be back soon. I don't think they've gone far.'

I didn't want to hang around though. I was extremely fatigued by now and the thought of waiting an unspecified time only to be told there was no room at the inn, appealed to me even less than moving on. The neighbour told me that there was a campsite a couple of miles down the road. I eventually reached my thankful destination but only after a painful detour of a mile. A man in his late fifties with a grubby striped shirt that might once have been worn with a suit was bending over his belly to fix a lawn mower.

I called over from my bike, 'Hello, excuse me, I was hoping to camp for the night. Is there a reception around?'

'I'm the reception.' The friendly gaffer booked me in on the spot and told me to go anywhere I liked. I chose a patch of welcoming green turf near to the toilet and shower block and set about unloading and setting up camp – it was six o'clock. As soon as I had pitched the tent, I dispensed with unpacking anything else, save my sleeping mat and pillow. I lay down to sleep and I was gone in a minute with the sound of birds twittering in the nearby trees fading to nothingness. Totally zonked for half an hour, I felt refreshed once I had shaken off the sleep and finished unpacking as the Trangia boiled up water for a coffee.

As I sat in the entrance to the tent sipping coffee still bathed in sunshine, the familiar signature tune to Coronation Street wafted across from a little caravan across the track and I thought about Cherie again. She loved Corrie. In fact, she had converted me to a zealous follower and we both sadly conspired to record the programme if ever we were away. I often used to lie on the settee while Corrie was on. Cherie would place a cushion on her lap and I would rest my head on it. For a full half hour she would gently run her fingers through my hair. How I missed her now.

It took five minutes for the knot inside me to ease and I was able to get my things together for the short trip to the shower block. Renewed and dressed relatively smartly, save for my disgusting squash trainers, I suddenly realised how hungry I was. I hadn't eaten since brunch in Ledbury. I had no option but to cycle to find something, as there were no shops around and the campsite had nothing to offer. Reluctantly pedalling and deliberately taking it easy along the back road to Evesham, I was surprised at the opulence displayed in the South Fork-like houses, each driveway sporting at least two very expensive cars. A mile and a half from camp, and now freewheeling down the main road to town, I saw the SPAR logo. It was an oasis in the desert to a man dying of thirst, except in my case it was desperate hunger.

By this time, opulence had given way to the characteristic shabbiness of so many council estates. The area looked rough, but I didn't bother locking up the bike in my haste to get to the food. As I quickly passed around the narrow aisles, I picked up everything I fancied. The end result was the selection you would expect from a ten year old who had been given a fiver by his granny, not the balanced and coordinated meal that would sustain a long distance cyclist. It was all thrown carelessly into a gossamer thin plastic bag by a disinterested teenage till girl. I left the shop like a hungry dog about to wolf down the dinner of the cat next door and sat on a low wall outside the SPAR shop. As I watched some dirty kids playing on a patch of spare tarmac, the dinner went down: beef pasty, followed by unspecified sandwich, followed by two mini pork pies, followed by prawn cocktail crisps and finally, a melted mint Aero chocolate bar. Easing the transition from one to the next were thirsty gulps from a two litre container of chilled milk. What a concoction.

I had a friend in university who had been brought up in Evesham by his parents who owned a market garden. I had never been before, and I knew I wouldn't have time to look around the next day; so, I decided to go and have a wander around. More importantly, I needed cash out of a machine if I wanted to have more than one or two pints of beer that night ... and I definitely did.

Thankfully, it was downhill all the way and I enjoyed the ride. I took the trouble to look in some shoe shop windows. I really did need something decent to put on my feet in the evenings. It was a half- hearted look though, and once I'd found a bank and taken out cash, I pedalled through the pedestrianised part of the town and then into the park to follow the riverbank path back towards the main bridge over the river. It was a beautiful evening and I was impressed with the way the rowing club members, practising on the river, overtook me with such ease. I'd seen these boats on TV, of course, but I was nevertheless impressed with the turn of speed they could muster. Once I crossed the river bridge I started the long slog back up the hill towards the campsite. I had reset the trip meter on the bike computer and, by the time I got back to the tent, it read five and a half miles. I could have done without it. It had been a long, hot, often painful day and I knew I would be back on the road for anything between six and nine hours the next day.

Worse still, the pub was almost a mile away. I decided to walk to giving my backside a rest. As a bonus, I would also stand a better chance of getting back in one piece after a few beers. Wednesday night, in a country pub, in a rich commuter village outside Evesham, on a beautiful midsummer's evening – the place was dead. It was just me and the barmaid. Having said that we did get chatting and, I would say we actually got quite close. After some time I told her about Cherie and she told me of some loved ones that she had 'lost' recently. There was no hint of chat-up, or any sexual connotations, but I did soak up her humanness, amplified perhaps, by my prolonged periods of solitude that day.

We were joined later by a couple of middle-aged men (what am *I*?). One bore a striking resemblance to Kenneth Clark, the then chancellor of the exchequer and after five pints, with the corners lopped off my inhibitions, I told him so. My eyes had not deceived me as he confirmed he had been told so many times before. He even sounded like him, but I had downed six or seven pints by then so I might have been wrong. I don't remember what we talked about, but I enjoyed the exchange of ideas and some banter before I set off at about midnight. The sky looked like the roof in a planetarium, the air was still warm and I meandered along the lane, back to the campsite. My thoughts were inexorably drawn to Cherie, so that when I reached the entrance to the site, I didn't want to go to bed. At the access lane to the campsite, I crossed to the opposite side of the road. There was no fence, just a drainage ditch separating the road from the field. I sat down with my legs dangling into the ditch and there, in the lonely quiet of the midnight hours, under the warm stars, I cried and remembered Cherie.

The Ride:

Ross on Wye to Evesham

Distance: 42 miles

Evesham to Brinklow

Thursday, July 5th

The first thing I had to do was follow my tracks into Evesham from the evening before. I decided not to bother to stop and look for shoes – I just wanted to get on. I was aiming for breakfast in Stratford, some sixteen miles away. The idea was to follow a similar pattern to the day before when I had brunched in Ledbury. No faffing around with breakfast in the tent for me. Apart from the hassle of having to go and buy all the stuff the day before, and finding somewhere to carry it on the bike, there was the time to cook it, the burden of fetching water, and the grand washing ceremony, or should I say, scratching ritual, of the soiled dishes. Sixteen miles was a good distance to get under your belt before the day, and more importantly the stomach, realised it had started.

The weather was already heating up and I thought about the phone call I had made to my mother the night before. By some magic, I had missed all of the stormy rain that had been around. South Wales and the South West had seen heavy, and strangely lengthy, thunderstorms and there had been a lot of flooding as a result.

I made Stratford in good time and picked up two post cards, one for Hafina, my youngest step-daughter, and one for Dennis and Margaret, good friends of mine. I asked a passer-by if there was a local supermarket that had a café. There would be, of course, in a place the size of Stratford on Avon, but the question was how far away? Luckily, the hypermarket was just a few hundred yards away, and I gratefully set off through heavy traffic, glancing over my shoulder before dangerously wobbling into the middle lane to turn right into the retailing compound.

On the one hand, it is good to see that the designers of these grocery temples are making an effort. ASDA for instance, have moved away from the architecture of the huge brick and incorporated some curves, at least into the exterior appearance of their stores. On the other hand, are they trying too hard? These new designs often feature little triangular roof adornments, and freewheeling down the Safeway access road into an ocean of cars the building at least, was reminiscent of Stalag 19. And talking of security and escape, I was not confident about the security of my gear if it was left on the bike. I thought about finding the store café by doing a reccy around the outside first, then propping the bike up against the window so I could keep an eye on it. Cherie and I used to do a similar thing with the motorbike but I was never really convinced then, as now, that it was the answer to the security problem, and logic dictated to me:

'What if the bike's pinched in the time it takes me to get around to the café, get a tray, queue up for food, get the condiments, cutlery, coffee, and pay. Or, what if a villain starts to break the lock and ride off as I look on helplessly from the other side of the window- maybe thumping the glass in a desperate but futile act of saving my trip. The simple fact was I would never have been able to give chase. By the time I'd legged it past the battery of checkouts, and dodged scores of loaded trolleys with their ambling pestilent pushers, the trail would have gone stone cold.'

So, logic now determined that I unload the bike. Logic did not however, suggest to me that any thief would probably be seriously thwacked by high-tension bungees if he had the strength to release the hooks holding my rucksack in place. And in any case, if the deviant was a spotty baseball capped adolescent, he probably wouldn't have the strength to pick the unwieldy rucksack up off the floor, let alone make off with it. And if the same youth tried to cycle off with the load still packed, he'd discover the laws of physics had changed beyond comprehension and he'd be on his backside as soon as his feet left the ground. But none of this occurred to me as I confronted the menace of the bungees.

'Sounds like a good title for a Hammer horror film,' I thought. *'The Menace of the Bungees.'* At the risk of putting my back out, I heaved and humped the rucksack and its attachments into a shopping trolley. The bike was locked – safe, with even the pump removed - and I could easily wheel the load into the store. I must have been the only one of scores of people milling about that went *into* the store fully loaded.

I ordered the traditional full English breakfast off the menu and sat down to enjoy it, my hunger by now nicely primed through the effort of the ride to Stratford and the passage of elapsed time since my last meal. I took time to read some of the complimentary newspaper and wrote my post cards so I could send them straight away. I took my post card promise very seriously, and I didn't want to get to the end of the day and discover there was no post box, no stamp, no time or simply no remembering after a few jars down the pub. It was a pleasant break that took the best part of an hour, but the time came to make a move, so I unparked the trolley and wheeled it back to my bike, filtering, rush hour style, with all the other trolleys now themselves piled high, but with very different payloads to mine.

I had to retrace my steps the short distance back to Stratford's town centre and I pulled up at a curb, a freestanding letter-box frustratingly just out of reach. An obliging passer-by helped me out leaving me to pedal off north eastwards along the A439 towards Leamington Spa and Coventry.

I didn't take too much notice of the scenery as I thought about Cherie's illness. It must have been about three weeks before she died, that she really started to lose it. The drugs she was taking at increasingly higher dosages were causing a lot of tiredness; and, Cherie felt frustrated that she was sleeping so much. It was ironic in a way: Cherie had always been very fond of sleep. On weekends, I regularly used to wake her at the crack of noon and serve up her ritual wake-up cup of weak tea with a single sweetener.

'Just wave the tea bag at it,' she would tell friends that didn't know her well enough to get it just right – she was very particular about the strength of her tea. On a workday, she was one of those people, like my brother Nick, who leaves the house at the last possible minute. Personally, I just don't see the point in all that frantic activity, first thing in the morning. I like to take my time, make a bit of breakfast, sip half a pint of strong black coffee, watch breakfast news and see to my ablutions before packing my brief case with a clean shirt and sandwiches and donning my waterproofs ready for the cycle to work. I would argue that half an hour's less sleep doesn't make any difference at all to the biological functioning of the human body. Of course, Cherie and Nick would disagree with a passion, and they used to join forces on the subject with camaraderie akin to the mutual bond between smokers or drunkards when the sanctity of their habit is challenged. But now that Cherie knew her time was limited, she had had enough of sleeping and wanted to be in the world of the living.

It came to the point where she had to be admitted into the cancer hospital at Velindre in Cardiff, so the doctors could get on top of the drug situation. She was assigned to the critical ward because there were no beds elsewhere. It really was a 'waiting for God' place – most of the patients were old and everyone was seriously dying, except for Cherie. Neither of us knew then she would be dead herself within a month. But Cherie, ever the pragmatic, said she preferred it to the ward she'd been on before. It was quieter and the atmosphere was more peaceful. A nurse gave her the option of promotion to a non-critical ward when a bed became available the next day, but she politely refused, content to be where she was. She was in for five days and every evening I visited and sat with her for a few hours. She found it hard to stay awake for the whole time; but, we had plenty of time to talk, either in the ward or just outside on the grass when the sun came out. When she dropped off to sleep, I took the opportunity to get a nap myself. If she was out for longer, I would open my briefcase and get on with some school work.

When the time came for Cherie to come home and the doctor was satisfied with her amended cocktail of drugs, the consultant, Dr Crosby, said he wanted a word with us. If we could just bear with him for a few moments he would try to find a room we could use. This was ominous. Every time this had happened before it was to give us bad news. So it was again. We sat in a small room with an old two-seater settee and several hard-back chairs. There was no natural light and a few chipped mugs scattered around told us that this was a sanctuary for the nurses on their breaks.

'Good news and bad,' said Dr Crosby. He really was a nice guy and we both picked up the transparent empathy he had for his patients. We wondered how a job so closely connected with suffering, trauma and death could hold any attractions for such a sensitive man. We could only surmise that he gained his satisfaction from helping people in their most dire of moments. He also took part in a lot of experimental research into how to alleviate pain, and prolong life for his patients. Ultimately, his work might lead to a cure for the black scourge.

'The good news: it doesn't look as if it's the stent causing any problems.' The stent had been inserted during an endoscopic operation where all the surgical instruments were fed down Cherie's throat guided by a tiny camera. Cherie's bile duct had become blocked due to the growth of a secondary cancer. She had exhibited all the signs of a failing liver, in particular, shocking yellow eyes, but she was fine once again as soon as the stent had been inserted. This time though, I knew the fact that the stent was working probably meant that something more serious was wrong. Dr Crosby was just trying to be diplomatic but I waited for crunch. Cherie doesn't have my hypochondriac tendencies and I don't think she saw it coming until Dr Crosby stated that this time, it probably was the liver itself causing the problems. Cherie's liver had been growing steadily over the previous month and now she looked well in to the term of a pregnancy. She was finding it increasingly difficult to get around and there weren't many clothes she could wear with any degree of comfort or decorum. It was so sad to see a once trim and fit lady transformed to a handicapped hobbler. Cherie was always proud, self-critical of her figure, and she would dither forever over what to wear. She loved shopping for clothes, her acquisitions a steady trickle of purchases over any given month.

Cherie now pressed Dr Crosby, 'How long have I got left?'

'It's hard to say.' This was the line that was usually taken – understandably. Dying of cancer is an uncertain business, so it not that the medics are avoiding the issues ... necessarily.

'Have I got six months, a year? Give me a rough idea.'

'Oh, it's not that long, I'm afraid.'

'What, not a year?'

'No, sorry - not six months.'

Cherie didn't quiz any further. I can only remember two, maybe three times, that she totally broke down and cried helplessly like a lost child. And this was one of them. All I could do was hold her as the doctor and the nurse respectfully left us in that pokey little room on the threadbare two-seater settee. Cherie cried for a few minutes, and then she was alright again. How she did it, I don't know. She amazed me then and she still does.

She counted six months forward, 'So we're looking at Christmas. We can get a few holidays in before then.' As usual, her optimism came naturally; but, of course, she was wrong.

Lost, in my thoughts, the miles slowly disappeared behind me. The temperature was way up, the sky was blue, and it was now mid-afternoon as I looked down at my trip meter to see I had nearly completed the target forty miles. I could start looking for a place to stay. More pressing though was the immediate need to get a drink. I think people can be split into two broad groups: those that get thirsty and those that don't. Normally, I fall into the latter category, and people who constantly go on about needing a drink often bemuse me. How many litres of water are you supposed to drink a day? – is it five? That seems to me like a huge amount. The largest volumes I ever consume are through the medium of beer, lager, stout or cider, and I have found that nine or ten pints is a giant amount. So, I confine my soft drinking to half mugs of black coffee. I probably consume six to eight of these a day, nothing like the required five litres of fluid, but that still keeps me peeing at irritatingly frequent intervals.

On the bike though, I suddenly realised I had a desperate thirst. I didn't want any amount of water though – I wanted something long, cool and alcoholic – on this occasion, it was Strongbow that I pictured in my mind's eye. I stopped to ask a local man if there were any pubs around. The time was about quarter to four. I was given directions for several; and, I set off down quiet B roads flanked at times by small linear villages. I was just a few miles east of Coventry by this time so these were probably commuter settlements.

I found the first pub – closed. The second, third and fourth were all shut too. Of course, it was Wednesday, more or less mid-week. What did I expect? This wasn't Greece or Spain, and it certainly wasn't UK holiday territory. I felt myself wilt at every bolted door - each disappointment a body blow. Just looking at each pub, I couldn't be sure if it was closed. The Gay Dog Inn back the other side of Pershore had appeared closed, but had pleasantly surprised me and in my hour of need had yielded two pints of Strongbow. So, I had to go through the rigmarole of awkwardly dismounting and finding somewhere to prop up the bike, before trying another closed door, drudging back disappointedly to the bike and clambering back on to push off once more.

I couldn't imagine there being any campsites in a place like this and I mused, 'What am I going to do - not touristy enough. It might have to be B & B or a cheap pub or hotel. Strewth - do I need a drink.'

I creaked another mile and a half that seemed more like five, and reached a crossroads. Again, I asked if there were any pubs around. There was, just a hundred yards up the road. Would it be open though? As I cycled up a slight incline along a straight section of road, I made a mental note of a chip shop on my right. Then, The Raven came into view. I embraced the mirage like a ship owner gazing at his galleon, sails billowing on the horizon with a hold full of bounty after years away at sea. But The Raven was a pub and it was patently open. People were seated on a small veranda overlooking the road with full pints in front of them, talking, laughing and joking. I took the trouble to lock the bike to a drainpipe but didn't have the physical or mental strength to take on the rucksack in unarmed combat, so I risked leaving it attached. I walked into the pub and felt instantly like a welcome guest amidst the hubbub clientele that filled the room. I ordered the fantasy pint of Strongbow and sat at a free table in the centre of the room. One of the cricket test matches between England and Australia was showing and I settled my weary body on the chair and started to watch.

The cider only lasted minutes; I was soon back at the bar. I exchanged a few pleasantries with the barmaid and as I walked back to my seat, a tall, oldish guy in a checked shirt started talking to me. I didn't really want to talk back though. I was interested in the cricket and I didn't feel like making the effort. What's more, he was on my deaf side, so I couldn't really just drop in and out of conversation. If I was in, I had to concentrate. The trouble was, if I wanted out, I would probably appear rude. He was likely to ask questions and I would stone-wall him, not through ignorance, but through deafness. Still, I tried the middle ground but it was impossible. I had to engage in conversation and hang the cricket. He quickly picked up my foreign accent and before long, I had acceded to his probing and he knew I was from Wales, on a pushbike and headed for the Shetland Isles.

He told everyone else in the pub, and I was given a definite psychological and physical boost by their responses. My second pint lasted longer than the first but not by much. I went to go to the bar for another but the check shirt man beat me to it and he insisted on buying me my third. He looked a fit guy, carrying very little weight. He had a longish face with a weathered outdoor complexion and shortish hair that looked as if it was coming to the part in the growing cycle when it would soon be cut. He was drinking Strongbow too, and this may have strengthened the blood brother affinity that often develops between afternoon drinkers, and explained his generosity.

More likely though, he thought, 'Come all that way on a bike - the poor sod deserves another drink.'

He came back and introduced himself as Chainy. He had a friendly and extroverted personality. I had noticed him holding court with the other afternoon drinkers before he'd got speaking to me. He was clearly a local character. His name came from his profession – he was a woodcutter of the old fashioned ilk, fifty-eight years old and proud of it. He chatted with me as he traded insults with some others in the corner. I slipped back to the bar and ordered two pints of Strongbow.

'I didn't buy you a pint so you could buy me one back.' The old drinkers' double think. Of course, he didn't buy for me with any expectation of a drink bought back; but, it is always nice to receive one just the same and it cemented the growing bond between us.

Travelling around in the mid-afternoon, mid-week and in un-touristed locations, you would expect to meet some strange characters - maybe on the dole, perhaps the sick or else too daft or lazy to hold down a job. But Chainy was none of these and before long it seemed as if we were the only two in the pub. This would have been partly explained by the fact that he was still on my deaf side so I was concentrating hard – unconsciously lip reading to compensate for words and syllables missed. But, as the fourth pint of cider slipped more slowly into me, the effects of dehydration, lack of food and expenditure of effort, must also have been combining to give me this 'world blanked out' sensation.

Chainy wasn't joking any more either, and the conversation turned to holidays. I don't know if he had ever been abroad, but I got the impression that he hadn't. He said he had worked all his life chopping down trees. He said that his holiday, if he could have one, would be to go to a big city. He cited London or Liverpool. His reasoning was that he spent all day in the countryside, chopping down trees, usually working on his own with no company for hours on end. Often in the middle of a wood or forest, largely isolated from the outside world, he often fancied himself wandering crowded streets and seeing the sites. It's hard to imagine he couldn't take off any time he liked and just do it – he was fifty-eight years old and only four miles from the edge of Coventry for goodness sake!

Whether he was having me on or not, I don't know. I was inebriated by now. I asked Chainy whether there were any B & Bs around. There was a place down the road and, on Chainy's command, the landlady phoned up for me but there was no answer. Chainy offered to put me up at his place. He lived a few miles down the road but he said I could chuck the bike into the back of his pick-up. I turned him down though. For a start, he had drunk at least four pints of Strongbow, and I suspected that it was probably quite a few more. I didn't fancy a ride with a drunken driver. Secondly, this guy was really still a stranger and I didn't relish the prospect of fighting off a raging homosexual attack, even though I seemed to remember Chainy assuring me he was straight. Also, the landlady had offered me the pub beer garden as a home for my tent and this seemed a less complicated option. And finally, from somewhere in the depths of my reasoning, I still had the notion that this was a trip I wanted to make under my own steam. Chainy had told me that his place was, '.... on the way'. That meant I would be cheating, just a bit, and in the end, that was the main thing that made me refuse his kind offer.

I left the pub, unlocked my bike from the drainpipe and manhandled the heavy rucksack up some stone steps to the garden. I put the tent up on the flattest piece of ground I could find, unfortunately still in full sight of the road. Having organised the tent's interior, it was time to sort out some food. I remembered the chippy a hundred yards down the road and walked still feeling half cut, to get my order in. The two fellas serving there looked as if they were from somewhere like Turkey. The cod in batter plus a portion of chips was ready in seconds. It was served so fast, I wasn't very confident that it would be any good. I was wrong though – this was the best fish and chips I had ever tasted. The cod was in a batter, not too crisp and slightly chewy and the chips were deep-fried to perfection. Of course, I hadn't eaten for hours, and I had used up a lot of calories travelling. Add to this the sharp edge that had been honed on to my appetite by four pints of Strongbow, and it might explain my perception of this meal as pure heaven.

Back at the tent, I had a short sleep, and then woke myself up with a black coffee. It was eight o'clock by now and still a beautiful evening. I sat just inside the entrance to the tent and started writing my journal. Chainy's talk of towns made me think of Cherie's views on the subject. She loved cities, not least because they contained so many shops. She quite liked visiting the countryside but she could never understand how anyone would want to live there. Apart from the lack of shops to go 'shopping', as in 'fun' shopping, you had to jump in the car if you wanted anything. If you fancied a beer, or a bar of chocolate, if you ran out of bread or eggs, or just felt like reading the paper, it was a trip in the car, or do without. Cherie was never one for the monster grocery shop either, so she was always running out of things.

A city girl at heart, she once classically commented, 'The countryside is OK - for keeping the towns apart.'

After about half an hour, I zipped up the tent and walked about twelve paces back into the ale house. This must have been a pub big on Irish music because it was playing through the sound system continuously. It did get me going and if I could have laid my hands on a guitar I would have enjoyed bashing out a few of the old classics – The Irish Rover, The Black Velvet Band, The Green Fields of France. But I had to settle for a pleasant chat with the landlord and landlady who had finished for the night and were enjoying a few drinks at a table. I can't remember if I was there until the end, but I must have drunk another three pints at least before I decided it was time to turn in. I took a short walk up to the local church and was surprised to see how magnificent it looked. It took me a while to realise that the light in the sky was moonlight. The church was artificially illuminated too and I went back to the tent to get my camera. The result was probably the best picture I took on the whole trip.

Back in bed, my mind wandered. On my bike earlier, I had really thought that I might have to spend the night camped out in a wood somewhere. But the landlady had been very kind in letting me stay in the garden. She even offered to make me breakfast the next day but I had politely declined. It felt good to be getting my accommodation totally free, even though I would have to go without a shower or shave in the morning.

'I'll just have to be smelly on the road tomorrow,' I thought.

'In fact, with the weather as hot as it's been I'm pretty sweaty after half an hour in any case.' I remembered my breakfast at the Safeway superstore that morning and was taken back once again, to Cherie and myself on our motorbike trips, tucking into cheap hypermarket breakfasts.

I cried for a while, but it passed and it occurred to me that I was feeling a bit fitter today. I was still getting a sore bum, more or less constantly, but my leg was holding out and seemed to be fine on the lower saddle setting. I thought about my current level of security. Anyone could see me from the road and jump me. I had thought the same earlier and been tempted not to go back into the pub for my second session.

Then I had reconsidered, 'To hell with it – I'm not sitting around here for hours, just to mind the tent. If I get done, I get done.' Any concern I might have had for my nocturnal safety did not keep me awake.

The Ride:

Evesham to Brinklow (3 miles east of Coventry city boundary)

Distance: 43 miles

Brinklow to Stamford

Friday, July 6th

In the beer garden, I found a place to pee that was hopefully out of sight of people going to collect their morning papers, then set up and lit the Trangia. I started to pack away the things inside the tent as I waited for the water to boil. It was too early for the day to have shown its cards, but it was overcast, dank and misty with not a breath of wind. It was the sort of weather that often precedes a scorcher once the sun has burnt through. I managed to get away by nine o'clock and covered the eight miles along quiet roads to Lutterworth where I picked up two postcards for MR and for Dominic and Helen, friends of mine from school. There was also a Safeway store in the town so I availed myself of a breakfast at their customary knock-down price including coffee – wonderful.

I then headed off for Market Harborough, twelve miles away, which turned out to be a bustling hive of a place. I pushed my bike through the pedestrianised part of the town half-heartedly looking for a pair of trainers, sandals or anything that would look better than the sorry articles I still sported on my feet. I actually ventured into one shop, slightly worried about my bike outside, but I just couldn't decide what sort of footwear I wanted. I also didn't relish facing the likely prospect of festering blisters to add to my other discomforts, so in the end I walked out, in my confusion only managing to mumble an unintelligible apology to the lady serving me, who had really done her best to help.

As I got back to the main road and the chaotic traffic, rain started to fall heavily for the first time since I'd left Merthyr. I wasn't really hungry but I felt I needed a rest and I had to stop to don my waterproofs. They were encased in a plastic bag that was bungeed on to the bike at high breaking strain. The little café I found on the outskirts of the town centre served the purpose. It was very small and family run. The tables didn't seem to fit into the room and making progress from one side to the other involved clumsily dancing with the chairs. The food in the display cabinet was clearly homemade but there wasn't anything there that I actually recognised. Perhaps not being a 'sweet' person didn't help. I ordered black coffee and something called a 'Chocolate Oatey' that turned out to have the consistency of a rotting brick and took just as long to chew and swallow. I must have spent the best part of half an hour in the place. The coffee was excellent and I ordered a second. On both occasions I asked for black but they insisted on bringing me a full stainless steel jug of chilled milk. So, after finishing each coffee, I emptied the milk into my cup and polished it off.

'It's all energy,' I thought as the time came to go.

Having awkwardly wriggled into my wet gear I went out to face the elements. My easterly route started to head more to the northeast as I struck out for Uppingham in torrential rain along the very pretty B664. After about an hour the rain stopped and the air started to heat up again. The smells were nothing short of mind blowing. With the past few days of dry hot weather, it seemed that the rain had opened a cask of perfume as the countryside hit my olfactories, stirring my emotions and taking me very much by surprise. The vista was of undulating hills; the fields were small, bounded by vibrant green hedgerows and with scores of deciduous copses scattered about. This was chocolate box Britain with intense fragrance to boot.

I was in two minds whether to go to Rutland water. I remembered learning back in school that Rutland was the smallest county in England and I seemed to recall someone the night before in the pub, telling me that it still was a bona fide unitary authority. I could see Rutland Water on the map and I felt confident there would be campsites there. It would have brought up the forty-mile mark and I was fairly sure the lake and its surrounds would be quite picturesque. Despite this, and with me feeling pretty good, thanks to ibuprofen, I felt I could keep going. I decided to just head straight for Stamford. That would bring me to fifty miles for the day and put me on the edge of the Fens. I also realised that it was Friday and it would be good to be in a town where there was a bit of nightlife. Not for the first time, I felt that I had been through some hard times physically over the past few days and I deserved to give camping a miss, for one night at least.

Although when I reached Stamford, I still felt I could have kept going; but, the seed had been planted and the thought of a bath, bed and nightlife won over. Stamford took me by surprise, a place I hadn't even heard of before. It was very oldie-worldie with a maze of little streets and alleyways filled with nick-knack shops. I was later told that the BBC series 'Middlemarch' had been filmed there. All they had had to do was cover the double yellow lines with grit, remove the street furniture and keep the traffic out and they were convincingly back in the nineteenth century.

After asking around and trying unsuccessfully to get accommodation, I eventually managed to find a rather grubby pub that had a room at the top of the house and a place where I could securely keep my bike downstairs. I humped all the gear up three flights of stairs and carelessly dumped them on one side of the room. Very little effort had gone into making this place look presentable. The carpet was threadbare and unsavoury brown in colour. There were, of course, no *en suite* facilities, although I did have a sink. To be fair, the bed seemed alright and there was a good view down to the street where a road cleaning vehicle was going around and around in circles, making a hell of a racket, as it cleared up the remains of what had been a Friday market. The stalls were nearly all dismantled or removed but the mess remained.

The most striking feature about the room was the cluster of televisions. You usually only see them like this in shops - in people's houses they would be in different rooms, naturally. But here there were three of them to be precise. The leads all mingled together like half-eaten spaghetti and there were two portable aerials of different designs lying on their sides by the biggest telly. It did look bizarre and none of them looked anything like 'state of the art'. They had all seen better days, were coated with dust and didn't look as if they would feature anything as advanced as remote controls. I wasn't bothered by their junk shop presence, and I chuckled to think that at least I would be able to watch Corrie that night.

I took the opportunity to wash some socks, underpants and a tee shirt. I had only slight feelings of guilt as I hunted down a few clothes pegs from a rucksack pocket and strung the items along one of the bungees that I now stretched across the sash window that I had managed to prise open. The flapping garments didn't enhance the appearance of my little grotto in any way and they looked a damn sight worse when viewed from the street as I realised later on. What would the Middlemarch producers have thought? I was just in time to do a bit of shopping. I was still keen on the idea of upgrading my footwear so I thought that, with half hour until closing time, I could easily do the archetypal 'man shop' – in - get what you want – out – job done. In the first shop, I found a pair of slip on shoe/trainers almost straight away. I quite liked the look of them and they were a bit different. They seemed to be comfortable enough although we all know the wicked lies that these inanimate objects will concoct just so as you will provide them with a home. Beds are the same. Taken together, new shoes and a new bed can ruin your life. How much of any twenty-four hour period are you either lying down trying to sleep, or on your feet, walking, running, climbing stairs or queuing. This went through my mind as I asked the woman what size the shoes were.

'Eights,' she said.

'Have you got any sevens?'

'I'll have a look.' But she didn't have any sevens – Sod's law. I tried both eights on but there was a bit too much room in the toe end of them. I wasn't prepared to take the chance but I thought I might come back if I had no joy elsewhere. I had a lack of concern about my appearance (functionality was more important) that might have allowed me to cycle in my vintage 4x4 squash trainers but it wouldn't stretch to going around town in them on a Friday night. But now time was running out, even if I was 'man shopping'. I descended along one of the innumerable alleyways that crisscrossed the town and hit the main thoroughfare - this was more like a conventional high street, pedestrianised as you might expect, but still pretty. A Millets store presented itself and I tried on a pair of sandals that I liked - a bit of a cross between sporty and Jesus, I thought. But I still had about ten minutes left so I thought I'd see if there were any sports shops around. I found one that yielded nothing but some assistants who were eager to pack up and go home, so I shot back to Millets to buy the sandals.

Back at the hotel, I lay on the bed, closed my eyes and fell into my customary late afternoon nap. When I came to, I headed for the communal bathroom and was relieved to find that nobody else had had the same idea as I: I locked myself in and ran a deep bath before descending into the warm water with a sense of eager anticipation. It seemed to have been a hectic day and it was such a treat to now experience some of the finer aspects of civilisation. I ran back over the main events of the day in my mind.

Sitting in the Safeway café that morning had reminded me of a whole afternoon spent with Cherie in a similar supermarket 'restaurant' in Poole, two years earlier. I remembered just how cool and patient she could be when crossed with adversity. We were on our way to Spain on the motorbike. We had left for Poole in plenty of time for the ferry crossing to Cherbourg at two o'clock. However, I had a nagging worry about having no chain to lock the bike to fixed objects on our travels. It's easy enough to lock a motorbike, but if it's not attached to something permanent like a lamppost, thieves just pick the whole thing up and cart it away in a van. My brother Nick had phoned the night before to say I could borrow his. He lives in Gloucester which is a bit of a detour, but I didn't think it would upset our schedule too much and it would save me fifty quid or more. So, fatefully, I decided to pick up Nick's chain.

Having reached Gloucester, it took ages to find a way of safely attaching it to the bike. By the time we eventually got on to the Poole road we were cutting it fine. When I realised what a tortuous route it was, I knew we would miss the ferry by at least half an hour. I shouldn't give the impression here that I made all the decisions without consulting Cherie. But she wasn't too hot on spatial awareness (at least out of a city) and she was happy to trust my judgement. When we arrived at the near empty ferry terminal, we concurred with a fellow –late arrival in a camper van. He kindly allowed us to use his mobile phone to change our reservation to the midnight crossing. We then had to face the prospect of a long wait. We couldn't sit and relax as you might in a car. We couldn't leave the bike out of our sight for fear of having luggage stolen. And to make matters worse, we knew that heavy rain had been forecast for the afternoon. On this occasion the weatherman was spot on, and we ended up in a supermarket café forlornly watching the puddles grow to the rhythm of the emptying skies ... for hours. A brief respite tempted us out for an exploratory ride, but more rain soon had us scurrying back to the supermarket.

In the evening, we found a pub where we could watch over the bike but, of course, I couldn't drink. Unbelievably, there was a further hitch. A chemical spill in the harbour delayed the docking of our ferry so we didn't actually board until half past one in the morning. We'd been kicking our heels for nearly twelve hours. All through this, not once did Cherie admonish me, nag me or moan. She just took the totally pragmatic view that the mistakes had not been made on purpose, that there was nothing that could be done and that what was needed now was to consider our next best option.

For all the cursing I directed at myself, she would simply tell me, 'It's Ok. It's all right - don't worry, Dear.'

In the bath I thought about my progress so far. Again I wondered whether I could make it all the way to the Shetlands and in particular, under my own steam. I knew exactly what Cherie would have said:

'I know you'll make it.'

She knew how determined I can be when I set my mind on something. On one occasion she stayed home when I decided I wanted to try a cycle ride longer than my usual twenty to thirty miles. We spent the night with my brother Nick and his wife Vicky in Gloucester. The next day, I went off to the London motorbike show on the back of Nick's ZZR 1100 and Cherie drove home. We had left my mountain bike in Gloucester, so I pedalled back to Merthyr via the Forest of Dean taking a scenic detour up the A40 before crossing the Brecon Beacons. The distance was around a hundred miles, and Cherie said she would stay at home so I could phone to be collected if I got into trouble.

I made it all the way but whenever we retold the story, Cherie always used that same expression, 'I knew you would do it.'

She always had so much faith in me, and the memory of that made the tears flow cool down my bath-warmed cheeks.

Now I wondered why I was making this particular trip. Yes, to get away from it all - to avoid the well-intentioned phone calls and house visits. Yes, to give me time to think. Yes, because I thought a physical challenge would be good for me. So was I doing the trip for myself? It couldn't be for Cherie I supposed.

'Cherie is gone now.' I didn't have to remind myself. Still, I thought that maybe I was doing it for the both of us. I knew that Cherie had thought that to cycle to the Shetlands was a good idea and the trip was giving me that essential element - time. Many memories of time we spent together had flowed into my mind as I had been interminably pedalling along.

'But, wouldn't I have had these thoughts had I stayed at home?' I debated.

'I'll still have plenty of time for that when I get back,' I answered myself.

I came to the conclusion that this trip was definitely something different. The fact that I knew Cherie would have approved was also another little way that I could carry out her wishes.

It occurred to me that the trip drew a line in the sand between Chapters Six and Seven in my life. Chapter Six – my life over the last eleven years with Cherie - Chapter Seven – whatever comes next. Chapter One was my early life growing up just outside Cheltenham in a caravan on a small site surrounded by orchards. Chapter Two was the move to the terraced streetscape of one of the less salubrious districts of Cheltenham itself. Chapter Three, the move back to rurality in the Vale of Glamorgan and my secondary school years. Chapter Four, university in Swansea. Chapter Five was my time with my first wife and the formative years of my two children. My life seemed to have been very episodic and I wondered whether this was the same for everyone. I thought not, if only because of the changing locations that were involved for me at each stage.

It seemed that thinking of my life as a book with chapters was quite apt. What was happening to me now did not make full sense without looking at the preceding chapters. But it could stand on its own and whatever happened next, would lay the foundations for subsequent chapters. I wondered what Chapter Seven was going to hold for me and whether it would be the last chapter.

I thought once more of the day's ride. Today had been the best cycling day so far. It had been surprisingly good to feel cool rain rather than the blazing sunshine that had accompanied me from Day One. Thinking back to the previous day, it occurred to me that I might have been suffering from the early stages of heat exhaustion. I was so relieved to find the Raven after all the other pubs had been closed. Today, I had felt much fitter and I wondered whether it was because I had struck a better balance between pedalling and walking. I climbed out of the bath feeling hot and sweaty as I usually do, and took in the view from the window for a few minutes while I cooled off. Then I realised it was time for Corrie and made moves to get the television on.

The first one didn't seem to work – a light came on but pressing buttons and twiddling knobs did nothing more. I swapped plugs in the sockets, untangled wires, plugged in various leads – all to no avail. I chuckled to myself at the irony of it all. I did want to see Corrie so I thought it might be an idea to see if the landlord was around. Whether I had failed to notice before, or whether it had just appeared, I can't be sure, but there on the landing was another telly. It had the same attic look as the others but I decided to purloin it and give a try. It came as a surprise to hear the sound of the pre-Corrie adverts but there was no picture. However, after fiddling for a while, a picture could be discerned through the snowy reception and it was, needless to say, fairly easy to follow the plot. Cherie would have been proud of me.

After a welcome coffee, made with the usual B & B sachets, and a half hour dose of Corrie, I prettied myself up and, on exit, tried unsuccessfully to lock my door in its flaky paint frame. Satisfied with hoping for the best (it's easy to be blasé if you've never been robbed) I set off down the rickety stairs and headed into the town. Cherie would have loved this I knew, as I passed once more through quaint alleys with nooks, little shops and art galleries. There seemed to be plenty of pubs and I couldn't decide which one to plump for. In the end I probably made the wrong, albeit interesting, choice. I was happy with my own company, but I had been alone most of the day so I didn't quite know what to do when a character came to sit by me and introduced himself through his hobby rather than by his name. The hobby in question was collecting shells from the beach in Skegness and he was overwhelmed with the brilliance of this unusual pursuit. Naturally, I found it difficult to share his enthusiasm, but I politely listened and nodded at what I felt were the appropriate times.

I noticed my new companion's tattoos, and in an old fashioned and snobbish way thought, 'What do you expect?'

After a little prompting, he picked up my Welsh accent, then went on to tell me a story about a lorry driver he used to know who was from Cardiff. The trucker in question seemed to have been OK but when he jumped up into his cab and put his hands on the wheel, my shell-collecting companion noticed that his hands shook all over the place. It turned out that the man had cancer from which he died quite soon after.

I finished off my drink and made my apologies. As I sauntered in search of the next pub, I thought about the man I had just left. He was definitely strange, but it was still fairly early and I concluded that I should expect some of society's more peripheral characters to inhabit near empty bars before the mainstream drinking hours. I went into two other bars and struck up less interesting conversations. It occurred to me that I could wander around Stamford all night and miss the sort of place I was looking for – fairly crowded with a mix of ages and some women as well as men.

In the event, the way I put it to the only other person in a rather hollow wooden floored bar was: 'Are there any oldies places around?'

He was younger than I, but he understood what I meant and gave me directions to The Crown. I found it easily and walked into exactly the sort of place I wanted. It reminded me of a pub in Merthyr that I used to go to with Cherie and also BC ('Before Cherie', as we used to call it). It was called The Wellington, referred to by everyone as

'The Wellie'. It was fairly small and more or less square in shape. The beauty of the place was that it was well run and it employed plenty of bar staff on busy Friday nights. There were quite a few seats but most of us ended up standing. The room would be shoulder to shoulder by half past ten as people made sure they got in before the door closed at eleven. A trip to the toilet took ages, not only because of the jostling bodies, but because every other person would be a friend, ex squash partner, colleague or stranger, equally fuelled with intoxicated sociability and all caught up in the general atmosphere of good cheer and just as eager as I was to engage in conversation.

The Crown could not be exactly the same for me, being a total stranger, but it did have the same happy feel about it. I didn't really want to stand and I managed to slip in to a seat as someone left. With my back to the wall, I had a good view of the rest of the room and I settled down to people watch for two pints worth of time – in effect about forty minutes. As I looked around, I couldn't help imagining Cherie walking into the room. She had excellent posture and she always moved with a deliberate sense of purpose exuding the confidence borne out of her fit athletic figure, good dress sense, careful preening and quite often, a striking hat, that everyone would want to try on – although they wouldn't have the confidence to wear it for real. Predictably, no woman came through the door to compare and I was warmed and saddened at one and the same time. My eyes fixed on a lady who was holding a large glass of red wine and stood near the bar. She was mature, I'd say late forties, and she was teamed up with another younger woman who had 'Done a Cherie' on me earlier on at the bar. Like Cherie, she was quite petite and she had used this to great effect in slithering through the crowd to the front, presumably catching the eye of the barman and unfairly cheating me out of my rightful turn to be served.

The two women moved to sit at the other end of the room and I wondered whether I should go and talk to them. I had been sat on my own for some time now and the prospect of female company appealed to me. Still, in a busy pub on a Friday night, I felt uncomfortable with the idea because of the obvious connotations that would be drawn. I suppose that these days the same inferences may well be drawn if I were to approach a strange man for conversation but that didn't occur to me. By this time, I had drunk quite a few pints of assorted beers, I'd say about five and it was this plus a resolve to bite the bullet, that prompted me out of my little cubbyhole.

'Do you mind if I join you for a while?' was the totally unoriginal line that came out, half expecting them to tell me to 'sling my hook', but the two women were fine - in fact they were very welcoming. I chatted to them for about an hour though I couldn't really remember much of it the next day; I'm sure they did send out signals that they were married, so perhaps they did think I was on the prowl. I remembered telling them about Cherie at some point – maybe this was because I wanted to talk about her – she had certainly been in my thoughts a lot. Perhaps it was to put them at ease so they wouldn't consider me a nuisance. But the main reason I told them was because I had already decided that I would not keep Cherie's death a secret. I asked her once, what exactly she wanted me to say to friends and people in work about her terminal cancer.

'Yeah - tell them – I need all the sympathy I can get,' was her response.

So I had decided that if it was good enough for her, it was good enough for me. Why try to hide the truth or bottle it all up? As far as these two strangers were concerned, I hoped they wouldn't mistake me for a fitness fanatic or worse, a sad freak with no friends and no life. With the love and support of all those around me over the past months, what could be further from the truth? I did enjoy the company of those two ladies that night, and it made a change to be in a bustling pub in a busy town with a real bed and a cooked breakfast to look forward to. All the same, it was a lonely walk back to the hotel.

The Ride:

Brinklow to Stamford

Distance: 50 miles

Stamford to Northlands

Saturday, July 7th

This was another day when I got temporarily lost. I imbibed in the full English breakfast that came as part of the hotel deal. It didn't really delay me at all because I didn't have to light up the Trangia to make coffee or pack up the tent. I was on the road just after nine. I had noticed a motorbike shop opposite the hotel; so, before I set off, I called in to see if I could get some fasteners for the faring on my VFR. A very friendly, older bloke ran the place. He was cast in the old-fashioned shopkeeper mould and we chatted for quite some time. After dragging myself away, and donning my waterproofs, I managed to get lost in the first couple of minutes of pedalling. I knew my way out of the town – or, so I thought - but it wasn't long before doubt got the better of me, and I halted to consult the map. I had indeed come the wrong way and had to retrace my steps, but I only wasted about ten minutes before I found myself, correctly, on the A6121 headed north for Bourne.

I was quite looking forward to this leg of the trip. The day before had been a good one; I was pleased with the ground I had covered and the fact that my body had stood up to the rigours well. I knew I was now entering Fen country and that the land would be as flat as a premiership pitch. This was the part of England sometimes called 'Little Holland' - it was even reclaimed by Dutch engineers back in the 16th century. I felt a surge of optimism; I thought I might even get further than the fifty miles I had covered yesterday. It wasn't long before the steady drizzle turned into something more serious – prolonged, heavy rain.

As I rode into the flat country, I soon realised that a lack of hills was not the panacea I had imagined. The pedalling was now relentless, with no relief. I still couldn't come off the saddle to pedal, as I might have done with an un-laden bike, and it wasn't that I hadn't got used to the new physics of balancing the bike with its load. The physics simply wouldn't allow me to pedal off the saddle. It made sense. If you watch someone pedalling out of the saddle, it's surprising how much the bike lolls from side to side. I had to make sure that I kept the bike as close to ninety degrees to the road as I could. If I threw the bike over just a shade, I could feel it starting to fall.

What made things worse was the straightness of the roads. They stretched like railway lines to a vanishing point, miles into the future. At least they would have, had it not been for the combination of mist and rain, which put up a curtain at about a hundred and fifty metres. Water was everywhere - not only above, but also on the road, streaming down the gutters and gurgling down the drains. And, every hundred metres the road would cross a minor or major field drain, basically a die straight river. The watery scene was completed with two other field drains that constantly kept the road company, one on either side.

Then I had an accident in a small place called Bourne. In the town centre, I cheekily filtered through a line of stationery cars that were waiting for the traffic lights to change. (I was mindful of the danger from a motorist's fist if I, per chance, scratched their pride and joy, in my attempt to aim the fat bike through slim gaps in the queued traffic). Pleased to be at the front when the lights changed, I led the procession of cars over the crossroads, typically crisscrossed with yellow paint. As I set off up my exit road, the A151, still conscious of holding up the file of cars behind, I spotted, too late, an enormous pothole. There was nothing for it but to hang on. In that split second, I didn't have time to predict the effects of the jolt but I sensed I was probably in trouble. I grimaced as the bike slewed off to the right. I couldn't hold it but was able to clumsily half stay on my feet as it collapsed underneath – after all, I wasn't going very fast and the height I had to fall was now a fraction of what it used to be due to my ridiculously low saddle position. The bungees securing the rucksack didn't fly off but couldn't stop the luggage falling to the side and the throwing the bike off balance. I was stuck in the middle of the road in the pouring rain with a big line of cars, lorries and buses tailing back across the junction. As the lights changed – gridlock! Travel in all directions was now blocked – by me! How many drivers heeded that old television public safety film which admonished, 'Good drivers do not enter the box until their exit is clear!'

It was a busy time of the day in a busy market town. Thank God for tinted windows. I looked back apologetically to car number one, but couldn't see anything through the windscreen. I was too embarrassed to even attempt to struggle to release the bungees, so I awkwardly succeeded in manhandling the whole sorry collection as far as the curb. The cars started to move along, correcting their steering to get around the obstacle that was still me in the gutter. I imagined the insults.

The bike prone, the rucksack underneath it, my metal thermos had rolled some distance away, and me in my untrendy waterproofs looking like the last kid left as the captains picked their football teams. Appearances though, were the least of my worries as I set about rectifying the situation.

I had come to dread packing the load on to the bike, and here, in this most public of places, it was worse. I had developed a sort of knack but it depended on finding a decent wall or a reasonably wide post. Then, I could hump the gear, as gently as was possible, on to the rack and hope that the bike would stay still. On this occasion, it was a shop window that kindly offered me the support I needed, and I managed to pack the load, for once at my first attempt, under the glower of scores of imagined bystanders. As I got underway, I resolved to get some more bungees. It would add to the rigmarole of loading the bike, not to mention the increased danger from flying elastic bands with metal hooks, but I didn't want a mishap like that again. Thank God I had been going slowly at the time. I imagined what it would have been like had I been speeding down a hill at thirty miles an hour whilst being overtaken by a juggernaut.

I settled back into the ride and picked up the unidentified, but nevertheless pleasant, fragrances of the countryside. As I trundled across the pancake landscape the rain continued to fall and I could feel its weight. By now I was getting wet – my waterproofs were good but they were lightweight with breathable fabric and they had their limits. The roads were quiet, especially as I got on to the B1180 and made my way towards Pinchbeck. It was an eerie experience and I could have been in a different world. Mind you, who the hell would have wanted to be out in weather like that? Even so, it didn't bother me, nor does it usually for that matter. I take the view that the world is by and large, a wonderful and a beautiful place. Being out in the rain, or the wind, or for that matter, in the middle of the night, should be savoured as much as any sunny spring morning or balmy summer's afternoon.

I remembered being out in the middle of Llandegfeth Reservoir, near Pontypool in South Wales, when I was a fledgling windsurfer. In those days, I was so keen on the sport I would turn up at the lake even if there was only a breath of wind. This particular day there was only the slightest breeze and as a result, pedestrian windsurfing. Suddenly, the sky darkened and the wind completely disappeared. I dropped the sail into the lake and sat down on my board. I was then sensually and emotionally overwhelmed by what happened. The lake had turned black and the rain now pummelled its surface – each drop producing a silver plume as it struck. In awe, I gazed upon a three hundred and sixty degree silver curtain of splashes. Flashes of lightning synchronised to deafening thunderclaps in a glittering finale. I felt totally alone but completely at peace. It occurred to me then as now, that most people would miss out on experiences such as this. I considered myself to be very lucky.

A main road and the sight of a pub that showed all the classic signs of being open interrupted my reverie. It was only about one o'clock and not time to start drinking, but I was in need of a rest and some refreshment, so I wheeled around to the back of the pub and propped the bike against the wall. There, in the middle of nowhere, in the pouring rain, I didn't see theft as a problem and I couldn't be bothered to mess around so I just left everything there, save for my map. The pub was fairly busy with little space at the bar and a sprinkling of people occupying many of the tables. It might sound a bit macho, but I truly do find it difficult ordering coffee in a pub. Nevertheless, I succeeded as a pool of water developed around me. It was the product of rivulets that gathered momentum and volume as they ran down my legs and on to the floor. A few friendly comments and quips from customers were directed towards me as I waited to be served, and these made me feel very welcome.

As I waited for my coffee, I perused the map and noticed that its protective waterproof pouch was not so waterproof - a puddle had developed on the inside and I had to break the Velcro seal, remove the soggy map and drain it. The atmosphere in the pub was surreal. In the middle of the day, it was dark enough to be night-time. The warming hubbub of conversation also made it feel like evening, but there I was, burning my lips on hot coffee (of all things) as I cautiously took the smallest of sips. And, I was so incredibly wet. What was also strange was that I did not feel alone. I ordered my second cup of coffee and felt completely at peace. As I sat on my own, drying out slightly, I was content to pore over the map and generally take in my immediate surroundings. But, contentment was evenly balanced with an appreciation for the need to 'get on'; so, I eventually pulled myself out of the wooden seat that had been so comfortable, and donned my very damp - though no longer dripping - waterproof gear. I was aware of the locals watching me as I togged up, and I smiled in their general direction as I left.

After a little confusion as to directions – was it left or right? - for once I took the correct option and struck out for Boston on the A16. Although it was a main road, it was fairly quiet and the Fenland landscape remained characteristically flat. A few miles from Boston, the rain eased off and the cloud colour faded to pale, rather than dark grey. Despite the light traffic on the inward journey, Boston was very busy. I found the tourist information centre in the middle of town and propped the bike up against the window so I could keep an eye on it. A street market had attracted hordes of people and I had to wait a while to be seen. There was a campsite about ten to twelve miles further north. The brochure indicated that it didn't have much in the way of facilities; in fact, it had no shower, which was quite a disappointment – a shower at the end of a long day made a big difference to my general feeling of well-being. I had every confidence in making the campsite, despite having found myself very comfortable in the pub at Pinchbeck. It would bring the day's journey to fifty miles and that was more than acceptable. I noticed on my bike computer that my average speed had increased over the last couple of days from nine to eleven miles per hour. This was a psychological tonic especially as it was coupled with the fact that I felt so much better physically.

I had a minor tour around the centre of Boston and watched a wedding at its impressive cathedral for a while. I stopped to take a photo of an old Rolls Royce that was being used as the bridal car in what looked like a big wedding. I could see the bride, groom and guests in the distance, having their pictures taken. Starting off on the final leg for the day, I wanted to get out of the town centre. I ended up bumping along some old cobbled back streets and had to ask directions a few times, on one occasion from the middle of a park I had been directed through.

I thought, 'How can I lose my way when my starting point is the town centre, and all I have to do is to get on the main road out - there are sign posts everywhere and I am the head of the geography department in a very large school?'

I suppose it has something to do with the way I see the world. I am guilty of not always taking account of my surroundings. I find I need to make a conscious effort to record landmarks so I can later find my way. Cherie used to do it naturally, town girl that she was – but she never knew where Scotland or France was. All the same, her type of spatial awareness was probably the most useful as far as everyday life is concerned. After dismounting and walking across a few roads via pelican crossings, I eventually found myself on the correct road, the A16 for Louth, and it was about twelve miles into the distance that I looked forward to finding my campsite.

All along, my intention had been to head for the east coast of England, because I was less familiar with it than the west. The shell collector in Stamford had extolled the virtues of Skegness, and I remembered two people I had met on my honeymoon twenty-five years ago telling me what a great place it was. However, I had received reports to the contrary, and although I had a serious internal debate about it, I eventually opted to miss out Skeggy and take the more direct route north. About six miles out of Boston, and starting to feel weary, I felt some gyp in my left knee. This was as ominous as the time I had felt the pull in my hamstring towards the end of Day One. I hoped that it was nothing serious and I thought it might just be a consequence of the relentless pedalling across the Fens. I began to feel disheartened and still had six miles to go to reach a campsite that had no shower, no village and, more crucially, no ale house within striking distance. It was about four o'clock as I cycled past a pub. It looked closed, but I was suddenly feeling at the end of my tether. I pedalled around the back and sought a secret hiding place, then walked into the bar. It was of the type that had previously been a number of rooms, but was now knocked into one large space. It was almost empty but there was a woman with a push chair and two young kids, a bloke on his own, two fairly old men at a table deep in conversation and a lady behind the bar who kept disappearing. Nearly always, when I stopped for a break, I took the map off the bike so I could see what was going on. Sitting on a bar stool and opening the map, I clocked my position as being just north of a village called Sibsey and close to a hamlet called Northlands.

    I had to wait a few minutes before the bar lady appeared again. I was still enamoured with Strongbow, even though the weather had turned sour, but there was no tell-tale pump.

    'This is the only cider we sell,' she said, 'but it's good and strong and, by the way, it's supposed to be cloudy.' She wanted me to understand this before she poured it. I nodded and affirmed my order with a single gesture. I was relieved to sit at the bar knowing I didn't have too much further to go. Suddenly, it struck me that I'd had enough. It was interesting how, in the late afternoon my resolve to camp seemed to dissolve, especially at the bar after a pint; so, when the landlady appeared again, I asked her about bed and breakfast in the vicinity. She kindly phoned a place nearby, but unfortunately it was full. On my stool, ten minutes passed before I got bored with looking around. I felt the uncomfortable twinge of being an intruder as I went to sit by an older bloke sitting at a table. Fortuitously, his mate had disappeared to the toilet so I had the chance to make conversation without butting in. At first the man seemed perplexed at my effrontery, but this quickly dissolved to affability and we settled in to conversation.

He was a fairly tall, well-built guy with plenty of grey hair left and rather large eighties spectacles masking a significant proportion of his face. His name was Samuel, and I quizzed him as to the origin of his unusual accent. He was originally from Canada but had lived in the UK for a long time. Further queries were needed to tease out his line of work, which he was reluctant to divulge. He was responsible for maintaining machines in an intensive poultry unit a few miles away. As I showed interest, he opened up more. He told me that the chickens were slaughtered when they were six weeks old; I squirmed a little - I am bothered by factory farming methods, but the pragmatism that I share with most others, allows me to lift chicken fillets off the supermarket shelf without too much reference to my conscience. Only now, confronted with the raw brutality (albeit still second hand), did the contradiction hit home.

He went on, 'The chickens are hung upside down by machine. At this point, fright causes them to relieve their bowels then they're dunked into electrified water which should kill them - but doesn't always. However, there is a man employed to finish them off with a knife if the water fails ... on the other side.'

Somewhere in the middle of this conversation, I had procured my second pint of local cloudy cider, and I was surprised to hear the landlady call out that that she was closing. A small quip from me invoked the response that she had never been open all along – just serving a few locals and doing me a favour. I left Samuel and went back to the bar glugging down the last inch of my cider.

Suddenly, Samuel broke the quietness, 'You can stay at my place if you like.'

A man had appeared behind the bar, but there were still just a few people in the room. All the same, I felt eyes burning into me. Clearly, this was a closed, small knit community in the Fens and an event had just happened.

Samuel continued, 'You're not gay are you?'

'No', I replied. 'Are you?'

'Definitely not.'

Our mutual heterosexuality confirmed, Samuel repeated his kind offer, and added that I could have a hot bath and that he would sort out a cooked supper for me. The way I felt about getting back on the bike left me little choice and I gratefully accepted, though eyebrows were still raised in the pub. The bar man asked if I had any form of identification. I produced my credit card from the bum bag around my waist, and he copied down my details on a pad. He was clearly aware that Samuel was laying himself wide open to this stranger that had appeared in their midst. He quietly warned me not to take any unfair advantage and told me what was already clear - that Samuel was a very decent bloke who was vulnerable, living as he did on his own. Samuel, who was still party to this conversation, perfunctorily commented that he had recently lost his wife. What a classic euphemism, 'Lost my wife.' I can understand why it's used – it's a way of avoiding the 'D' word. If you think about it, it sounds a bit daft - rather as if you are talking about a dog that's gone astray but with hope of it finding its way home.

Someone said to me back in Merthyr, 'I'm sorry you lost your wife.'

Of course, I appreciated the sentiment but I replied, 'I didn't lose her, she died.'

I wasn't trying to be awkward but it helps me to cope better if I hit the nail on the head. Using the words 'died' or 'dead' brought home to me the finality of Cherie's condition; it helped me internalise never being able to see her again. I didn't much consider whether I should divulge my own situation to Samuel but in this case, I sensed it might allay some of his anxiety.

'My wife died two weeks ago,' I said. 'That's why I'm doing this trip.'

Samuel gave me directions to his house which was only a couple of hundred yards away and off down a side road. Meanwhile, he got in to his car and was waiting for me by the time I had clambered back on the bike and cycled down. I parked the bike against the wall of his semi-detached house which had a large garden at the back.

'My wife was the gardener,' Samuel drew an arc with his pointed finger. 'I do my best, but I can't keep on top of it.' The house was clean and tidy but had the obvious look of a place two decades out of fashion. It's easy to understand I suppose. When you're young, you spend time and money sorting out the house - buying furniture, decorating and collecting knickknacks such as paintings and kitchen knives. Once you have it how you want it, time passes, and as you drift through middle age, you don't notice that things have moved on. You are unaware that your little nest has become a bit of a shrine to the seventies or eighties, and the fact that you have lost the decorating habit means it doesn't occur to you to do anything about it.

I followed Samuel upstairs, half carrying, half dragging the rucksack and its add-ons. Samuel showed me into my room for the night which was decorated in keeping with the rest of the house, with a double bed that Samuel's son and daughter in law used when they came to visit. Samuel repeated his offer of a bath, and I gratefully said I would take him up on it.

He went out to do some gardening but conceded half to himself and half to me as he disappeared, 'I don't think I'll make much of an impression.'

I looked around the bedroom - an old-fashioned carpet and two freestanding dark wooden wardrobes with a matching dressing table. I peeked through the net curtains to see that the room overlooked the front garden. Just the other side of the road the countryside opened out into the distance – flat, flat, flat. I ran the bath deep and the water started to run cold. It looked as if I had used up all of Samuel's hot water.

I felt a bit guilty but thought, 'If I'm going to have a bath, it may as well be a good 'un – I'll make sure to tell Samuel that I've used all the hot water.'

I wanted to give my leg a good soaking in the hope that it would sooth my knee. Yet again, I had a sense of foreboding that it was going to put an end to my cycling. I stayed in that hot, deep, hippopotamus bath for nearly an hour – initially just my eyes and nose breaking the surface. After a while, I heated up to a point where I had to drape my arms and legs over the sides in an attempt to cool down.

When I eventually left the bathroom, sweating profusely, I could hear Samuel in his own bedroom having a snooze, his snoring combining with voices from his portable TV.

'Now is the time for me to get a nap myself,' I thought. I woke, twenty minutes later and put on clean clothes. Downstairs, Samuel was busying himself about the place. He had prepared a cooked dinner that he now put into the microwave. As he served it to me, on a tray, I had the distinct suspicion that this was, in fact, his evening meal - one that he (or more likely someone else) had prepared for himself earlier that day. The food was set out on a plate with cling film covering it.

Samuel, is this your dinner?' I quizzed him lightly.

'No, no. No, indeed. I had my dinner while you were sleeping.' I didn't believe him. Samuel put the television on for me; and, after I had finished eating, he came into the room and we started chatting. He told me how his wife had died suddenly, before his eyes, only six months previously. Just before Christmas, they were getting ready to go out for the evening when he heard a thump from the next room. He went to investigate and found his wife lying on the floor. He dialled 999; but, by the time the ambulance arrived, it was too late – there was not a lot they could do and she died. As Samuel told me the story, I started to cry. Not just a snivel or a tear or two - it all came out - a total loss of control and an outpouring of grief that had not happened since before Cherie had died. Samuel understood and he quietly left the room.

A little later he began to talk about his past. He seemed to have been unlucky in love. He told me how his previous common law wife, a Belgian woman with whom he had a long distance commuting relationship, developed a secondary cancer and died. Before that, his first wife had been caught out when Samuel arrived home a day early from a business trip. He walked in to find her with another man, so that was the end of that. We talked about our respective situations for quite some time before going back to the pub.

As Samuel described in detail his current state of mind, I felt grateful that I at least had had the time and the opportunity to say goodbye to Cherie. We always talked about everything with no holds barred: what was going to happen to her, fears about pain (though not about dying), annoyance at missing out on the rest of the 'party', our feelings for each other and, sometimes, just touching and holding each other. Cherie always had a wonderful touch and she used it, almost without thinking. I would often lie on her lap and she would stroke my hair as I dropped into my power nap at the end of the afternoon or in the early evening. What bliss it was to feel my consciousness and all its turmoil slip away as I felt her closeness, her touch, her love. When we stayed in for a night in front of the TV, I would often gravitate to the floor, and if I rested my arm on her leg, she would nonchalantly play with my watch, a curiously comforting massage. When Cherie was ill in hospital, if I rested my hand on her and she would start to play with my watch.

Samuel, undoubtedly, would have had similarly endearing and comforting memories, but he hadn't had the chance to say goodbye, and it was this that caused him the greatest anguish. Coupled with the suddenness of her death, he kept imagining that she was still around. I have heard that this is common. Certainly my mother felt the same about my father when he died five years ago. A colleague of mine had asked me if I planned to sell the house when Cherie died.

'Why?' I replied.

'Too many painful memories,' he said. He was right in a sense - our house is full of Cherie. She had a wonderful eye for colour and loved designing décor, so apart from all the happy times we spent together in our home, each room is now a visual jolt.

But, as I said to my colleague, 'Memories are all I have left now – I cherish them.'

Cherie wasn't content to pick something off the shelf from B&Q. She knew what she wanted and she was prepared to pay twenty pounds a roll and wait two weeks for it to be delivered. I understood this and I used to switch off as she flicked through book after book of wall coverings in the local Fads store, occasionally offering a suggestion that may or may not have met with her approval. Now, I have to content myself with softly laying my lips on the wall and kissing the paper she chose.

It was very clear that Samuel was going through a lot of turmoil, and I felt a great deal of sympathy for him. I'm not sure, however, how empathetic I was. I suppose I should have been. In many respects we were in the same boat, but I didn't really see much of a parallel beyond the inescapable fact that we were both recent 'widowers' - what a horrible word that is. In a strange way, maybe that explained the difference between us – he was a widower and I didn't feel as if I were. It might just have been a generation thing because Samuel was quite a bit older than me but I thought it more likely that I didn't see things the same as he did – perhaps he saw himself as a victim whereas I didn't view myself that way. Because she died from cancer, I considered Cherie the victim and was used to feeling sorry for her rather than myself. At least for now.

We eventually made our way to the pub and bought each other a few drinks. Samuel said he quite liked playing pool so we had a couple of games; however, Samuel wasn't much competition for me (and I'm pretty useless), so there wasn't a lot of point in playing. Nor was there much atmosphere in the pub; or, maybe the emotional strain of the evening was taking its toll. Around closing time, we went back to the house, and Samuel turned in. I made myself a cup of coffee and settled down to write my journal. As I wrote about the day's events, I cried again.

However, as I did so, the thought kept coming into my head, 'Am I behaving this way because I feel I should be? Like an actor unable to escape from his role?'

Wasn't it strange? In the throes of despair, a part of me wouldn't let vent to honest emotion but instead, sought to interrogate the integrity of my feelings and my conscience. My thoughts went back to Samuel, his bereavement and his kindness, and I resolved to write him a note before leaving in the morning. He had 'had it tough', as they say, but he had helped me immensely that night.

Once I had finished the journal, I wrote the letter and propped it against a jar on the windowsill. I must have been more under the influence than I realised because I had the notion that I would be up at the crack of dawn and gone before Samuel stirred. Thinking back, the note may have sounded a bit corny, but I know I wrote from the heart when I thanked him for his trust and his hospitality. I cried again as I expressed my gratitude for being able to let my feelings out, and I wished him peace in the difficult times I knew he had to face in the future.

I must have been whacked, but I still didn't quite feel ready for bed. I unlocked the back door and went out into the garden. It was very black, and I fumbled my way around trying with little success to dodge the branches hanging from numerous trees. Having finally found my way to the back of the garden, I looked out across an open field. There was not a sound to be heard, and I stayed there for some minutes, rotating 360 degrees to take in the monochrome tranquillity. After everything that had happened since meeting Samuel, I was in melancholy spirits but curiously at peace too, as I decided that the day was done.

The Ride:

Stamford to Northlands (about 5 miles north of Boston on the A16)

Distance: 44 miles

Northlands to Wrawby

Sunday, July 8th

A cock crowing, and crowing and crowing, awoke me early. I had experienced roosters at dawn before, but this was unbelievable. In the end, I got up and went downstairs. Samuel was already up making coffee. I noticed the note had gone.

When I sheepishly referred to it, he just mumbled, 'Oh yes, I saw something.'

I was quite happy to leave it at that. I had said all I wanted to say in the note, so I changed the subject.

'What the hell is that cockerel playing at?' Samuel told me the story. A house a few doors up had kept hens for laying eggs but the house had caught fire a couple of years before. The hens had escaped out into the fields opposite and had become semi wild. The house was either unoccupied or had changed hands, so no one was interested in the poultry except a rogue cockerel who had appeared from nowhere. He, of course, was very interested indeed and was taking his duties as master of the harem very seriously. Every morning, he would crow his nuts off and all the birds would come out of the fields to answer his call and do his bidding. Talk of the devil, even as we spoke he started up again – it was deafening. No wonder, the little monster was now in Samuel's front garden. Wielding a broom, Samuel set off after him with a rather awkward and gangly gait exuding what might be best described as gentle fury. Of course, he stood no chance of catching the cockerel, but at least the racket now faded as the bird hopped off down the street, still defiantly making noises like a ball-kicking kid sent packing from a parade of lock up garages.

Samuel returned but didn't seem to have taken much satisfaction in his minor victory. He may have won the battle, but it looked like the war would go on for a long time yet. After a short conversation, I started to get my things together from upstairs while Samuel went out again to tackle the garden. He returned to steady the bike while I loaded up. I told him if he ever wanted to visit Wales he would always be welcome to stay with me, and I reminded him that I had left my address and telephone number on my note. With a 'Cheerio', I set off up the ruler-straight road just catching Samuel's wave in my peripheral vision.

'What does he make of me?' I wondered – we were two very different people and I doubted whether he really would want to visit me, and indeed, whether I would want him to.

The weather was quite cool, overcast and threatening to rain, but it managed to stay dry. I was still in Fenland with its long endless, bendless roads, but I noticed a slight incline, perhaps indicating that I was on my way out this huge shallow basin. The wind was against me, and it was a plodding slog for the first fifteen miles to Horncastle. Worse still, my left knee was still aching. The hot bath and the rest had not done the trick. Being Sunday, everything was quiet, and the back roads I was travelling on were virtually deserted. It was quite surreal and I started to feel lonely, almost as if I were the only person in the world. Maybe I was missing the hustle and bustle of the busier roads I had been on before – roads that always had a sprinkling of villages and towns, and streets full of people going about their business. My route now was as rural as I had encountered to date, and the only real feature of the landscape was its lack of features – interesting in itself, but only for a while. So, I noticed less of the scenery and found myself concentrating on the grind of pedalling, mildly irritated by the unfavourable wind and very much worried by my aching knee.

'Ow!' I cursed aloud. It was my knee. Momentarily wracked by a sudden searing pain, I thought it was going to seize up. Gingerly, letting up on the effort, I kept on pedalling. To my surprise, far from getting worse, the discomfort and pain actually seemed to ease. It was as if something had been released. However, I didn't put too much faith into this miraculous recovery, and I stopped to lower the saddle once again. I must say that it did improve things; I definitely felt a lot better. If my knee had packed in, I was in the middle of nowhere.

My thoughts turned to what I would have done: 'Dial 999, I don't think so. Get to a house? Get to an A & E department?'

Every option would signal the end of my journey. I returned to my resolve of Day One - if it was just pedalling that was the problem, I vowed once again to walk and freewheel. The prospect of catching the train still deflated me immensely and the thought struck me that I needed a rest day.

I had been cycling for just over an hour and a half when I started to feel hungry. Rounding a bend a garage came into view strategically placed at a T junction. It was the first sign of life since leaving Samuel's place; and, to my delight, it was open. It made sense to take advantage of this fact, because I had no guarantees, on a Sunday out in the sticks, where the next meal might come from. It was a mistake - a horrible sandwich (where was Cherie with her purloined stash of service station condiments?), a tasteless cheese pasty, a bottle of Lucozade (for its purported energy) and a Kit-Kat for desert. It wasn't even cheap.

'Remind me not to do that again,' I chided myself. After squirming around for a while, I managed to get my bum comfortable on a low wall outside the garage overlooking the road. Occasionally, a car passed. An uncanny chill was carried on the wind and a sense of desertedness engulfed me, as did my feeling of loneliness.

Not for the first time, I told myself, 'No one said this was going to be easy.' It gave me a little strength, but it didn't lift my spirits as I set off once more.

About ten miles down the road, I came to the village of Wragby. There was a pub at the crossroads, and I parked up the bike and went in. A few people were dotted around quite a small room. It didn't come over as a particularly friendly place though, as once again I resisted the strong urge to order a pint of something alcoholic, opting instead for a coffee and some crisps. Why I went for crisps I don't know - I rarely eat them. I must have fancied something savoury rather than my usual chocolate, although chocolate does go rather well with strong, unsweetened black coffee - crisps definitely do not. As I sat down in a corner, I was just in time to see Tim Henman go out of Wimbledon. I was hoping to stay a while and enjoy the latter stages of the match, but it ended all too soon.

The afternoon cycle was still a grind, but I felt a lot better, physically and spiritually. My knee held up, and I just kept going. I wanted to reach Brigg. Paradoxically, Brigg was a place I had never visited but knew quite well. Being a geography teacher, I often used Ordnance Survey map extracts from past GCSE examinations and one of these was of Brigg. Seeing an area only in map form naturally gives a different perspective. But after studying an area on a map, visiting the place in the flesh produces a *deja vu* effect. Put another way, it's a bit like looking into the future and being able to fortune tell. I have made a point of travelling to places I have only seen on a map, a number of times before.

One of the most memorable was a visit to Buttermere in the Lake District after interpreting the map with a group of thirteen and fourteen year olds. I hadn't long been seeing Cherie and it was one of the first trips we ever made together. The trip was only for two full days, but it is seared into my memory as if it were yesterday rather than eleven years ago.

We had camped at Buttermere for two nights. The first day, the weather was beautiful and we had had a long walk around the surrounding ridges, having scaled the steep valley side up to Red Pike. We were treated to magnificent views of Buttermere and Crummock Water, as we climbed up and up, taking regular breathers and turning around to admire the vistas. We regretted very much our decision not to bother to bring food and drink. On the second day, we went for a long bike ride. We had studied the OS map the night before and decided to hire mountain bikes from Keswick. We didn't want to be over ambitious. I hadn't cycled in a while and Cherie, although fit, had hardly been on a bike at all. So we planned to skirt the Lake District proper with its nasty hills and busy snaking roads, and follow a route that took us along quiet country lanes finishing at a pub where we guessed we'd be able to get some lunch. For the second day, we were lucky again with the weather, and we cycled off in high spirits. It was the first time either of us had ever used indexed gears on a bike and we were both very impressed with how slick the gear changes were. The gradients we did encounter posed no problems thanks to the low gear ratios featured on these 'new to us' mountain bikes. We made good time, unexpectedly with little effort, and reached the pub early. A table outside was chosen and our food was ordered as the garden began to fill up around us like a popular beach on a fine summer's day. There the similarity ended. As we waited for our meal to arrive, enjoying a drink without having to worry about drinking and driving, we started to get cold. It wasn't that it had become less sunny – the sun had been coming and going all morning. It was more that we must have cooled down now that we had stopped exercising; but, it was the chill in the wind we felt most, a wind hitherto unnoticed. We had been pedalling with the wind imperceptibly at our backs. No wonder the going had been so easy.

By the time lunch was finished, our shoulders were shrugging with discomfort as the cold started to penetrate bone - we didn't need further invitation to start the trip home. Only when we began pedalling did we really appreciate the strength of the wind. We had been cycling for some time, struggling against it, when we hit the main road and saw with horror, the signpost,

KESWICK 13 MILES

We had probably taken the wrong option in coming back along the main road, rather than the quiet country lanes we had used before. Although there were fewer hills, there was no respite from the wind that was effectively funnelled dead against us and stronger now, with no trees, bends or hills to act as windbreaks. That journey seemed to take forever. Both of our backsides were so sore, we had to stop every five minutes and take a rest. We ended up walking a lot of the time. Were we glad to hand those machines back when we finally made it. No more the wonderful mountain bikes with the superb gears – they had turned into monsters. Typical of Cherie though - no complaints were directed at me. I had been struggling, so she must have been suffering a lot more – we both moaned bitterly about our bums though. Those two evenings in the

Lake District were topped off with hearty meals at the pub in Buttermere, washed down with a fair amount of ale. Thoroughly deserved, we thought.

Now I was on my own. Nevertheless, my 'fortune telling' with the OS map in school had stirred my curiosity, and I was looking forward to reaching Brigg – had I been on foot, it would have put a spring in my step. As it was, I bowled along at a steady pace, forgetting my discomfort. I reached Brigg at about four o'clock and cycled into the main pedestrianised thoroughfare. Up and back again, I couldn't see anywhere I might get a cheap night's accommodation. I stopped a young couple to make enquiries. They told me there was a campsite about two miles up the road - it had a pub and only charged £2.00 a night. I had sort of set my heart on a bit of luxury that night, but two quid and a pub on the doorstep was enough to entice me to carry on a bit further. I became aware of how much I perked up towards the end of a day's cycling. It must have been psychological rather than physical.

'I can make another two miles - that's only about quarter of an hour - just take it easy - you can always get off and walk, Billy Boy.' The other consideration was the fact that the campsite was on my way to the Humber Bridge – I would actually be covering some of tomorrow's ground. That thought clinched it, and I ignored the temptation to test my fortune-telling out on Brigg. Setting off, I soon had to dismount and was forced to walk up the hill towards Wrawby.

The directions from the young couple were accurate; the pub soon came into view on my left. As I approached, I felt a huge surge of relief. The weather was beautiful now and the patio area of the pub was full of families enjoying a drink in the sunshine. Raised voices, banter and laughter filled the air and I imagined eyes following me as I self-consciously dismounted and propped the bike against the wall in full view. This was probably the best form of security under the circumstances. I exchanged friendly comments with a group sat at a nearby table and went into the pub. The room was long and busy and at the far end, I could see some trestle tables with what looked like the remains of a buffet on them. I had to wait a while before getting served. Having ordered a pint of lager, I enquired about camping.

'Two quid a night for a small tent ... and there's a shower, clothes washing facilities and a tumble drier ... you might want to take some fifty P's with you.'

It looked as if I had made the right choice to camp after all – two quid for all that! Maybe taken in by the pervading aura of bonhomie, I cheekily asked about the buffet.

'Is that food going to waste down there?'

'Yes it is - help yourself if you like – no problem.'

The place had obviously been very busy until quite recently. There was a mess on all the un-cleared tables. Ashtrays were full of ash, nips and crisp packets that had been crumpled up but had now re-sprouted. On the previously polished surfaces was spilled beer, more ash, fag packets and semi peeled soggy beer mats randomly scattered beneath half-finished pints and other assorted drinks. I set my pint down at a table that looked slightly less cluttered and dirty. I discovered that where the tables weren't wet they were sticky – not the ideal spot to satisfy the hunger that now enveloped me. I wandered down to the end of the room and the trestles, feeling I was being watched but not really caring what people thought, as, tramp–like, I gathered together a staling meal of sandwiches with their corners already turned up like pirate's hats, quartered pork pies, flaking mini sausage rolls and one or two hardening cubes of cheese impaled on cocktail sticks. Luckily, I found what looked like an unused paper plate and carried my stash back to the table.

Despite the bright sunshine outside, it was gloomy in the pub as I started to wolf down my catch, unaware that I was indeed being watched. Despite my initial hunger, I gave up on some of the pirate-hat sandwiches and a pallid vol-au-vent, and sat back to drink my chilled Stella. I wondered about the future and my way forward.

Three important things occurred to me. First, Cherie was the epitome of pragmatism. If the boot had been on the other foot, and it had been me that had died, she would have, as she always did when crossed with adversity, 'just got on with it.'

Secondly, I had said to Cherie twice, maybe three times, that I would absolutely have swapped places with her. Given that I am generally self-centred and hedonistic, that was quite something – the hypothetical offer was from my heart and I meant it. I would have gladly laid down my life in order for her to have carried on. I had already lived five years longer, and I had achieved so many of my ambitions. Cherie was just setting out on many of hers.

Lastly, I remembered my thoughts of a few days ago – my life as a book. This was the end of Chapter Six – Chapter Seven must go on come what may. I think I was trying to rationalise and justify the fact that I was feeling good. I had overcome some pressing physical and mental strains that day, and I must have been experiencing a sense of achievement as I relaxed my weary body.

A minute or two later, and seemingly out of nowhere, she appeared and sat next to me.

'You're not really eating that are you?'

'Yes, I suppose I am,' I answered back in slight defiance.

The woman was of medium height, not too overweight, but tight fitting jeans and a tee shirt that hinted at ample breasts exaggerated her plumpness. I noticed she had a couple of kids in tow as she continued her line of enquiry.

'What you doing eating that?'

'I was hungry and it was there.'

'You must be mad.'

We settled into a conversation. Her name was Melanie, and she soon learned that I was on an extended bike trip. I can't remember if I told her about Cherie – I don't think I did, probably because she didn't ask the 'Why?' question. The two kids sheepishly smiled in the background as we chatted, and I grinned back. In fact, the conversation was quite short, and it was brought to closure by a stark invitation.

'Do you want a proper meal?'

'I wouldn't mind.'

'Come around to my place in an hour and I'll cook you a meal – chilli con carne.'

'Are you sure?'

She was quite genuine in her offer, and I accepted. As she told me her address and gave me instructions, I noticed her tattoos. I'm not a lover of them at all – it's the permanence of the things. I know piercings can leave marks, especially on the eyebrow but at least the scarring tends to be quite minor. However, tattoos are like graffiti on the body, except with graffiti you can forget about that garage door or that sub-way wall. But you can't escape your arm, your back or the eyes stamped one on each cheek of your backside (apologies to my brother, Chris!).

Melanie must have taken pity on me, and I was touched by her generosity and kindness. After she had gone, I was left to ponder. I thought about the wisdom of inviting a total stranger back to your house. Of course, Samuel had done the same, but this lady had two kids as well as herself to consider. There can't be many people who would take such a risk, and I wondered why fortune was playing into my hands. It seemed to come down to the startling prospect that either I must be Mister Handsome or Mister Charisma, or she must be Missus Goodie Two Shoes or Missus Bonkers.

I had an hour, so I thought I'd better avail myself of some of the luxuries of the site. I finished my drink and hurried off to do a bit of washing. I didn't have time to wait for the drier, but I put in my money and decided to pick up the laundry later. If someone wanted to pinch my socks, pants and tee shirt, it was a chance I was willing to take. I phoned Viv, a friend of mine from school, then had a shower and spruced myself up (in so far as I could) before setting off for Melanie's place.

It was only a five-minute walk and I politely arrived slightly late. One of the kids answered the door with a beaming face and let me in. Melanie showed me to the living room and made her apologies as she returned to the kitchen to finish cooking the meal. I stayed in the living room and talked to the children. They were very friendly, articulate and curious, and I enjoyed their company.

I genuinely like children and, for the most part, I enjoy working with them. I have never regretted following the vocational instincts that picked out teaching as my chosen career as early as thirteen years of age.

In Melanie's large square living room, I nestled into a deep soft armchair asking and answering questions until she called the kids to come and get their food. The eldest brought me my chilli con carne on a tray and we all settled down to eat. The meal was very welcome – I'm sure my earlier 'dinner' would not have sustained me for long. After I had finished, I entertained the two children with a few riddles. I collect these and try to commit them to memory. I can usually keep youngsters gainfully occupied for half an hour with just one of these lateral-thinking problems as I listen to their elaborate theories and commend them on their cleverness. Then I break it to them that they haven't quite hit upon the right answer - dashing their hopes, before feeding them with a clue to set them on to a different line of enquiry. On this occasion, it was the story of a man travelling towards the top of a mountain with a rucksack on his back. When he gets there he knows he is going to die – how come? In between listening to the kids' theories, I talked with Melanie.

'I have very strong religious beliefs,' she said. 'That's why I asked you come around for dinner.'

'Thanks. It was very generous of you, but you know, I'm not religious at all.' Melanie didn't mind and went on to talk fairly non-stop. I didn't feel any need to interrupt her as she told me that she was renting the place and had moved around quite a bit. She made her living as a vocal entertainer singing with backing tapes, and she gave me a demonstration - she was what is sometimes described as 'a belter'. Melanie went on to say how she seemed to be at odds with the local community who had failed to accept her. This had not been helped by the fact that she had once performed in the local pub where we had met earlier. By her own admission, her act is rather loud and raucous and it did not go down well with the village locals. Melanie spoke in contemptuous tones about some of these people whom she saw as small minded and blinkered - not the most religious of thoughts maybe.

I told her that I had been on the pub/club circuit myself and mentioned that I played a harmonica as well as a guitar. In no time, one of the kids produced a harmonica and pleaded with me to play. To their delight, I gave a short rendition of 'Oh Suzanna'. I pointed out to them that a harmonica is a very easy instrument to learn, especially when played in the 'first position'. This means that the melody is played mainly by blowing rather than sucking. Put another way, when playing with another instrument such as a guitar, if the song is in the key of G, then a G harmonica would be used. There is no need to buy a book on how to play like this. With bit of practice blowing and sucking most people will get to play a simple tune intuitively, without thinking - very much like the way we learn to whistle. The kids must have been convinced because they quibbled over whose turn it was next, handing the harmonica back and forth and sharing dribble whilst not quite making any recognisable tune. When they offered it back to me for another demonstration, I tactfully declined.

After dinner, I must have spent about an hour chatting before the kids were told to start getting ready for bed. I carried on, mostly listening to Melanie who stuck to the same themes – religion, her show, and the small-mindedness of the local people. Nothing was said directly, but I had the feeling that Melanie would have liked me to stay longer, in fact, until the morning. I wasn't interested, and I felt I needed a change of scenery; so I thanked everyone sincerely for their hospitality and took my leave.

I didn't get very far. The pub was only around the corner; since I wasn't ready to turn in, I was sitting at the bar within minutes. It was fairly quiet but the landlord and landlady were there and we soon got into a conversation. My trip inevitably came up and the people around the bar were very interested to hear my story. I don't remember buying many drinks, especially as the night wore on and we started tucking in to a few whiskeys. My revelations about Cherie's death, prompted the landlord Peter, to lay his own feelings open. His main problem was with his estranged children who had been poisoned against him by his ex-wife.

'Such a familiar and sad tale,' I thought.

Through tears he said, 'It's breaking my heart not being able to see them. What's worse, I can't even tell them how much I love them.'

I told him about how Cherie would write to me (even though we lived together) on the occasions when we had had a major falling out. She realised she could express her thoughts and feelings with the pen in a way that wasn't possible face-to-face. She was able have her say unopposed and detached from the heat of the argument. In turn, I was able to digest her point of view and re-read her letter several times. Whenever Cherie employed this tactic, she made sure she wasn't around. It made me want to hold her, kiss her, make up and tell her I loved her – I couldn't wait until she got home. As we faced each other across the bar, both Peter and I had tears rolling down our cheeks.

The conversation turned to other subjects but eventually came around to Melanie, my hostess earlier that evening. The landlady spoke of her in very unkind terms and decried the show that she had performed in the pub. I defended her,

'It's not easy settling in small village a long way from home. I know she's a bit unconventional but she's been very kind to me. Her kids are lovely.'

Peter agreed with me as we argued the point, but his wife seemed unconvinced. Poor Melanie was not going to crack this one. It was interesting that I had enjoyed hospitality and friendship from both sides of the feud. What a shame they couldn't see eye to eye when they lived in the same small village.

I had been toying with the idea of taking a rest day which I mentioned to Peter.

'Great,' he said. 'We'll show you around. There's a lot to see and you can have lunch with us.' I liked the idea of spending more time with my new friends, but I didn't commit myself. I knew then that, despite the booze in my brain, I probably wouldn't stay another day. The Humber Bridge was on the agenda for the next leg. In my mind, it marked the boundary between the south and the north of the country and I wanted to get there. It was way past closing time by now, so I said my goodbyes and plodded off to my tent, miraculously remembering to pick up my stuff from the tumble drier on the way.

The Ride:

Northlands to Wrawby (just east of Brigg and 10 miles south of the Humber Bridge)

Distance: 50 miles

Wrawby to Scarborough

Monday, July 9th

Considering I'd been to bed so late the night before, I managed to get going early, having already discounted the idea of staying and meeting up with Peter and his wife. With coffee brewed and drunk and the tent and everything else packed up, I was off by ten to nine. Rather than cycling, I wheeled my bike across the loose chippings on the car park, wisely deciding that to slip on this stuff would at best mean re-packing and at worse cause me injury, even more likely as I could still feel the effects of the alcohol from the night before. The weather was fine and I was looking forward to picking up breakfast somewhere. I had looked at the map, and decided to head for the Humber Bridge via the main road. There were quieter roads but they were less direct, and it was likely they would have involved more ups and downs. Considering I make my living from geography, I only recently noticed how much engineering goes into grading a main road - a motorway even more so – where the hills that have been sliced into cuttings are followed by sections that have been raised up on embankments giving good views across flood plains.

Luckily for me, a greasy spoon appeared on my side of the road, just two or three miles into my day. Apart from the slight hangover, the cycling was made difficult by a fairly stiff breeze that was dead against me. I leaned the bike against a storage shed and stepped up into the port-a-cabin. Two blokes were well into their breakfasts as I ordered a full English for myself. I sat down at a corner table and started to read one of the complimentary papers. It seemed that in no time at all, breakfast was served. And what a breakfast it was – huge – a truly massive greasy spoon. As I tucked in, the two men finished and disappeared, so I had the place to myself. I disjointedly read the paper chasing beans around the plate, surgically removing fat from the bacon and tucking into sausage, bacon, toast and black pudding. What a feast, topped off with an enormous mug of hot black coffee. Through the steam, I must have spent half an hour half watching the passing traffic out of the small port-a-cabin window.

I chatted for a few minutes to the owner, a lady in her middle years. She told me she was from Grimsby and that she had operated that particular pitch for quite a while. She said she was quite well known by locals and regular passers-by, and she said it was surprising how people would talk to her. They would let her into their inner most secrets and ask for advice. Apart from making a few bob from the business, the lady (whose name I never asked) described how she loved her work and how she took her role as an ad hoc counsellor very seriously. If she had lived in California, she might have made millions as a shrink.

As I pushed on, in heavy traffic for the Humber Bridge, I felt pretty good; but, on and off, my left knee was hurting and in the back of mind it was a constant worry. I had taken two paracetamol and an ibuprofen tablet so I was aware that any damage might be worse than it felt, masked as it was by the painkillers. As the Humber Bridge came into view in the distance, I felt a sense of relief at reaching this personal milestone. In my mind, this was my first real achievement. If my body gave up now, I had at least reached somewhere that was a respectable distance from Merthyr. I was quite impressed with the bridge, although it was similar to the old Severn crossing that was very familiar to me. I got off to walk the 'up' side of the bridge. The slope wasn't that steep but lofted high above the Humber River, it was very exposed and the wind against me picked up. Although I was on the pedestrian walkway, traffic, particularly lorries, passed very close by. I felt even more diminutive as the road level was about a metre above my pathway making the trucks look even taller. I remounted on the downward leg of the bridge and passed at least two parties of junior school children who must have been 'on a trip' to the Humber Bridge. They had a teacher in front and another at the back and they all carried little clipboards. It's a pity they weren't walking in crocodile formation, because I had to wait for some time as they passed by like a shoal of sardines in a David Attenborough documentary.

As I left the bridge, I followed, with some confusion, the pedestrian walkway signs, dropping down steeply into the Humber Bridge car park with its visitor centre. There I bought post cards for Hafina and Ken and borrowed a pen from the shopkeeper so I could write them there and then. I also got myself a drink and some chocolate and took fifteen minutes to wander around making sure I kept the bike in view as my bum and legs enjoyed the rest.

I checked the map and headed off for Beverley but missed the town centre completely, as I was inadvertently side-tracked along its bypass. By the time I realised what had happened, I couldn't be bothered to make a detour. I didn't particularly want to stop in Beverley, but it would have been nice to have seen it. As I continued on towards Driffield, I gradually experienced a change from upbeat travel mode to downbeat slog mode.

When I finally reached Driffield, I was surprised how busy a place it was. By now I was fed up with the hard work, and I decided to refresh myself in a pub. I found one with a spot at the rear to park up the bike. Sitting on a high stool, I shared the bar with one other bloke, who was a scrap metal merchant, and ordered a pint of Strongbow. Soon we got into a conversation in which he gave me some bad news. I couldn't have studied the map too carefully because I thought it was only about another fifteen miles to Scarborough.

'Sorry mate, it's at least twenty-two, and the road's a bit of a bastard an' all.'

'Are you sure?'

'I should be; I travel it often enough.' The bringer of extremely bad tidings called the barman over to seek reinforcement, which he promptly got. My expression must have given away my despair because the scrap metal man went on,

'Why don't you stay here or just go as far as Bridlington – that's only ten miles away?' I was tempted, especially as I was already coming to the end of my second pint of Strongbow; but, I had set my mind on reaching Scarborough and had promised myself a rest the next day, having completed exactly one week of my journey. I also thought Scarborough would be an interesting place to spend a free day. I liked the idea of being on the east coast at last, and I knew Scarborough was quite big so there should be a few things to explore and do. I thought I might even go and see where the hotel had fallen into the sea a few years before. I didn't make the scrap metal man aware of these other considerations, so he continued to wisely underline his argument,

'You're not in any rush are you? What's the point of overdoing it? Stay here or just get up to Bridlington. That Scarborough road is a bugger – there's some huge hills.'

But, I had made up my mind. I said cheerio and walked along the street to find a cash point machine. I took out £80 instead of the usual £40 thinking I would probably spend more in Scarborough on a rest day. Despite the long queue, I decided to go into the bank to transfer some money from a savings into my current account. It was surprising how much money I was getting through. In a business-like mood, perhaps brought on by the two pints of Strongbow, I remembered I needed a phone top up card. Next, I needed something to eat so I found a Greggs bakery. Again there was a long queue but I waited patiently, eyeing the illuminated pasties through the glass cabinet like a starving dog as his 'Chum' gets opened.

Still waiting behind two or three people, it hit me. The Greggs ladies all had white trilbies, exactly as Cherie used to wear when she worked in the school kitchen and where occasionally, I would visit her as she served the children. I suddenly had a crystal clear picture of her in front of me. There she was, her 'Term 3' white uniform hugging her curves and a pair of Doc Marten's boots that would have seen her right on a trek over the Brecon Beacons. Her red hair was mostly hidden under the white, netted trilby. Also, very clear was her movement – I could see it - busy, busy with short steps, quickly multi-tasking – smiling at me, calling me 'Dear' and asking me if I wanted anything to eat. That look on her face – she was always so pleased to see me – she would raise her brows, her eyes would brighten and she would break into her smile. In the busy street, I stood outside the shop trying to eat my pasty with tears rolling down my cheeks. I don't know if anyone noticed the state I was in – I didn't care. Cherie had just touched me with her presence.

As I ambled around to the back of the pub to pick up my bike I felt curiously elated, but also drained emotionally. Now, I really didn't relish the prospect of twenty-two miles of hard slog. Which is exactly how it turned out, especially for my knee which was now causing me a lot of pain and felt very weak; a bit like a plastic supermarket bag carrying too much wine, I expected it to give up on me at any moment. I had to walk a lot of the way, but the terrain demanded it anyway. I should have listened to the ex-scrap man in the pub and changed my plan. I estimated I would have done nearly sixty miles by the end of the day; and, with a heavy load through difficult terrain and a wind mostly against me, that was too far. Two-thirds into the slog, I was torn between taking a rest and delivering some calories to my withering body, and keeping going so there would be an end to it. I opted to stop at a garage and sat on a wall, eating chocolate and drinking Lucozade, alternately gazing back up the hill I had just whizzed down and up the hill I had to conquer next.

I was in contemplative mood,

'No one said this was going to be easy'. This was becoming a mantra.

Not feeling at all rejuvenated, I resumed the trudge. After an age, I reached the brow of the final hill and stopped for a few moments to thankfully cast my eye over the plain before me. Then I pushed off and freewheeled down for a mile or two before hitting Staxton and the main A64.

I was in for a nasty shock. I had miscalculated again. I thought I would be able to coast from the top of that hill and triumphantly enter Scarborough like a benevolent general liberating an oppressed town. The signpost informed me otherwise.

Scarborough 6 miles

'Oh no!' I cried out loud in desperation. I was absolutely knackered, but I had no choice. I pushed myself onwards with great effort. Despite the flat terrain, I still had to keep getting off to walk. My knee was giving me a lot of pain and I felt totally 'done for'. The traffic was heavy as it was now rush hour, but I finally came to the outskirts of the town. Even then, there was still some distance to go before I eventually reached the town centre. All the time, I had been keeping a keen lookout for campsite signs; but, to my dismay, I didn't see any. At last, I reached my destination at about six o'clock and realised that Tourist Information would be closed. That didn't bother me too much because I had every confidence, based upon past experience, that 'Pub Information' would be just as good.

I found a likely looking alehouse and parked up, as usual, out of sight. The pub was once again fairly empty as I ordered a pint and struck up a conversation with the barman.

To my disappointment, he didn't seem that knowledgeable on the campsite question, but he very generously said, 'You can stick your tent up in the garden if you want to. Sorry there are no facilities, but you're quite welcome.'

I was tempted. The pub was very central, and I was totally spent. I didn't fancy the prospect of any more travelling that day. The trouble was, the garden opened out on to the main road and there was no fence or wall for most of its boundary with the street. I was prepared to take some risks as far as theft was concerned, but this would be asking for trouble. In truth, I would have had to stay with my stuff and I didn't want to be chained to my tent all night. The other thing was that I really needed to freshen up, so I needed some basic creature comforts. The barman prompted the other drinkers for some suggestions; and, after a short debate, I was given instructions on how to get to a campsite with all the gubbings a couple of miles out of town and up a big hill.

'Great,' I thought. Finishing my drink, I sincerely thanked the landlord and retrieved my bike. In fact, that pint, plus the knowledge that it really would only be two more miles, revitalised me a little and as I walked up the long hill following directions for Pickering on the A170, I experienced a surge in my spirits. One thing about completing that hard and painful journey was a strong feeling of satisfaction and achievement. Far from being a burden, the fatigue I now felt was a physical manifestation of my conquest of sixty gruelling miles, and the significant crossing of the Humber Bridge was an age ago.

I saw signs for the campsite but they were posted early; it was still some time before I eventually wheeled the bike up a driveway, past tents, caravans and camper vans, looking for a 'Reception' sign. I rang a doorbell on the porch and waited for an answer. After a while and several attempts, a young girl opened the door and showed me through to a small office. Everything seemed well organised.

'Two nights, no problem - one tent and a pushbike. That's ten pounds a night, so twenty pounds please.'

'Twenty quid - that's a bit steep. I'll only use up a small amount of space.'

'But, we've got all the facilities, and you'll want to use those, I expect.'

'Are you prepared to come down a bit on that price?'

'No, sorry Sir, those are our charges.'

If I hadn't been so knackered, I would have looked elsewhere. As it was, I just wanted to get my tent up, get a shower, and have a rest. And it wasn't as if I were on a budget. I'd already forked out quite a bit for good equipment and spent a considerable sum on booze every night. But, I did begrudge paying ten pounds a night when most places charged me between two and four pounds fifty.

'Can I pay by card?' I had the cash, but I couldn't face going to the machine again and in any case, handing over a twenty-pound note – real money - would have added insult to injury. It's funny how paying by card softens the blow. It's easy to understand how people get into debt. I'm a lot better these days, but I have a long history of credit card debt.

I still quote with a misguided sense of pride, my bank manager's comments when he called me in for a lecture (in the days when bank managers used to do that sort of thing): 'Mr Hill – you have a cavalier attitude towards money.'

How right he was. My ex-wife and I had guessed we were in trouble when he asked to see us. However, his attempts to make us see sense backfired somewhat.

'Do you realise, with your combined income you are in the top 10% of wage earners in this town. No way should you be in this financial predicament.' His face reddened and sweat beaded at his hairline – his exasperation was genuine as he drove his point home.

'You should be going on two or three holidays a year and buying a brand new car every three.'

As we walked out of his office and into the street, he may have despairingly heard us through his open window as we yelled out in unison, 'We're rich!'

It only takes a small twist to make a big turn, and it is so easy to stray off the path of righteousness especially when righteousness is not where you want to go.

I left the office and set up my tent under a tree. Once my sleeping mat was inflated, I lay down and fell into complete sleep. I awoke, groggy, and made a coffee before getting down to the shower block to clean away the day. I had been so determined to get to Scarborough; but, now that I was there, I argued with myself as to whether I should go down and explore the town. 'There's a bar on the site – I can go there and leave Scarborough until tomorrow.'

'But it's a beautiful evening – I reckon I can manage a walk – it's downhill all the way. Maybe I can catch a bus - I can always get a taxi back.'

In the end, I decided to check out the bar but it was lifeless except for a few kids running riot in the poolroom, so town it was. I made a few enquiries and discovered that the buses didn't run past the campsite. I was in for some more exercise but the thought of cycling didn't even cross my mind. I set off walking down the long hill towards the town centre, my body still creaking but pleasantly relaxed as I caught glimpses, through breaks in the trees, across a pretty valley to my left.

Still some way from the actual centre, I stopped off in what looked like a typical 1970's pub. Like most of the architecture then, it was bland on the outside and bland on the inside. I sat at the bar watching other people and felt quite lonely. This didn't look like the sort of place where someone would come and say hello. I was glad that I had only ordered a half rather than a pint, and I left. As I came into the town centre proper, I needed to find some food. I didn't pass any chip shops but another pub presented itself. This time I had a pint but I don't think I was really up for it. I was probably too tired. In the pedestrianised centre I wandered around for a while looking for a cash machine. Charged up again with a modest amount of money, I noticed the familiar logo of McDonalds and decided to go in. This was most out of character, as I would usually go hungry rather than exchange cash for a cardboard meal served up in a cardboard container and a drink in a polystyrene beaker. Hunger held sway over discretion.

I sat on a piece of street furniture in the pedestrianised zone, absentmindedly dipping my fingers into the punnet to pull out chip sticks, alternately taking bites out of my tissue-cradled bap. Milling around there was a sprinkling of people of various ages, but they didn't help me feel less lonely and tears started to well up. Down at the end of the thoroughfare paved with pseudo-cobbles I could make out some archetypal seaside railings shimmering through my watery eyes. The street seemed hollow, and at that point so did my world. The McDonalds gone, I had to do something so I went to look for a welcoming pub. I dropped into one but walked straight back out – too quiet. I tried another and stayed for a pint but despite the fact that it was reasonably busy, I still felt isolated. The phrase, 'Alone in a crowd', sprung to mind and I realised that I had felt most at home in those pubs where there were just a few people, sometimes only one. On this night though, I don't think any sort of pub was going to be to my liking.

In the end, I got the message. It was time to go home. There was no way that I could face the long two mile walk back up the hill to the campsite, so I found a taxi rank and took the easy way out. Back at base, I should, of course, have gone to bed, but the light was still on in the site bar.

'I'll have a last pint here,' I told myself and my alter ego didn't put up a fight. Perhaps because I was feeling down and lonely, any last-ditch chance of some companionship was worth a gamble. Or maybe it was my lifelong aversion to going to bed (lust aside) which I put down to my upbringing. My parents must have found their four young kids very wearing and bedtimes were set in stone. I remember like yesterday, being six or seven years old and going to bed way too early when we lived in a caravan just outside Cheltenham. Lying wide-awake and gazing at curtains printed with a pattern of green, red, blue and yellow bottles, all arranged at jaunty angles (which I bet explains my love of alcohol!), the summer sun shone straight through the gossamer fabric and I lay awake for hours. To make matters worse, my Dad insisted that when we went to bed, we went TO SLEEP. We were in trouble if we talked, and I often used to sneak a book under the bed covers. I managed to read, sometimes with a torch, but was ever vigilant and ready to drop the covers and feign sleep, should Dad appear. I don't hold any of this against my Dad but BEDTIME was to shape my life into the future.

For a start, I never introduced my own children to the concept. When I felt they needed to go to bed, I would encourage them to go upstairs; but, I would always go and read to them or allow them to read to themselves for as long as they liked. I don't think they knew what bedtime was. Furthermore, to this day, if I can stay up I will, and this explains how I ended up in the campsite bar ordering a pint of Guinness.

There were two other blokes, one either side of me on bar stools. The one to my right looked seriously weathered and judging by his deeply lined face he must have been in his sixties, of slight build and rather overdressed. He was wearing black trousers, a white shirt with fancy embroidery and glittery bits attached, all topped off with a black waistcoat.

The glittery shirt man wouldn't have looked out of place in a cheap gambling joint in mid-western cowboy country. He was amiable enough though, and we quickly struck up a conversation. He was a professional musician, albeit an ageing one, whose instrument was the keyboard, which explained his apparel. My bike ride soon came into the conversation, and he said that he was familiar with the Orkneys.

He told me the story of the Churchill Barriers, which was all news to me. These had been built on Churchill's orders during the second-world war. They were stone causeways that were constructed between the islands on the eastern side of Scapa Flow, a large inlet where the British fleet was holed up taking advantage of its sheltered waters. The idea had been to prevent the incursion of the inlet from the east by enemy U boats. According to the musician, the locals advised that the barriers were being built too low, and that on one or two occasions during the year, high spring tides would completely submerge them rendering them useless as a defence against U boats. What do locals know? The ministry took no notice. But one night, on a very high spring tide, a German U boat audaciously crossed over the barriers and torpedoed a British cruiser. Two thousand men were onboard, the ship sank and it is now a permanent war grave. Even today, from time to time the ship still loses oil. The U Boat got away Scot-free, but locals reckon it must have scratched the paintwork on its underside getting out.

I can't remember the musician's name, but he told how he had played all over the place including Iceland and Finland.

He asked me, 'Have you ever heard of Bert Weedon?'

Of course I had. Bert was famous for his 'Play in a Day' guitar tutor books. As an aspiring thirteen year old guitarist who couldn't tune the thing let alone play any chords, I was singularly unimpressed with Bert's book which, if I remember rightly, taught you how to play a tune with just single notes. Even if I could have read music, it would have been boring.

My companion went on, 'I played a season with him in Skegness about six years ago. He kept wrecking every bloody song – I don't think he had a clue about diminished and augmented chords. In the end, I plucked up the courage to tell him.'

'What happened?'

'He told me to fuck off! The Great One then went on to say, "I've been doing this for thirty years and I ain't changing now".'

I was surprised that Bert should take such a simplistic approach to his work when on stage. Even I know how important chord nuances are. Still, many of the world's greatest guitarists claim to have started off with Bert's books, including Eric Clapton and George Harrison. I'm probably falsely judging 'Play in a Day' as a foil for my own ineptitude on the instrument.

We carried on talking, mainly about music. The musician then changed the subject to warn me about the next leg of my journey up on to the eastern edge of the North Yorkshire Moors. There was no way of escaping a daunting climb. It didn't look as if the weather was going to do me any favours either – the forecast for Wednesday was awful: heavy rain and gale force winds.

'Should be interesting,' said my new friend. I studied his face again. It really was a totally 'lived in' face – maybe 'lived out' would be a better way of putting it. And my initial impressions were inaccurate. Far from being a sad old man in out-of-place razzmatazz clothes, this guy had certainly seen a bit of life and he was very interesting to talk to. In fact, when he got off his bar stool to leave he was quite tall, close to six foot with slightly bandy legs. He took interest in me too, and he suggested that I write a book based on my trip. I modestly disclosed my fears about not making it to the Shetlands.

He sympathised with my knee problem but urged me,

'Get where you're going, provided you've got the money, even if it means taking the train.' After he had left I thought that both ideas, the book and the train, were good ones.

Talking of lived in, my fairly healthy tanned face had turned into a haggard one now. As I looked in the mirror, having attempted optimistically to empty my bladder for the night, there I was - drawn, with bags under my eyes and skin looser than I had noticed before. My hair was positively 'Lester'. Lester was someone I had been thinking about on the road earlier when I was considering letting my hair grow during the trip. Lester was short for Lester Fontaine. Probably eight or so years before, he was a character in Coronation Street. He was an ageing showman who was an old flame of Vera Duckworth. She had rekindled her affections for him after a chance meeting in Blackpool, but she never quite got to do any really dirty deeds with him. I think her husband Jack found out. The point was his respectable head of hair was distinctly bouffant. Cherie and I were amused by the storyline with its inherent humour and its characters, especially Lester. Shortly after that, Cherie noticed my hair had grown longer and had taken on more than a passing resemblance to Lester Fontaine's quiff. From that day on, the term 'Lester' was our own private shorthand for describing my hair when it needed a cut – it always made us laugh.

Back at the mirror, it didn't look as if I was losing weight, despite all the physical exertion.

'Too much Guinness, Strongbow and bitter,' I thought. 'Not to mention greasy spoon breakfasts, choccy bars, fizzy energy drinks and fatty chip suppers.' As I crawled into my sleeping bag and warmed up, I fell asleep looking forward to my first day off the bike since I'd left Merthyr exactly a week ago.

The Ride:

Wrawby to Scarborough
Distance: 58 miles

Rest Day

Tuesday, July 10th

I had a disturbed night's sleep despite having drunk quite a few pints. Actually, that was partly the cause – I had to get up three times in the night for a pee. Each time involved having to first realise that I was in a tent and not a bedroom, then work out where the door was, before fighting my way out of my tight fitting sleeping bag, fumbling for the tent zip and finding something to put onto my feet. I then had to assess whether I could walk across no man's land in just my underpants and a tee shirt, and finally I needed to locate the key to the toilet block (two pounds deposit paid) that I had cleverly placed into a corner of the tent so I could find it easily – but which corner? The whole process had to be reversed when I eventually got back to the tent. After three of these performances, it was no wonder I didn't sleep too well.

Also, I had a strange dream. I had turned up at what seemed to be a cross between a hospital and a doctor's surgery, and caught an admin person, rather than a nurse, in the act of 'tidying up' Cherie's body. She hastily stopped when she saw me like a schoolgirl found doodling on a desk. Then Cherie was gone and the hospital now looked like an assembly line in a huge factory. The massive rectangular structure was subdivided into several large partitions that ran the length of what now seemed more like one of the connecting annexes at an airport terminal. I anticipated an echo, but it was silent and there was no one around except me. I spotted Cherie's body moving down the length of the central partition. She was on rollers that reminded me of the conveyor system in a matchbox toy car factory where I used to work. For some reason, Cherie was not in a coffin, but wrapped in a shroud and again I caught somebody shiftily tidying her body. I was still alone, but then suddenly joined by another person whom I didn't know. I slowly realised it was mourner and that this was Cherie's funeral. We waited and waited for the rest of the congregation to catch up, imagining that we had somehow got ahead of the crowd. In the end, we came to the conclusion that we must have come the wrong way. That would explain how we came to be following Cherie in her shroud. I was sure that we weren't supposed to see that.

We kept walking down the never-ending building until we did finally get somewhere – a crematorium, although its credentials for being such were as tenuous as those of the 'hospital' we had just left. I discovered that 'due to all the delays', the cremation would have to be postponed. I was distraught. Then I caught two undertakers carrying Cherie's body in the shroud, and to my horror, her head was momentarily exposed. With that, they bundled her head first, into – I wasn't sure what – a sack, a coffin? At the same time, I was both distraught and furious. I stormed up to the hospital admin department to complain. As I vented my anger, no one even listened to me, let alone acted – if I had been on television reading the news, I would have had more chance of making contact with these people.

After I had finished ranting, I was kindly asked by a woman, 'Do you want something with salad?'

I was then told that it was common to hallucinate after bereavement. That was too much, and I lost my rag with them again. Gradually, I calmed down and started to secretly wonder if I had imagined the whole shroud thing. Certainly, a lot of what I saw had been very fleeting.

As I came to and realised that I was, in fact, in a tent, I was puzzled that I hadn't been able to escape the dream and was immensely relieved and comforted to realise that Cherie's funeral had been far from a disaster. As I boiled up some water and settled down to drink my coffee, I hunted around for my notebook and wrote down everything I could remember about my strange dream. Like most people, I often have clear recollections of dreams that may stay with me for hours; but, by lunchtime, I've forgotten everything. I wanted to record this one, even though I had found it most disturbing. The reasons for it were obvious I suppose, but the postponement of the cremation was almost certainly a re-enactment of preparations I had been making for Cherie's funeral.

She had told me that she would like something different – what a surprise. So, I had canvassed the opinions of a few friends, and Cherie's sisters and her children. One possibility had been a horse drawn hearse. Another was to take up the offers made by two different people who owned horses, to have a horse drawn carriage of some description. Cherie had adamantly specified that she didn't want a hearse so we dropped the first idea. The other plan was seriously investigated. I remember feeling a lot of pressure at the time. On the one hand, I wanted to give Cherie the unusual send-off that I knew she had wanted. On the other hand, I was stressed at the thought of getting the whole thing together. A horse would have to be brought from fifteen miles away in a box; the carriage (or whatever it was) would have to be brought separately. How was this all going to be timed?

Then I considered the trip to the crematorium. I know less about horses than I do about designing a nuclear bomb, but I figured that any Dobbin would have one hell of a job pulling a trailer up Swansea Road – a distance of something like two miles and uphill all the way. The total journey was more like five miles. It might have been a better idea to sort out the horse and carriage at the top of the hill, but that would have meant transferring Cherie from a car - what a palaver. The window of time for cremations is a small one and ours was not even the last slot of the day. If we weren't there on the button, there would have been huge embarrassment and goodness knows how much heartbreak and stress for all concerned – Cherie's family from Liverpool, the kids and, of course, me. I could see the whole thing turning into a terrible farce. I talked over the ideas for the funeral with my friend Dennis. He confirmed my doubts before I voiced my own misgivings and that was that. The horse idea was abandoned.

My first rest day. I started to make a mental note of things I had to do. Have my hair cut; buy, write and send post cards; write a letter to Rina, my daughter; phone Richard, my son; activate the phone card I had bought; see a chemist about something for my knee; and, get some shaving gel. I went for a shave and ablutions, cleared up around the tent and was then ready for a trip into town. I knew that no buses stopped on the road passing the campsite, so I had to walk for about three quarters of a mile before I reached the first stop. I did consider walking all the way; but I wasn't really in a hurry so I decided to wait and chill out - it seemed that I was forever on the go, so why not take it easy for once. Waiting for the bus, the weather was dry with just a few clouds and it was quite cool. Time seemed to stand still as I occasionally looked at my watch. It must have been on the third or fourth glance that the penny dropped, and I realised that my watch had in fact stopped. Watch battery – another thing to add to my shopping list.

I wasn't accustomed to using public transport and, as had been the case in Ross on Day 1, the wait for the bus seemed more an act of faith. As I sat on the bench, I considered the musician's suggestion from the night before – to write a book. So far, I had only kept a log, but now I considered all the hours I was spending each day, on my own and lost in my thoughts. Thoughts about what I'd seen and who I'd met and what I was going to do next. And a lot of the time I thought about Cherie. My mind ran like a video recording in which past events played out in full colour with sound. And the video would make me smile, laugh out loud, make me sad, and even cry. I thought about my past – before Cherie – BC. I even went back to my childhood. Then there was the future – what was going to happen to me?

The more I thought about it, the more I felt a book would be a good idea. Not that I knew the first thing about writing one, but I didn't think that that really mattered. It was unlikely anything I produced would make it into print, but for two reasons I felt that it was still a good idea. Number one, the process of writing the book would be good for me - a way of focussing my thoughts and a cathartic tool to help me cope with Cherie's death. Secondly, I was conscious of the fact that I was very much alone on my trip. Although I had met people on the way and had indeed, formed fond associations with a number of them, these acquaintances were just that - acquaintances. They weren't sharing my trip, every mile of the way, as Cherie would have done had she been alive. They were transitory, like a distant mountain observed from a speeding train window. I thought that writing a book would be a way of sharing my experiences with friends and family, even if publishing was a pipe dream.

The original idea of keeping a log to provide me with a written record of my trip would be a third motive, but the record would be that much more complete if I could do a proper job of writing it as a book.

A hundred yards away the bus appeared from a side street like an apparition and grew in size as it approached. I alighted in the centre of town and made a mental note of where the bus stop was. I wandered around for about an hour, during which I got a haircut (no Lester Fontaine for me, Cherie) and enjoyed some friendly banter with the hairdresser before finding a chemist where I asked for some advice about my knee. A helpful lady fished out a knee support bandage, and I regretted not bringing the ones I already had at home with me when she told me the price - they're not cheap. I asked her about pain relief for my knee and she recommended ibuprofen.

Simple pleasures but I did enjoy the social interaction with the hairdresser and the chemist. After dropping off a film to be processed, I got a new battery fitted into my watch then decided to take a look around Scarborough. I can't say I was particularly impressed. The main street was pedestrianised, like so many other town centres. I had no objection to that, except that it did make Scarborough look like any other place. Mind you, I suppose all towns looked similar before they were pedestrianised. I wandered down to the promenade and bought myself a baguette. Foregoing a pasty, pie or sausage roll, I was pleased with myself for choosing this healthy option. I sat on a slatted seat eating my breakfast when suddenly, a young toddler fell head over heels as he passed by with his mother. It was a bad fall and junior's face was the first thing to hit the pavement. His mum picked him up and brushed him off as he justifiably wailed.

I smiled in believed wisdom as she caught my eye and I passed comment,

'Where there's blame there's a claim.'

She laughed, and I suddenly wondered what it must be like living with her. I made her laugh. Cherie used to tell me the same. The pair disappeared. I crumpled up the wrapping from the baguette and found a bin for it, then ambled down to the sea front and noticed that a lift was installed to get people down to the beach.

'What a posh resort!'

I had considered seeking out the place where the hotel had fallen into the sea. Perhaps I could take a stroll along the beach to it. But now I felt lonely and decided not to bother. I suppose, being a rest day, I didn't have the goal of a destination to reach and the lack of focus was not doing much for my sense of well-being. Enough time had elapsed for me to think about picking up my photos so that's what I did. I also bought some post cards and decided that a pub might now be a good idea. I could write my postcards and my letter to Rina and, although I didn't consider it at the time, be amongst people. I sauntered into a Wetherspoons, ordered a pint of Guinness and found myself a seat after looking around for quite a while - the place was very busy. I looked at the photos I had just had developed. These were the first of the trip and I wanted to write notes on the back of them before I forgot where they had been taken.

As I opened the envelope I was quite taken aback - Cherie was sitting on our settee - a head and shoulders photo. She was in her dressing gown, hair blonde and so short it must have just been cut. She was smiling, but that was not the most striking thing about the picture. For some reason, the shot was over exposed so that Cherie's face was lit up, ironically giving her a ghostly appearance. But it didn't scare me – if Cherie was a ghost I had faith she would be a friendly one, especially to me. The image did upset me though - it was the last thing I had expected.

Most of the other shots were of the bike trip to date, but there were a few of Cherie's wake with our kitchen as a backdrop, crowded with friends and family. The centre of the room was dominated by Cherie's casket and at one end of it on the lid, was a black and white photo of Cherie as a baby, with two big kiss curls on top of her head. On the back it says,

CHERIE

Born March the 24th 1960

Eyes - Green

Hair – Brown

Another copy of it had been in my briefcase ever since I had taken it to work to be photocopied. I hadn't intended for it to stay there, but somehow it did. Every time I look at it, I gaze into the baby's eyes and kiss its face. Sometimes it makes me cry – it always makes me sad.

The child looks back at me and I think with sorrow, 'I know your destiny little one'.

Tragically, Cherie never had the chance to grow old, and I remembered talking to her about Lady Diana. The world saw her as such a beautiful woman; and, with her untimely death, they would never have their image of her tainted by the onset of old age.* So it was with Cherie.

Wetherspoon's had the large floor area typical of modern pub interiors – former walls that had created smaller rooms had been designed out as an essential part of the refurbishment. There was lots of wood with sturdy balustrades, heavily panelled walls and a massive long bar, behind which an army of young staff slid back and forth like ducks in a fairground shooting gallery, only visible from the waist up and in matching livery. The floor area was covered with wooden chairs and tables, and the relatively small windows were incapable of illuminating the ballroom within, creating a pervading gloominess only slightly brightened by some inadequate wall lights. The main activity seemed to be eating rather than drinking and I felt a little guilty having taken up a whole table to myself. Amidst a background of melded conversations, cutlery chinking plates and a sporadic piercing squawk from a young woman who only seemed able to shout, I arranged my few possessions on the table and made space for my paper.

    I was aware of a few curious eyes, but they either got bored or I forgot about them as I started to write, first the post cards to Nick, my brother and MR, my stepson. I also used the photo of the Brigg signpost as a post card and sent it off to Graham, my fellow geography teacher at school - I knew he too would appreciate the significance of Ordnance Survey Brigg. I then wrote my letter to Rina. Rina had just graduated from Exeter University and was taking a working holiday with the Camp America scheme before going on to do the Bar Vocational Course in Nottingham University. She had left for America before Cherie had died but had said her goodbyes and more or less knew what the score was. I wrote Rina a long letter and got quite upset a number of times. I must have been in the pub for at least two hours, and I had sunk three pints by the time I had finished.

    I left the pub and wandered the town for another hour. I was not in high spirits, and I still felt lonely. Whether it was seeing Cherie's picture, or the emotion of writing the long letter to Rina, I don't know, but I was very sensitive and there were triggers to upset me as I walked around. Like every time I passed 'New Look', the clothing retail chain. Cherie used to buy a lot of clothes in their Merthyr and Cardiff stores. Then a street musician played an instrumental version of 'Nights in White Satin'. Cherie liked the song, and I had spent hours learning to sing and play it back in our early courting days.

My lack of talent was evident in her forthright appraisal of my efforts,

'It doesn't sound as good when you do it.'

However, the musician did do a good cover of it, which opened the emotional floodgate again. The triggers kept coming. I found myself noticing women and assessing if any of them looked like Cherie and if not, comparing them in any case. It occurred to me as I followed this sad pursuit that I was not looking for a replacement for Cherie – I wanted Cherie. I wondered what it was going to be like when I got back home, and I felt that things were now getting harder, especially over the last couple of days. Was it that the novelty of the trip was wearing off? Was it because I had taken a day off or was it because, save for the hairdresser and the chemist, I hadn't had any real conversations with anyone yet today?

Something useful came out of my amblings around Scarborough though. I remembered that, so far, I had been fairly lucky with the weather. The sleeping bag, that didn't fit inside my rucksack, had been ok strapped to the outside encased in two top to tail plastic bags. However, I doubted how long this makeshift arrangement would be successful; and, I had caught the weather forecast for the next day – gale force winds and heavy rain. I decided to find an outdoor shop and see if they could supply me with some kind of permanent waterproof bag. A passer-by gave me directions and I soon found the shop just as it started to rain heavily. Inside, I learned that what I needed was a 'stuff bag'. Luckily, amongst the stock was a shop-soiled stuff bag that the owner kindly sold me for a fiver.

'Bring it back if it's too small.'

'Let's hope it's not,' I thought. If it was, it would mean a big detour into town next morning upsetting my whole schedule for the day.

I had been very pleased with my healthy baguette earlier on, but I spoiled it all now by picking up a big portion of chips and two jumbo sausages. In the rain, I ate my dinner as I made my way to the bus stop. Luckily, there was one waiting and within a few minutes we were off. I soon remembered I had forgotten something – shaving gel ...

'What the hell.' At least I now had a way of keeping my bed dry.

The chap in the outdoor shop had told me, 'You can send these things floating down a river and the contents will still be bone dry. Just make sure you fold the top over five times before you fasten the snap buckle.'

Back at the tent, I organised my gear and came across the charger for the mobile phone. The name 'CHERIE' was gouged in wonky writing, probably crafted with an implement from one of the kid's geometry sets. It wasn't an anti-theft measure - it's just we had so many different 12 volt chargers for a host of appliances. But, the sight of Cherie's name jumped out of the black plastic and again triggered the melancholy that had been with me for most of the day. Settling down for my early evening snooze, I resolved to get an early night and worried about the next day's weather. The forthcoming gale was forecast to bring winds from either the north or the west. That meant the winds would either be directly against me or hitting me from the left side, possibly blowing me into any overtaking traffic.

'Heads you lose, tails you lose,' I thought, and I reluctantly considered staying another night.

Half an hour later I awoke from sleep and felt better. I couldn't face going back into Scarborough though, so I decided to stick with the early night plan. This didn't mean I couldn't get a few drinks in the campsite bar. The two men from the night before were already sitting on tall stools. The musician's name turned out to be Dave Griffin and I talked with him for a long time. The other man was a Scottish guy whose name I can't remember. He heard me talking about Cherie but didn't say much for a long time. Eventually, he told his own story. His wife had suffered from cancer for nine years. He described the long journeys he used to have to make to visit her and said how difficult it had been. He didn't say how she was, and I left it for a while, trying to find the right moment before asking him tentatively,

'Is she OK now?'

The reply came back, 'I lost her in the end, two years ago.'

I said how having time with Cherie before her death had helped me say goodbye and perhaps prepared me, and I told him about Samuel and the sudden death of his wife.

My companion started to cry and when he had composed himself a little he said, 'We never mentioned my wife's illness – not at any time during the nine years she suffered.'

I felt I had put my foot in it - as if I had a monopoly on grief and the right to spout out my own version of coping without a thought for how things might have been for others. This poor man must never have got to say and hear the things he needed to say and hear. I couldn't see how that was a good thing.

Back in the tent, I put on my ACME elasticated head torch and started to write up my journal. I lasted about twenty minutes before flying insects noticed the light and told all their friends. Perhaps it wasn't such a good idea to pitch under trees. Final thoughts wafted through my mind at the end of what had been a difficult day.

'By all accounts, tomorrow is going to be a stinker - but I'm only going to go forty miles - and there'll be a campsite there - so I'm told. Time to sleep.'

I hadn't managed an early night after all.

<u>No Ride:</u> (rest day)

*In dreams I still retain my youth,
Awake the mirror shows the truth
The channelled face, receding hair,
The figure wrecked beyond repair
This image is not poor design
In fact, the likeness is just fine
A portrait of one in decline.

So tell me, since you tell no lies,
Why are these sacs beneath my eyes?
Why sprouts the hair from ears and nose,
While on my scalp it scarcely grows?
The torso once so well-defined
Its sculpture now is realigned
And all foundations undermined.

Stripped bare I see that you're no liar
My once spare waist's become spare tyre,
 Strange how I've filled a second chin
Yet arms and legs have surplus skin
The onset of my mortal's fate
Reflected in my stooping trait,
And reaffirmed by stiffening gait.

Aching sinews, shrinking pains,
Legs all strung with purple veins,

Brown aging spots become apparent
And opaque skin has turned transparent,
Flaccidity where once was muscle,
Lethargy where all was bustle
And sometimes I can hear the rustle
Off dried leaves in my blood.

Scarborough to Guisborough

Wednesday, July 11th

Wind, bloody wind. I knew the forecast was bad with heavy rain and a gale predicted. I also knew the wind direction - it would be hitting me on the nose or trying to knock me off. It turned out, that with the twists in the road it was an unhappy combination of both for most of the day. I had a fairly restless night's sleep, despite the Guinness; but, I made a rather difficult decision before going to bed. I didn't want a repeat of the toilet dance routine from the night before. This sounds disgusting, I know, but I wasn't using my Trangia cooker for anything except boiling water up in the kettle. There were two pans as part of the system. Why not use the smaller pan that stacked on top of the larger, as a potty? I could wash it out every morning, and, as I said, I didn't use it for its intended purpose anyway. It was settled and I employed my new toilet facility for the rest of my trip. It meant I could sleep, as I was accustomed to doing, in the raw and now my habit of drinking substantial quantities of liquid in the evenings would no longer conflict with the subsequent and inevitable functioning of my bladder. Why didn't I think of this before – sorry, Mum!

The rain lashed down most of the night, and the wind buffeted the tent keeping me awake for long hours. As I tossed and turned listening to the elements and wondering about the next day's ride, I came to the clichéd conclusion that discretion was the better part of valour. I would have to stay in Scarborough another day. It was just too dangerous to risk my unstable bike on a main road in howling gale. Thinking about it though, I had been impressed with the behaviour of drivers in general. I'm not sure whether it was the result of education and an enlightened attitude towards cyclists, or just an instinctive reaction to the sight of me from behind, wobbling along a meandering course. But 99.9% of all vehicles gave me a wide berth as they passed me by. Lorries, especially, would even move into the opposite lane to get by. Not that this made me complacent - I still always tried to stick to within a metre of the curb.

Then the usual thing happened. Just as it was getting light, I fell into a deep and much needed sleep. When I woke up, I lay in my sleeping bag for some time trying to gauge the wind strength. Although it was still gusting, it didn't seem so bad – plus the rain had stopped. Reversing my nocturnal decision, I decided to push on. I boiled the kettle and started to pack up as an unholy row developed between two campers. I'm not sure if it was my defective hearing but I could only make out a few of the actual words and most of those were expletives. Loud Voice versus Even Louder Voice – Even Louder seemed to win – predictably I suppose – he certainly got in more 'f' words per second.

Disappointingly, the waterproof sack I had bought for my sleeping bag was too small. Very disappointing in fact, because it meant I would have to make a big detour into Scarborough to change it for a full priced one. Worse still, I'd have to come back up the hill. I decided to try the sleeping bag without its own stuff sack and this made a big difference – it now fitted into the waterproof bag albeit with a bit of persuasion. Better still, I could get my fleece into it as well, provided I patiently expelled the displaced air as I went, and this made packing the main rucksack a lot easier. As I loaded up the bike and propped it against a tree, it fell over and I had to release the bungees and start from scratch. Finally, I got everything strapped on securely and walked up to the site office to return their blessed toilet key and retrieve my two pounds deposit. On my return, I pulled the bike away from the tree, cocked my leg over and pushed down the right pedal - there was no resistance.

'Damn!' Looking down I could see that the chain had fallen off when the bike had toppled over. It was just as well - despite the fact that I was now going to get oily hands - because, as I put the chain back on, having re-propped against the tree, I noticed that a bolt had come off one leg of the back rack. The leg was still in place and temporarily held by the pressure of its load, but if I hadn't noticed, it could have slipped out of position a few minutes down the road. Down being the operative word. I would have been bowling down the long hill towards Scarborough. The leg of the rack would have jammed into the spokes of the back wheel and I'd have been off. It could have been very nasty accident, and I now breathed a huge sigh of relief. I searched for five minutes in the grass looking for the bolt but to no avail.

This was now going to delay me for hours because I couldn't ride the bike into Scarborough. I would have to walk and bus it there and back and find a bike shop. Come to think of it, I would have to take the bike with me so they could try it for size, or remove the bolt from the other side – what a potch.

The campsite was a big one so I hit upon the long shot that there might be some sort of workshop around. That being the case, they just might have what I was looking for. I went into the site shop and made enquiries and the lady called out,

'Steve!'

A tall, thin man in his early thirties came from the back room and told me he might be able to help. I followed him, pushing the bike, up to some out-buildings where he started to hunt around various boxes and containers, eventually coming up with a bolt of the correct size and length – what luck! As he proceeded to fit the bolt, he told me that in the past he had done a lot of cycling himself. He was into road racing and had reached quite a high competitive standard until he broke his hip twice in two separate accidents. He was unable to cycle at all now. Steve pointed out that he didn't have a locking washer for the bolt and strongly advised that I get one as soon as possible – without one I ran the risk of the same thing happening again. All in all, the job only took quarter of an hour, and I considered myself very lucky to get it fixed so soon. This was the first technical hitch I had encountered in over three hundred miles so I couldn't really complain. I thanked Steve, who refused to accept any payment, then pedalled off the campsite and freewheeled down the long hill.

The ride to Whitby along the A171 was a lot better than expected. There were lots of hills that took me up on to the North Yorkshire Moors but the wind was hitting me sideways and slightly from behind giving me a bit of a push if anything. Downhill though, the wind had a destabilising effect and I couldn't whizz down the hills in the usual fashion. I made a discovery in sight of breakfast at a greasy spoon I could see on the brow of one of the high spots. I knew I needed a pee and I didn't want to spoil my meal by having to hop about like an infant school boy about to wet his pants. The heather was spectacular, but there were no trees this high up on which I could lean the bike. I tried supporting the rucksack and then laying the whole bike on its side. It seemed to work – everything stayed in position and nothing slid off. I scrambled down into a gully and relieved myself, almost out of sight of passing traffic, as steam rose from the heather. I clambered back up the short embankment and was pleased to find I could successfully right the bike by using the reverse procedure – basically, supporting the heavy load and letting the bike look after itself.

I continued up the hill in a straight line until I reached the burger van parked up in a lay-by. It wasn't one of those you could sit inside, like the one just outside Brigg with the cook-come-counsellor; unfortunately, I had to stand outside in the wind, overlooking the bleakness of the moors under a grey sky that started to rain. I had a hot coffee as well as a bacon and sausage jumbo roll wishing I were seated somewhere warm out of the wind.

I made Whitby by two o'clock but stayed on the by-pass. As I crossed the River Esk, I could see boats below me to my left, cocked at random angles in the mud, the tide having sucked the sea out of the channel. To my right and across the road, I could make out the town itself, the harbour and what looked like a ruined abbey on a hill, silhouetted against the sky. Wobbling over the river bridge I came to the bottom of what I later discovered to be a very, very long hill. The road bore left and westward, straight into the wind and I saw a sign for Guisborough – 22 miles. My speed dropped to less than six miles per hour over this leg of the journey. The hill must have been nearly three miles long – it went on forever. At times, there were slight respites in the gradient and I tried cycling but it was pointless. I would have to walk this one. The wind was so strong it seemed to add weight to my legs as I leaned into the bike in my efforts to shove it up the interminable slope. I could feel the strength being sapped from me. It started to rain again and I put up my hood to keep the stinging shards off my face. About three quarters of an hour up the hill, I noticed a pick-up truck parked across a minor road junction a few hundred yards on.

'Funny place to stop,' I thought, assuming that the owner was taking a break or on his mobile phone. As I passed, a man wound down his window and said something but I didn't catch it. I took down my hood and wheeled the bike closer to him.

'Do you want a lift up the hill, mate?'

I realised that the bloke must have passed me and taken pity – it wouldn't have been difficult to see that I was struggling.

'How far you going?' I asked.

'Not far, just a few miles up the road, but it'll get you to the top of this hill.' It would have just been a case of supporting the load and cradling the bike into the open backed truck. It would have been so easy. I was sorely tempted, but something held me back. So far I had made every single mile, every yard, under my own steam. I just couldn't accept the lift.

From the expression on my face, this Good Samaritan understood and he said, 'You've got to do it on your own?'

'Yes, I have. But, thanks a lot for the offer – I really appreciate it.'

The pick-up pulled back on to the main road and as it got smaller I thought, 'I must be mad,' but I knew that if I didn't make this trip on my own muscle power, it wouldn't be because I'd taken a lift for a few miles when the chips were down.

In any case, it wasn't so much the hill now - I hardly noticed the end of it - but the wind. At times, the noise from it was deafening and it was there, in my face – big time. On the whole trip so far, it was the only thing I could think of that had really annoyed me. And while getting angry at the wind (of all things) was totally pointless, it didn't stop me cursing and swearing at it. Wind was not like hills – it was alive! And it was organic - ever changing. Just when I thought I could start cycling the gale would once more flare up with a vengeance and I would again have to dismount. The afternoon journey from Whitby can only be described as a total *battle*.

'Wind, damn wind!'

It was not only against me – it was against *me* – it was personal. I vowed I would not be beaten by it. The miles ticked by so slowly on the bike's milometer that I changed the mode on the computer to 'time' rather than 'distance', so at least I could get some notion of progress. Eventually, eleven miles from Guisborough, a mobile greasy spoon came into view at a typical location - a desolate lay-by on the top of an exposed hill. As I made inexorable progress towards the van, the thought of a hot cup of sweet tea seemed like the closest I was going to get to a deep hot bath or a cwtch (homely Welsh word with no English equivalent - 'cuddle' is the best approximation) in front of a glowing fireplace. In this most vulnerable of spots, the wind turned up yet another notch. The burger van was sensibly orientated so that its open side was out of the wind. As I parked up the bike and took refuge, the buffeted van looked and sounded as if it was going to blow over. A solitary lady was manning her post and she served me up a delightful mug of hot tea and a Mars bar. Naturally, we talked about the weather and she must have felt sorry for me because she refused to accept any money for the tea, only taking for the chocolate. Ten minutes later I pedalled out from my sanctuary and back into the maelstrom.

As I steeled to my task, I thought to myself, 'You'd better get used to this– what's it going to be like when you get to Scotland?'

Even at the end, I couldn't freewheel off the moors into Guisborough – downhill, the wind raged against me and I had to keep the pedals turning. I passed signs for a campsite two miles before I reached the town, but I had already decided absolutely, that tonight, I would seek out a bit of luxury. The first pub I came to was called The Fox; I was heartened to see that accommodation was advertised. I hid the bike and went to make enquiries, only to be told that all the rooms were booked. There was some element of confusion though. The night before, a local woman had booked in having told her husband she was leaving him after a blazing row. She had made a reservation for two nights and was supposed to confirm with the proprietor her firm intentions for the second night.

The landlord said, 'I haven't heard a peep – and she's taken all her stuff. But I can't let you have the room 'cause she might come back.' He pondered – clearly he didn't want to let down someone he knew but neither did he want to lose custom.

'I'll see if I can get her on the phone.'

'Don't worry,' I interjected. 'There's another place down the road I can try.'

'Oh Lord, you don' want to stay there!' He seemed very bothered I might book in with a rival.

'He's dead right!' a voice from a burly man with a pipe from the other end of the bar. 'That's a bad place to stay.'

They didn't realise, that compared to a night in a tent anything would have been a palace to me, especially after the physical trials I had endured that day. It seemed as if there was some sort of feud going on. The landlord eventually bit the bullet and allowed me to take the room.

'She promised - it's her fault for not confirming.'

I was relieved to be 'home' for the day, but the pub a few doors down would have been my very next port of call had the decision gone against me. It later turned out that the woman had succeeded in giving her husband a jolt and they had sorted things out. Everyone's relationship is different, but I'm thankful that Cherie and I were nearly always on an even keel – I don't think I could have coped with melodrama.

I had a long beautiful, hippopotamus bath and thought about the day's events. I felt a great deal of personal satisfaction having reached my goal for the day and I relived the hardest sections again. I felt a need to talk to somebody and I missed Cherie. What was it going to be like in the future? I tried to be positive and considered how much time any of us spend with our loved ones.

In the course of a typical working day, after taking a cup of tea to Cherie in bed, I would have 6.30 a.m. until 8.30 a.m. 'own time'. Then I'd be in work until 4 o'clock, before getting home to see Cherie for the first time really in the day. Even then, how much time would we actually spend together during the evening? Much of the evening would really be own or working time as well. I often would spend any number of hours doing school related work. At other times I might be playing music in a different room, going out to play football, watching football, etc. Cherie, of course, would have her own interests. There in the bath, I couldn't be bothered to work out the mathematics but it was an interesting analysis. Sleep Time takes up most of the night. What proportion of time is left in each other's company? The upshot of all this was, would I miss Cherie as much as I imagined?

But then I started looking at it from the other side of the coin. We often watched TV together, sharing the experience and talking about it afterwards. Cherie would often explain things that I had missed for one reason or another. In many respects we enjoyed the same sorts of TV programmes – drama, and film in particular. But we also had our own niches. Cherie loved cookery, holiday and home improvement programmes and I watched football, documentaries and current affairs. I was so glad that I had thought to install satellite television when we found that Cherie was ill. She really did enjoy *Ready Steady Cook, Changing Rooms* and *'Wish You Were Here'*. And of course, what about all the weekends, our walks together in the Brecon Beacons, trips down to the boat, pub crawls, preparing for dinner parties, shopping in ASDA. The list was endless. How was I going to be without her? What was I going to be without her?

I watched Corrie after my bath, and as Gina threw her flat key back at Dev and the signature tune played out the episode, I turned to my imaginary wife and said in unison with her,

'Ah haa!' the second syllable rising in mild exclamation - our usual response to the climax of the show, as we sat facing each other at either end of our settee with legs entwined.

I needed to get myself some food. I hadn't eaten since the greasy spoon on the way to Whitby – my breakfast really. I went for a wander around Guisborough. The place had loads of pubs and I went into three of them in fairly quick succession, just ordering a half pint in each with the intention of perhaps returning to the best of them later.

As I sat at the bar of the second pub, there was a photograph of a woman on the wall. There was a sub-title on the picture:

Only the good die young: 1957-1998

The woman serving behind the bar told me that the lady in the photo had been a bartender there.

'What did she die of?' I asked.

'Dunno, some sort of bowel problem – she was only 41.'

'Hell of a coincidence,' I thought.

Of all the places to go in Guisborough, I end up at this particular end of a deserted bar staring straight into the face of a woman who died of exactly the same thing as Cherie at exactly the same age.

The next pub I visited had a few more people in it, most of them were staff. Again the conversation was about death. The subject was one I had not really heard of before – closed coffins. Apparently, if someone has died with severe facial injuries or even decapitation, the coffin is permanently closed, for obvious reasons. I wasn't too upset by either of these unhappy coincidences, but they did bring me back to how I was going to be without Cherie. I thought about the wonderful support given to me by my friends and family, but it still didn't answer the fundamental question.

The third pub was again pretty empty with a few old men sat around the bar. I quickly drank another half pint and wondered why I had bothered. After finding a chip shop, I returned to my temporary home, The Fox, as it seemed to be the best pub in town. After fetching my journal from my room, I settled with a pint of Guinness at a table to write. Although there was a convivial atmosphere with plenty of people, and the décor was homely as familiar pop music played in the background, I felt quite down. I had become used to being able to cry briefly and recover, but this seemed more like depression. I felt lonely in the midst of these people and I had no inclination to go to the bar where I might get into a conversation and perhaps snap myself out of it.

When I'd finished writing my journal, I just sat in my seat and occasionally filled my glass until the closing bell rang. Once more, I thought about what I would do without Cherie. Would I get out and do lots of things – follow interests and hobbies? Perhaps I would get back into the music scene and re-establish past musical acquaintances. I thought about getting involved with sailing again – maybe doing a 'Day Skipper' course down at Swansea or Cardiff marina. Or, what about writing and recording some more songs or more hill walking. Not surprisingly at this point, more cycling didn't occur to me! One thing was for sure: I didn't want to stagnate and I thought I'd better keep away from pubs and booze unless it was to share it with family and friends.

When I got back to my room I noticed one of the hotel staff had kindly tumble-dried my washing for me. I had only hand-washed it so it still looked grubby but at least it smelled clean and it was dry and warm. I spent a few minutes looking at the map and thinking about the next day's route before turning in relatively early, still in a sombre mood.

The Ride:

Scarborough to Guisborough

Distance: 42 miles

Guisborough to South Shields

Thursday, July 12th

For fifty percent of the time the weather was sunny. The rain came in the form of showers and I sheltered from them rather than donning my waterproofs. I got away from the hotel by ten to nine but there was a twenty minute delay while I called into a motor spares place to get a locking washer for my back rack. I noticed the errant device was already losing its bolt again. After picking up a pasty for breakfast at a bakery and calling into a chemist for a mini shaving gel, I stood on the main street as the day came into full swing - mothers popping into the shops having dropped the kids off at school, delivery vans with their back doors open being unloaded and an old man trying to park. It was a busy little place.

Having felt a bit down the night before, I was now in much better spirits, possibly the result of a fairly early night without too much alcohol. Perhaps it was down to the fact that I had deliberately slept in, knowing that the shops wouldn't be open until nine o'clock. Or, it may have been just the natural way of things. I'm lucky in that I don't generally suffer mood swings but from time to time when I feel a bit low, I tend to feel refreshed as a result of it – usually the next day. As I stood under the overcast but dry sky, I thought about that warm comfortable bed. After languishing in it for half an hour, I had enjoyed a couple of cups of coffee whilst watching breakfast TV. It was a real luxury compared to my usual morning routine and I actually received the weather forecast from the horse's mouth rather than second hand from a stranger. Having said that, my gear was good enough to withstand anything the summer weather could throw at me, so I was unperturbed.

As I finally got cycling, I found the going very hard again. The wind was still strong and dead against me. I hadn't exactly forgotten about yesterday but this now brought it all flooding back. I had to fight against it for about six miles until I changed course from west to north and headed into Middlesborough. The wind actually helped a bit then, caressing me from the left hind quarter as I headed up the A171. I could see from my map that there was a toll bridge across the River Tees to the east of the city centre. My plan was to cross the toll bridge, more or less missing the city, and head for Hartlepool and the coast road to Newcastle. As I hit Middlesborough around ten o'clock, the traffic was heavy. The roads were wide with at least four lanes at times. It was very unsettling getting into the right hand lane to follow the route straight ahead as I was dwarfed by lorries, buses and cars speeding past me to my left and my right. 'Lane discipline' was not a concept that seemed to apply to me on my bike at that moment. I didn't feel I could include Stratford upon Avon so this was the first real city I had encountered on my trip. I was hugely relieved to get onto a slip road and I parked the bike up to don my waterproofs as it started to rain. Two minutes later, the rain stopped and I had to pull up again to take them off as I began to overheat. I had in fact, made a detour of about half a mile in order to get off the fast multi-lane road. From the vantage point of the flyover, crossing the carriageway I had just left, I could see the transporter bridge in the distance – its characteristic shape the same as the one in Newport, South Wales.

I cycled through a rather dilapidated industrial area interspersed with houses before eventually getting to the bridge. The trip from Guisborough had been either hard work or downright scary, so I was really dejected to see the sign at the bridge:

Bridge Closed Due to High Winds.

Retracing my steps, I had to do an even bigger detour to cross the Tees via the main road bridge on the A19, losing my way at least twice in the process. As I was now further west than I had planned, I decided to abandon the idea of the coast road through Hartlepool and Peterlee and opted to follow the main A19 up to Seaham. I didn't imagine it would be very pleasant, but with all the hassle so far that day, I wanted to make progress northwards.

The manager in the pub the night before had described the A19 dual carriageway between Middlesborough and Newcastle as seeming slightly uphill all the way, at least that was his impression from being at the wheel of his car. I knew that Middlesborough and Newcastle were ports and both at sea level, so I had more or less dismissed his theory as bunkum. But, he was right. Perceptibly, the road just kept going up and up and up. Not a steep gradient, but enough to make it hard work on the bike. Fortunately, the wind was giving me a bit of help, but it was not pleasant being on a straight, busy dual carriageway for mile upon mile.

I picked up a cup of real coffee at a garage, although the drinking of it was preceded by an intelligence test. I'd never come across a machine like this before. The coffee itself was in a type of cassette. I didn't realise that the machine punctured the seal so I spent a good few minutes, my fingers in a fight with the cassette, before eventually gaining access to the coffee. Only then did I realise the role played by the machine and I surreptitiously discarded the now useless cassette into the bin. I hoped the attendant wouldn't notice, or that at least if he did wouldn't tackle me over it. Second time around I managed to get a delicious coffee from the confounded gismo.

Seaham was a bit of a detour; however, I once briefly dated a girl from the town when I was in my first year at university. I realised that the odds of getting in touch with her were very slim, but I thought it would be an interesting distraction. A sizeable group of my university friends have stayed in touch and we still meet up regularly, if infrequently. Alison is not one of these, so I thought it would be a real coup if I could establish contact after all these years. It is sad to lose friends simply because people have moved around - like a 'Pooh stick' disappearing around a riverbend. If I can, I stay in touch, even if it is only an occasional visit or a Christmas card.

I stopped off in a café and had a cup of coffee and a scone and asked if I could look at the local phone book. Unfortunately, phone books don't seem to be as ubiquitous as they used to be, so I had to rely on word of mouth. I asked in the café and later in a grocery store as I bought a couple of bananas, but I was told that there are millions of Andersons in Seaham - they must have originally come across the water from Scandinavia - which put an end to my short lived, half-hearted attempt to make contact with an old acquaintance.

Just a few miles north of Seaham I hit the forty miles mark and started looking for some accommodation. I reckoned I would probably have to book into bed and breakfast again as I was now entering Sunderland. I thought about another university friend of mine, Dave, but any remote chance of me turning detective again was scotched by my failure to remember his surname. As I rolled down one of the main roads towards Sunderland city centre, I came to some temporary traffic lights that had been installed to cut the two-lane road down to one so that road works could be done. There was easily enough room for my bike and I could always wander into the largely empty road works area, so I ignored the red light. If it had been green, the chances were that it would have changed to red before I'd managed to pedal to the other end in any case. The driver of the road washing machine didn't see it that way and he angrily blasted his horn repeatedly at me. I smiled at his mate, who was in charge of a shovel, and he shared the little joke with me – there really was nothing any of them could do about my mild law breaking.

I kept my eye out for bed and breakfast signs but was surprised to see none. As I arrived in the middle of Sunderland, I could see that I wasn't going to find anything suitable, so I decided once more to plump for Pub Information. I found a near empty pub amidst a busy road junction and the barmaid instructed me to bring my bike into the bar. It was just as well because there was nowhere to hide it. In the absence of Strongbow, I ordered a pint of Scrumpy Jack and then quizzed the girl about somewhere to stay. She directed me to pass over the Wear River Bridge and said I should make my way to Roker, then head for South Shields along the A183. Apparently, this was typical British seaside territory and there was sure to be plenty of accommodation. Furthermore, she was fairly certain that there was a campsite in South Shields and she thought she had seen tents there as well as caravans.

I finished my drink and opted to press on rather than ordering another. I looked at the map and estimated that I probably had another five miles to go, and I was already feeling very tired. I negotiated some busy roads but found my way to Roker and the A183 without any difficulty. What the barmaid had told me was absolutely true. This was the archetypal British seaside. I was a little surprised because I did have a perception of the Northeast coast of

England being dominated by heavy industry. But it was all there: a beach stretching out beyond the obligatory tubular railings, a wide promenade, cheap gambling joints filled with one armed bandits and penny falls machines and lots of chip shops. I took the opportunity to get my evening meal at one of these and fortuitously took shelter from a rain shower in the process. The place was more or less deserted, probably due to the poor weather, the fact that it was a Thursday and also because the school holidays had not yet begun. Still, window and door frames with faded paint and rotting wood bore testimony to the demise of this and most other seaside towns, and their fifth rate standing amongst the general paying public, who would much prefer to go to Goa, Orlando, Turkey or Benidorm, probably in that order.

It didn't take me long to get fed up with the cycle lane so thoughtfully provided by the council who must have felt a little ripple from Agenda 21 and the 1993 Rio Earth Summit. It was there that cycling was deemed to be a sustainable and desirable mode of transport, to be encouraged by all nations of the world. The British Government signed up to the dictate and it has cascaded down to the unitary authorities who are under obligation to demonstrate their commitment in their local plans. Cycle lanes have appeared in many of our towns and cities but too often they are just a sop to Rio rather than a functional utility. There's one on my way to work which is only eight metres long! This one along the northeast coast was interrupted by numerous side streets so I went back on to the road proper.

As I passed the sign for South Shields and clocked up exactly fifty miles on the computer, to my left I saw the campsite through railings, rising gently up on to a low hill and flanked by what looked like a council estate. I found the gate and wheeled the bike up to a port-a-cabin that I assumed was the reception. I was very relieved to see tents, as well as caravans – the barmaid had been right. The woman at reception was extremely friendly and helpful. She insisted that I have a fresh cup of tea before setting up my tent and made me sit down 'in the warm'. I was grateful, and even more pleased when I discovered that because it was a municipal site, the fee was only £3.50. Furthermore, it had full washing and showering facilities. And, as a special bonus, there were two pubs within walking distance. The kind lady added more credence to the reputation Geordies have as warm and friendly people, by providing me with chocolate (not just ordinary) biscuits with my hot tea.

I phoned Richard, my son, and Sylvia, my ex-wife, to let them know where I was. I also resolved to write Richard a letter to tell him how proud I was of him achieving his degree. I had made the difficult decision not to attend his graduation which, unfortunately, had coincided with my trip. Although I had discussed the matter with him, I still wanted to write to him formally and I felt that a letter would be something he could keep in a way that a phone call, or indeed, actual attendance, could not.

It started to rain just as I finished pitching my tent. After my nap, I wrote my journal and then went for a shower and shave before heading off to the pub just after eight o'clock. During the ten minute walk to the pub, the sky brightened as the sun set and I took what later turned out to be a very dramatic photograph with the housing estate silhouetted against a blue sky with more than a scattering of ominous black clouds.

What an interesting interlude the pub turned out to be. Like most of the ale houses I had been into, there weren't many people around. I sat at the bar on a stool and got talking to a barmaid (again). I didn't actually drink that much, even though I stayed until closing time, not for any health conscious reason, but because I had run short of money. I could have paid for my beer with my bankcard, but I had left that back at the tent and it was too far and too late to go back by the time I really needed it.

Having said that, I wrote in my journal on my return from the pub, and I must have been a bit tiddly because the entry in my log reads:

'Whoops! It's just started raining – tip, tip, tip on the tent'.

As I wrote, I realised I did not have to wear my Dalek light as there was enough illumination from the nearby toilet block. Hunched on the floor with my thermomat doubled for extra cushioning, I felt that I deserved a cup of coffee, but I had to risk boiling up just inside the entrance to the tent on account of the rain. I'm sure that drinking alcohol then setting fire to a stove in a tent are not sensible procedures when camping, but I was aware of the danger and took care. The flames were accentuated in the dark but Trangias are wonderful bits of kit – they never seem to go really bonkers – one reason why they are used with children on expeditions.

Earlier in the pub, I had talked with the bar maid for quite a while after she had finished her shift. She was in the process of following an access course before hopefully going on to university to eventually become a junior school teacher. She asked me about my trip and told me about a foot ferry that went between South Shields and North Shields. It would be a convenient and novel way of crossing the Tyne and it would keep me away from the city centre and the main arterial roads. This sounded good to me because I didn't fancy a repeat of my lane swapping experiences in Middlesborough. Although the bike would add an extra eighty pence to the fare, I judged it to be comfortably within my budget!

'The trip only takes a matter of minutes,' the girl told me. It was a pleasant chat, but Suzanne soon left with her boyfriend who had come to pick her up. I was left at the bar with another barmaid called Steph.

She surprised me by saying, 'I want to go and live in Cwmamman in South Wales.' This is in the next valley to Merthyr and only a few miles away.

'Why's that?'

'Because that's where the Stereophonics are from, so it must be a nice place.' I didn't quite follow the logic.

There was a small group of people sat further along to my left and separated from me by a narrow pillar. The nearest of these was a slim man who had his back to me. I could hear him talking and I picked up his accent even though I couldn't make out what he was saying. I swung around on the bar stool and with my confidence bolstered by a few drinks, I broke the ice.

'I thought Geordies were hard to understand?'

The man turned, looking a bit surprised at the intrusion, but then replied, in a Geordie accent,

'They are, but we're posh Geordies down here! Go to Newcastle and you'll not understand a single word they're sayin'.'

The bloke's name was Brett and he told me he used to be a confectioner on luxury cruise liners. That was quite a coincidence because that's what Cherie's father used to do. In fact, Cherie's Dad had been involved in the evacuation of Singapore during the war but it was always difficult to get him to say much about it. Perhaps it holds unpleasant memories for him, maybe he's forgotten, or, he simply doesn't find it a worthwhile topic of conversation. Brett was also involved with war – the Falklands campaign, and as he started to talk about it, he began to tear up.

I said sympathetically, 'You don't have to talk about it.'

He replied that it was OK, and went on to tell me some interesting tales. He told me of one particular cock-up where six men were killed in a mix up between the SAS and the SBS.

He talked about the Sir Galahad tragedy and about the guy in charge, who apparently said, 'I'm not evacuating the ship unless I can get everyone off in one go.'

Of course, the ship was a sitting duck and was hit by a missile killing and maiming a large number of our men. He also told me of a disturbing practice on board his merchantman. It seems that all the troops were issued with breathing and fireproof gear but the civvies were not. In the event of a missile attack, the value of a civilian volunteer was obviously less than that of a paid up soldier. Brett got more riled as he related his accounts. His most harrowing experience had been his involvement in the rescue of victims from the Sir Galahad and he clearly still hadn't gotten over it. He told another story of how one of his friends, who was a sort of a motorbike courier, had his leg blown off when he hit a land mine. He finished off by telling me how the Ghurkhas would know who to kill at night, by the way soldiers tied their shoelaces.

'Just as well I was not involved,' I thought, 'with my absentmindedness.'

Brett said he no longer worked on the ships, but it was nothing to do with the Falklands war. He was now chef at the pub. It seemed that everyone else in the room was too, or if not a chef, then bar staff, cleaners, chambermaids or dog's bodies. Eventually, I ran out of money but a woman I had not even noticed, kindly offered me a pound to help me out. I gracefully declined but Steph the barmaid served me up a half pint on the house. Brett said he would have bought me one, but I had the feeling he was watching his pennies and was not too well off himself. Given how open he had been with me, I decided to tell him about Cherie. He really did empathise and he was not the first person whose eyes filled with tears when I told the story. That brought me to tears as well, and the atmosphere was already emotionally charged when he said something that would later become ingrained in my mind:

'You know who you're doing this for don't you?'

I said with some confidence, 'Yes, me.'

'No, you're doing it for the one you lost.'

It really got to me and I cried openly. Brett apologised, although he needn't have, and left me for a while on my own. When he came back he told me that he knew for certain I would make it to the Shetlands. It was a nice thing for him to say and it did cheer me up a bit and strengthen my resolve.

Brett went on to tell me that he also used to work at sea on coasters and I discussed with him the possibility of catching one back home.

'What do they carry?' I asked.

'Anything – sand, scrap – anything that will make money. Give 'em a few quid and they'll probably take you.' He continued,

'There's no way you'll want to go 'round the Hebrides though,' and he described the awful weather and the rough seas of that region. I told him I'd like to try it once and that I'd always loved the sea, boats, ships and the like. Indeed, it was my first choice of profession and I may well have pursued it had it not been for my hearing defect.

The subject changed and Brett told me of an interesting pub that used to exist just down the road. It used to be called 'The Grotto' and it was built into the cliff in a natural cave. There used to be something like 393 steps leading down to it, plus a lift for the feeble-legged, feeble-lunged or lazy. Until a few years ago, it used to be an absolute magnet for locals and tourists alike until geography intervened. An offshore rock with a natural arch collapsed. You could still walk to the rock at low tide but the council blew up one of the stacks because it was in danger of falling down, possibly on to someone's head. Brett reckoned that this had changed the tides (I thought waves) so that erosion of the area around the pub was made worse and it was forced to close.

Two others in the group, one before and one after Brett's monologue put it more simply, 'It needed doing up and it cost too much.'

I enjoyed my evening in the pub and my conversations with Brett especially. He had suggested to me earlier that I take more time on my trip.

'Why stop only one night in each place? Why not stay here tomorrow?'

Back at the tent I dwelled on what Brett had said earlier.

'You're doing it for the one you lost.'

There's that word again – *lost* - but it didn't bother me as I gently cried myself to sleep.

The Ride:

Guisborough to South Shields (Newcastle)
Distance:50 miles

South Shields to Powburn

Friday, July 13th

The forecast was rain, heavy rain in the morning and drier with a little light drizzle in the afternoon. I woke at about six thirty and went to visit the adjacent toilet block. I wasn't sure if it was the Guinness or the salt in my tears, but my eyes were bloodshot to hell with dark Boris Karlov bags under them. It was late enough to get up, but given my macabre appearance, I decided I needed to get back to sleep. When I got up it was raining and I decided not to bother to shave and shower – I had sorted myself out the night before and I was about to embark on another day of toil, so there wasn't much point. Thinking about it later, it was a bad move. If I had the chance to pretty myself up, I needed to take it because I never knew where I was going to be at the end of a day's cycling. What I didn't want was to turn up in a pub, bewhiskered, and looking and smelling like a tramp whose self-respect had long since been washed away down the gutter.

In South Shields, I pedalled through the main shopping street and was surprised how big the place was. As usual, the main thoroughfare was pedestrianised with wavy bricks underfoot and a hubbub of people going about their daily routines. With some new money from a cash point machine I queued to buy a filled roll from a bakery. I hungrily devoured my breakfast, taking shelter from the rain just outside the door of the shop, watching the tide of people as I chomped. It made a very pleasant change from my usual pasty and I pondered over my illogical addiction to them.

'Yes, I used to like them, but of all the ones I've eaten lately, how many of them have been any good?'

Breakfast consumed, I asked for directions to the foot ferry the girl had told me about the night before. Before long I saw it signposted and soon I arrived to see a queue of people awaiting the arrival of the next shuttle. It was clearly a popular service, and I could see why looking at the map. For anyone just wanting to travel across to North Shields, a considerable detour would be needed to get over the River via the Tyne Tunnel. Newcastle itself was about six miles to the east, but I wanted to press on north and didn't feel I could take the time or spare the energy to visit the city centre.

On the ferry, I had a chat with an elderly local man. I had leaned the bike precariously against a bulkhead, but I had little confidence it would stay put especially on a boat. In the event, the trip lasted less than ten minutes and I tried to fathom out what was going on through the windows. They were small and scuffed with years of use and my view was impeded. It seemed as if we were going the wrong way. The old man said,

'Everyone says that'.

By the time we docked, I still hadn't figured it out.

I had to ask for directions to Morpeth and as I looked around, I feared I might lose my way. I had been dropped off in an area of old housing that had an aura of decay. No main roads were visible, just the usual pre-war grid-iron pattern of terraces with some gaps where buildings had been demolished and weeds now taking advantage of the new open space. Almost straight away, I had to ask a man for some directions because there was no obvious route out of the labyrinth. Eventually, I found myself pedalling through an inter-war council estate. Again, I stopped to ask for directions from some builders.

'Turn off this main road and down that side-street, then keep going.' It did occur to me that they might be having an early morning laugh at my expense, a bit like kids deliberately sending strangers the wrong way. I convinced myself that all adults grow out of that particular form of behaviour, so I took them at their word and after a while, ended up on the main A19 headed for Morpeth (thanks fellas).

It wasn't really my first choice of route. There were two other main roads heading north that would have been far less busy, but having found my way on to this one, I didn't want to mess around searching for the alternatives. The dual carriageway was busy, but I was lucky that there was a semblance of a hard shoulder. It was only about a metre wide and it was strewn with small chippings flung from passing traffic, along with scattered pieces of glass, and drains regularly spaced in depressions that I could just about dodge without meandering into the main carriageway. However, despite the hurdles, that metre wide strip still offered a sanctuary of sorts from the heavy traffic that trundled or sped past.

The cycling itself was not too difficult, but it continued for twenty miles in what was now very heavy and continuous rain. Still, it was so much better than fighting against the wind which had now thankfully died down to a gentle breeze. My body didn't register any real complaint as I noticed my speed on the computer – sometimes 13 mph, but mostly 11 or 12. That was good going, and I flicked the button on the computer to compare it with my average trip speed of about 10 mph. Also, I was very pleased that I had managed to dodge Newcastle city centre by using the foot ferry, and all things considered, my spirits were high despite the appalling rain and traffic.

Half way along the dual carriageway, I called into a McDonalds, typically located near a large roundabout. I propped the bike up against one of the goldfish bowl windows, grateful that I would be able to keep an eye on it. Perhaps a 'young' and a cool thing to be seen in McDonalds - but not with the outfit I had on. Pushing through the swinging cowboy doors, I padded to the counter leaving a trail of water on the floor behind me. I ordered a coffee in a polystyrene beaker, and sat by the window for ten minutes watching the traffic through the rain, before getting my backside into gear once more. Later, I stopped off in a garage and had another coffee from the same type of cassette machine I had encountered before – this time though, I knew how to operate the confounded thing.

By the time I reached Morpeth, it was still pouring down. I guessed that in a place that size, there must be a café where I could get a sit-down meal out of the wet. It was only after a second pass through the town that I found a place in a side street. I was doubly pleased that it had a large window area where I could again prop up the bike in full view. I opted for 'beef in a bap' with gravy and chips and a cup of sweet tea – I was fed up with unsweetened black coffee. The interlude gave me time to dry out a little, as I listened to a succession of hit songs from the 1950's. I was there long enough to hear the sequence come around again. So were the youngsters serving me, who happened to be very outgoing and friendly, which, in my experience, is not always the case.

They questioned me about my bike, 'Where are you going?'

'Scotland.'

'Where have you come from?'

'Merthyr Tydfil.'

'Murth –a- tud-vull.' Carefully enunciated, it still didn't sound right with a northern accent.

'Where's that?'

'Wales, South Wales.'

They were very impressed, and melded with the good food and music they gave me a big boost. In a feel-good frame of mind, I reflected: certainly, I had covered a lot of ground since my tentative departure from Merthyr, but there was still an unfathomable distance to go. At least I had lost the fear of failing totally, and I felt that even getting this far now represented a reasonable achievement.

Cycling through the Northumberland countryside, the rain eventually stopped and I started to really enjoy the scenery. Ping-ponging ibuprofen and paracetamol throughout the day, for my leg and my bum respectively, had definitely helped to ease the continuous discomfort and pain. My knee felt a lot better but I had to shift my seated position all the time - I was still very saddle sore.

The rain triggered memories of Cherie in The Ambulance. This was a 1974 Ford Transit ex-ambulance converted to a rather large ungainly camper van, painted by a previous owner in horrible two-tone brown. Some people give their campers names like Daisy, Bessie or Homer. Despite puzzled looks from people, we always referred to it as The Ambulance.

'We'll have to go in the The Ambulance.

'The Ambulance has broken down again.'

'Where can we park The Ambulance?' The simplest of statements caused confusion. Most of the time, we were oblivious to this.

Cherie would be cooking and I would be sat at the table reading or just keeping her company. It was a big van but a very small kitchen so there was no chance that preparing a meal was ever going to be a collaborative event. Over the years, we spent a lot of time together in that old ambulance, often in the pouring rain. I was never a meticulous maintenance man and I adopted with negligent verve the maxim: 'If it's not bust, don't fix it'. But when the rain started to drip into the habitation part (sleeping quarters at night – dining table by day), something had to be done. My solution was predictably slap dash and impermanent. I climbed the ladder at the back of the vehicle and attached a bin liner, folded to the approximate size, to the leaking skylight and secured it with a bungee. It looked pretty gross from the outside but it worked. Another time, the rain started leaking through the main windscreen as I was driving along. As luck would have it, the rain only dripped on to me. This was good because I put it down to just one more thing going wrong with The Ambulance and neither of us wanted to mess about trying to fix a leaking window when we were away and wanted to have fun. Cherie got hold of a bath towel and tucked it into the neck of my tee shirt so it now resembled an oversized baby's bib – how thoughtful! As I remembered those times, I once more marvelled at how she coped with problems in such a matter of fact way. So many people treat trivial mishaps as major crises, but the two of us would simply breeze through – together. We shared a common perspective on life and I loved her.

Again, I pondered,

'Who am I doing this trip for?'

It wasn't exactly an obsession – it was just a question that kept popping into my mind I couldn't shake it off.

'How could it be for Cherie?'

Maybe it was because I knew that *she* thought the trip was a good idea and that *she* had faith in me – *she* believed I possessed the determination to get to the Shetlands, whatever the obstacles.

Then I countered with, 'Of course - I'm doing it for me – to get away- time to think - a physical challenge - maybe draw a line in the sand.'

I couldn't say that I felt anger at Cherie's death, although I knew that anger was a common reaction to bereavement. When I climbed steep hills or battled against the wind, I didn't feel that I was venting anger. Maybe, subconsciously I was, but I can't know that. Occasionally though, I would notice an old couple walking along, or even an old man or woman on their own, and I would fleetingly get thoughts about the unfairness of Cherie's illness. I had experienced a similar thing when my father died. I often mistook grey haired gentlemen for my Dad, but would then realise in a second it couldn't be, which was instantly followed by an awful feeling of loss (no wonder people say they've lost someone!), followed by anger.

'Why should that old codger, struggling to even walk, be alive when my Dad is dead - he was only fifty-seven?'

Then I would admit, 'These old people do *deserve* to be alive – but, why? Because they are good? Because they have never smoked? Because God has favoured them, maybe because they go to church?' I dispensed with all of these. 'They were lucky.'

The more I came to terms with seeing 'undeserved' characters walking the streets, sitting on benches, propping up bars or complaining, often complaining (about anything under the sun), the easier it became to accept the nebulous but comforting adage,

'That's life'– or perhaps 'That's Living' was closer to the mark. I could understand that, in life there is no absolute order, and an Irish folk song that I used to sing sprang to mind. Called, 'Isn't it Grand Boys'*, I first heard it played live in the place where I cut my performing teeth – a pub called 'The Bruce' in Dowlais, Merthyr.

There was a sort of mathematical logic to the chorus, 'And always remember the longer you live, the sooner you bloody well die'.

But Cherie hadn't lived long and she was 'bloody well dead'. Neither of us were naturals at mathematics – just our luck that the norms should not apply for us.

By now I was feeling the weariness percolating into my muscles and I started to get concerned about finding a spot to camp. I didn't have any information and settlements had become something of a rarity. I came to the cross roads where the A697 met the B6341. There was a shop/post office there and I parked up to get some fuel for my body and hopefully, some intelligence on the camping front. Working in the shop was the friendliest bunch of people you could imagine. The man, whom I assumed was the owner, was dressed in traditional grocer garb with a striped apron protecting a checked shirt with collar and tie. He was busy unloading supplies from his pristine van parked outside. Totally in character, the van was sign written with his name and the proud title, 'Grocer'. It reminded me of one of those retrospective dramas like *The Darling Buds of May* or *Heartbeat*, where every vehicle has a showroom shine and every person is well turned out in the fashions of the day.

I had a laugh and joke with the lady assistants; in the midst of the banter, I sought information about camping or bed and breakfast establishments in the area. They knew of a pub a few miles down the road that might have accommodation and they seemed to think that the garage, about six miles away, might accept tents. I said cheerio and hung around outside the shop eating the few miscellaneous items I had bought and hopefully boosting my energy levels with Lucozade. I had covered close to forty miles and the fifteen-minute break had lasted long enough to let my body think its day's work was done.

Back on the saddle, I couldn't decide whether to take a slight detour into the hamlet of Glanton and try the pub for bed and breakfast, or stick to the main road and hope that the garage did indeed take tents. Glanton was 'sort of' on the way and a pub sounded a better option than a garage, so I took the detour despite the fact that I could see it was going to involve a fairly steep climb. I pushed the bike up the hill to the village only to find that the pub was closed.

'Now what?' I backtracked to an antiques/bric-a-brac shop that seemed to be open. Inside what I assumed was a family run business (though where the trade came from in this most rural of settings I couldn't imagine) was a collection of people apparently sorting some things out. I wasn't sure if they were actually open as I wandered in.

So far on my trip, I had encountered so much kindness and met so many good spirited people, I now had raised expectations. The folk there weren't rude but neither were they friendly. They told me that they didn't think that the pub had any rooms and turned their backs.

I think I heard a gruff, 'Goodbye.'

I was knackered - it was the end of my day and I'd come a long way, but of course they didn't know that. Any offer of help or advice was not in their minds as they busied themselves, oblivious to this insignificant man on his bike. For me, the detour had been a waste of time and now I had to pin my hopes on the garage. I had mentioned to the grocer that if I couldn't find a campsite I might put my tent up in a field, but he reminded me of the current foot and mouth epidemic and said that, with access restrictions in force, if I did I could be in trouble. This removed from me a very important bolthole - my tent was small, could be rigged in a couple of minutes and plonked virtually anywhere. I had planned that if I got stuck I could always camp rough but it now looked as if I might have nowhere to stay – what now?

All across the UK, foot and mouth disease was wreaking havoc and large tracts of open land were now 'no go' areas for the general public. It struck me how these restrictions stimulated a yearning for what was now denied. I'm sure many of us don't go into the countryside on a regular basis, but once we're not *allowed* to go, we feel a desperate, almost spiritual need to get out there. Now, restricted access to the fields and woods had a practical implication rather than an aesthetic one. What the hell was I going to do if this garage didn't offer camping? I would have to secretly camp under cover of darkness, SAS style. I knew I couldn't cycle any further.

Thankfully, the dogleg back to the main road involved a downhill 'wheee!' and I soon saw the garage coming into sight at the bottom of a dip in the road. As I pedalled onto the forecourt and leaned the bike against a wall, I couldn't see any tents. I went into the garage shop and it was more like a well-stocked SPAR. At the counter, I tentatively asked about putting up my tent and was greatly relieved to hear an affirmative response.

'You can go in the children's play area; but, you'll have to wait a bit, because Thomas is in the middle of cutting the grass.'

'Have you got anywhere I can shower?'

'Sorry, we're in the middle of sorting the shower out, but there are washbasins and hot water. The door doesn't work yet though so you'll have to come through the shop. Make sure you're sorted before ten o'clock because we close then.'

It wasn't great, but it was far better than the SAS option. I went outside to examine the site and, sure enough, Thomas was busy at work making a hell of a racket with a strimmer and wearing full protective face and ear gear. I waved to him and he stopped the machine.

'I won't be a minute.'

In fact, he was about ten, but I took the opportunity to wander around and picked up some bits and pieces to eat. Outside I feasted on my assortment of savouries and sweets and was reminded of the SPAR dinner I had had as I sat on the wall on the outskirts of Evesham. The end result was the dissipation of my hunger but no real pleasure.

Returning to the play area, Thomas was finishing off at the far end so I started to make camp. The area was rectangular and the measurements of a good-sized garden with a hedge separating me from the weathered, pot holed concrete of the garage complex. On the other side of the garden was a damaged fence that failed to prevent access to a small steep gully with a stream. At one end of the patch, there were kids' climbing frames and several wooden 'all in one' bench-tables dotted about. It looked as if the owner of the garage had successfully diversified, making the most of his scattered rural market and the transient tourists that passed by on their way to or from Scotland on the A697. The garage was a supermarket, the caravan site accepted tents and the vehicle workshop was the size of an aircraft hangar suggesting a fair throughput of business – oh yes – and they sold petrol.

The tent erected and organised, I settled down for my late afternoon snooze. I dropped off for a while but was soon disturbed by the arrival of other campers. Despite my best efforts to ignore them, I couldn't get back to sleep. They were a large group and in high spirits as they tried to get to grips with erecting an old frame tent that they had borrowed. They noisily wrestled with scores of poles that used to have coloured tags but with years of use and abuse these essential prompts had weathered away – an engineer would have struggled. As they giggled, laughed, hooted and shouted banter, I couldn't help being irritated as I tried to rest. Eventually I gave up and surfaced. I wandered over to my new tribal neighbours, more out of curiosity than any need to make peace (not that they knew they were at war). They turned out to be an affable bunch attending a wedding party. There wasn't room for them to stay at the house so, rather than draw straws to select a driver, they had decided to camp. I chatted to them for a while then dug out my washing gear and traipsed through the shop with my toilet bag, towel, and clean underwear to get to the washroom.

The facilities were grim - a temperamental shower that successively burned and froze with the slightest of adjustments, a flow rate that wouldn't have bothered a stranded spider, chipped tiles and the accumulated grubbiness that comes from a long period of neglect (I had forgotten that the shower was in the middle of being "sorted out"). I wished I'd had a shower in South Shields before I'd left and vowed not to miss an opportunity like that again. Despite the lamentable facilities though, I was pleased that the site had only cost me two pounds for the night. The big attraction of the place was that there was a pub a hundred yards up the road, and I headed there as soon as I'd made myself look decent. I didn't get out of there until quarter past three in the morning. Even then, there were quite a few people still going strong. I had arrived at about eight o'clock and the place was already in full swing. It was a Friday but I hadn't seen any villages in the area. The pub must have been tapping into the same source of revenue as the garage entrepreneur.

The barman had an accent I couldn't make out, a big bushy beard (very much like Buster Merryfield, the uncle in *Only Fools and Horses*), and an overall scruffiness epitomised by the weathered leather flip flops on his otherwise bare feet. At one end of the long room was a roaring fire and next to it, there were a few small round tables that were empty. I couldn't resist going to sit by the fire but once I had been there a while, relaxing as the flames danced on the coals, I wondered whether I should have stayed at the bar. It was at the bar that I had met most people on my trip. As I sat at the table, a group of women of various ages sat near the opposite wall, laughing, joking and screaming. One or two of them were quite attractive but too young for me. Most of them were too old and none of them were Cherie. They soon left to go off to some do, maybe the same wedding as my fellow campers. At the same time, I noticed a spare bar stool and decided I had had enough of my own company.

I soon got into conversation with a couple at the bar. The man was a chemistry teacher and his wife an NHS administrator. They were a very pleasant couple; but, as usually happens when teachers get together, I found myself getting drawn into a discussion about education - I needed to change the subject. I told them I was on a long cycle trip and that was enough to steer us on to hobbies. Their passion was collecting old Austin A35s and they had about four of them that they had restored to mint condition. One of them was the standard saloon, another was the van version and they also had a pick-up. They didn't drive them very often but they attended rallies and took them for a spin when the weather was fine. They also collected butterflies, as well as participating in an unusual game which involved tracking down objects on Dartmoor.

As I talked to the couple, I became aware of some of the other people in the bar. My curiosity was aroused because they seemed to be rather out of the ordinary. I politely wound down my conversation with the couple and swivelled a little on my stool to bring me into hearing range. A pause in the chatter gave me a chance to ask a question that let me into the group. Two of the men and a woman were local, but two other men were sheep shearers from New Zealand. I chatted to one of them, a bloke called Raiff, for some time – in fact I followed him back to his table to carry on the conversation.

'There's a whole gang of us here in Northumberland – we travel around all the farms shearing sheep.' I was surprised how nomadic these guys were.

'We've just come over from Canada. Before that, the season was back home, in New Zealand.'

Apparently, this world tour was a regular occurrence and a fair amount of money was to be made from it. Raiff told me he usually earned £100 a day. He finished his drink and took me up on my offer to buy him another. We talked a while longer but it was hard going as he spoke quickly with a quiet voice and a very strong accent. He told me a bit about himself and I noticed his leg nervously tapping the cross rail of his high barstool. He liked his work and the travelling but his family life was a disaster and his wife now didn't want to know him. From the way he spoke, I could understand why and he didn't stir any sympathy in me. What's more he broke the drinkers' code – he didn't buy me a drink back. After a trip to the toilet, I didn't return to the table but made my way back to the bar.

At the bar I started talking to a young guy who I later found out to be twenty-eight, although he didn't look it. Of medium height but very slim with an outdoor complexion, he was a shepherd who had been doing the job since the age of nine. His young son was now following in his footsteps and he used two sheep dogs and a little Jack Russell that he said, 'Woke 'em up'. It seemed strange to be talking to a modern day shepherd, especially one I thought was so young, but despite his high spirits he started to tear up when we got on to the subject of farming. The tough time that farmers have been having is always in the news. It's been getting steadily worse for years as the government and the EU have tried to grapple with the conundrum of supporting agriculture whilst reducing food surpluses and cutting the cost of the common agricultural policy. To make it worse, the country was now in the grip of a foot and mouth epidemic having only just bumbled through the BSE crisis. The young farmer was genuinely upset over his present plight and I felt bad for bringing up the subject.

The Buster Merryfield look-alike had finished his stint behind the bar and other staff had taken over. He was a sheep shearer too and he seemed a lot more interesting than Raiff. I must have been getting drunk as I said, pointing in Raiff's direction,

'I'm not very impressed with him.'

I don't think it was very wise of me to slag off Buster's compatriot and fellow sheep shearer – I was just a stranger. Still, he took no offence and immediately bought me a drink to prove that Kiwis are not all like Raiff.

Stood near the bar, by now into the early hours but still buzzing with activity, we were joined by another shearer. When the subject of my bike ride came up he bitterly started to complain about the loss of his driving licence on account of a cyclist. He had been involved in a collision with a bike. It wasn't his fault but the police became involved. It transpired that he had been drinking and was over the limit.

Tact now definitely deserted me as I stupidly pointed out,

'But you shouldn't have been drinking and driving in the first place.' He'd been upset at the start and now I stood before him - a hated cyclist, inflaming an already volatile situation.

As he homed in on me, through a boozy haze my self-preservation instincts must have kicked in, and I relented, 'Sorry, yeah – I can see what you mean... especially when it wasn't even your fault. Crazy, I dunno – they didn't have to ban you did they – bloody mad, eh?' I managed to patch it up with him and, I think, saved my skin in the process.

I don't particularly like losing an argument and I'm not bad at holding my own even when I know my viewpoint has dubious validity. But this was different. Already with aching knee and sore arse - imagine adding to my list: bruised all over, black eye and worse still, broken bones.

Although I spoke to lots of people in the pub, and I was there for quite a few hours, the place didn't seem as friendly as other pubs I had visited. I sidled away from the drunken drink-driving, cycle-hitting, sheep-shearer from New Zealand and found an unoccupied bar stool. Alone in the crowd, I wondered whether I should have stayed quite so long. There were quite a few women dressed up but none to match my classy Cherie. I noticed that I was now by the side of an old man who had passed me on one of my frequent trips to the loo.

Out of the blue he said to me,

'You don't have to be totally negative do you?'

This was delivered in a broad Geordie accent and I was taken aback a little. Thinking back, perhaps my darkening mood was in truth reflected in my face, but I couldn't fathom out his comment at the time. I caught his attention and told him about Cherie. I must have thought that the sod should know the full facts before he started firing verbal bullets at complete strangers, but mentioning Cherie's death was a cheap trick and I soon regretted it. Not only because I felt her memory shouldn't be used in this way, but also because the sod would not leave me alone after I had told him. He harassed me off and on for the rest of the night with big hugs and heavily laden sympathy. It was not what I wanted and he made me feel very uncomfortable.

By now the room was starting to thin a little and the owner of the pub, who had relieved Buster Merryfield earlier on, now crossed to the punter side of the bar and I started talking to him. I said what a surprise it was to find so many foreign sheepshearers in the place and he filled me in on a few more details.

'I do good business with 'em – some of them spend nearly all their wages in 'ere! A few of 'em actually sleep here in the bar – on the benches over there. I cook 'em breakfast in the morning.'

He had seen the old man embracing me and was curious, so I told him what was going on. He started to talk with great affection and fondness about his own wife. He pointed her out to me. She was middle aged and was one of the women I had been watching as I sat by the fire earlier on. She had been debating with her friends whether she should put her hair up or down and she had left with them for the party. Now hours later, she had returned.

Her husband clearly thought the world of her and I said to him, 'Why don't you do something really special for her – totally out of the blue, not to mark any occasion, but just to show her how much you really love her. It doesn't matter if it's cheap or expensive – just do it.'

We exchanged views on the subject for a short while but his line didn't falter, 'She knows I love 'er - I don't need to do anything like that.'

I couldn't win him over, but I sensed him thinking on it. It's such a cliché, but how true are most clichés. We do take each other for granted – why can't we shake ourselves up and bloody do something about it. I hoped the landlord would do something special for his wife and I wished she could have been a fly on the wall listening to the way he was talking about her. Did I ever *really* do anything like that for Cherie? I think I did, but now I wished I had done more. I half staggered the short walk back to the garage sobbing all the way. It didn't take me long to get into bed and it was sleep that arrested my sorrow.

The Ride:

South Shields to Powburn (Northumberland)
Distance: 45 miles

*Just look at the coffin, with golden handles

Isn't it grand boys, to be bloody well dead?

Chorus

Let's not have a snivel, let's have a bloody good cry

And always remember the longer you live the sooner you bloody well die

Chorus

Just look at the flowers, all bloody withered,

Isn't it grand boys to be bloody well dead?

Chorus

Just look at the mourners, bloody great hypocrites
Isn't it grand boys to be bloody well dead?

Chorus

Just look at the widow, bloody great female
Isn't it grand boy to be bloody well dead?

Chorus

Powburn to Lauder

Saturday, July 14th

Yippee! I rode for just under a mile not looking where I was going, save for the odd glance. By coincidence, I had flicked the bike computer on to 'odometer' to see how far I had come since leaving my house in Merthyr. I didn't know when it had clicked on to its present reading of 499 miles, but I childishly wanted to see it mechanically change to the milestone of 500. It must have only just changed because I seemed to be going for ages gazing at the damn LED display, afraid to look anywhere else lest I should miss the grand event. Eventually, it happened and was predictably anticlimactic, but at least it meant I could now concentrate on looking where I was going again. I started to think about the significance of the distance I had covered.

'Am I half way? I can't be far off. I'll have to check on the map tonight.'

The significance of the achievement hit me, and I felt a rush of euphoria and a deep sense of satisfaction as I realised I could now return home having at last accomplished something of magnitude, at least by my standards.

That morning hadn't started off well. It had been bad enough not having any showering facilities, but I had to walk through the busy garage shop carrying my toilet bag and my towel to find that only the cold water worked. I was a bit hung-over after my night in the sheepshearer's pub, but at least I didn't have a headache or a bad gut as such. The main way the drink got me was the manner in which it took me an age to get myself into gear. Everything, even the simplest task, like putting the Trangia on for my morning brew took an age.

Given that, I was surprised I had the presence of mind to think about bike maintenance. It had occurred to me the day before that I needed to get some lubrication on to the chain, and I had noticed as I locked the bike to a rustic garden table that the tyres needed air. I ambled over to the hangar-like garage and mooched around looking for someone. After a few minutes, a man appeared and kindly loaned me a can of WD 40. I had noticed a white motorbike and I asked him about it. He had sold it that morning and the buyer was due to pick it up later on. In my rather imperceptive state I hadn't realised that it was exactly the same motorbike as my own – a Honda VFR 750. It was even made in the same year – 1989. Had it been the same colour, black, I might have made the connection but being white it just looked like a different bike until it was pointed out to me.

'Why are you selling it?' I asked.

'Dunno, it's a really good bike. I just fancy a change – something newer and sportier.' He was going to get a Fireblade.

I continued the conversation, 'I'd rather stick to my VFR I think. It does everything well – touring, blasting, cornering at speed - not that I'm that bothered about belting around bends.'

I could never understand the sense in treating ordinary roads like a racetrack just because you're on a motorbike - and yet all the motorcycle magazines display religious zeal in promoting speed around bends and regularly feature articles with titles like, 'Go Faster Around

Bends' and 'Take the Right Line'. As far as I'm concerned, you never know if there's a tractor or a broken down teenager hidden around the corner fully equipped to instantly send you into the next world. But, as a rather mature, born again biker, I'm probably missing the point and, as a result, the real thrills of motor biking. Still, I always remember the ageing racing driver Stirling Moss being interviewed.

In answer to the question, 'How do you drive on ordinary roads?' Sterling replied, 'When I was younger I used to drive like a nut-case. Then one day I suddenly thought to myself, "What would happen if I met myself coming the other way?" It was a Eureka moment and from that moment I was a different driver – on roads of course!'

I went back to the play area to sort out the bike then returned the WD 40 with a thanks and a goodbye. My tyre was topped up with air at considerable expense of effort. The pump basically was not up to the task even though I had honed my technique over the years. I also tried a new way of packing the bits to the outside of the rucksack that made it feel more stable. By the time I had done all this, it was a late start and nearly 11 o'clock before I pedalled back on to the A697.

Almost immediately, it started to rain and I stopped to don the wet gear. Despite the weather, cycling through the Northumberland countryside was again a very rewarding and pleasant experience. By a twist of fortune, I had taken the Coldstream road rather than the coast route or the A696 to Jedburgh that would have taken me over the Cheviot Hills. In so doing I had taken the flattest way. The hills were gently rolling and I was able to pedal up most of them, easing off for a few hundred yards as I traversed the crests, then relaxing as the weight of myself and my load allowed me to coast down the other side, usually at a speed of sixteen mph or more. It was an understated green world that slowly passed me by, but I took in very little of it. Nor did I think about my route or the host of other practical matters that so often preoccupied me. It was turning out to be my most introspective day yet and it was stories from the past that played out in my mind.

It must have been the white VFR and the chat with the guy in the garage that triggered the first. Cherie was overly cautious in many ways. On the motorbike she would politely prompt me to slow down, or take the corners easier. On the boat, she'd deliberately sheet out the jib in the gusts so the boat wouldn't heel so far over.

But, in other respects, she was the opposite. She decided to take her CBT (compulsory basic training) on a motorbike because she wasn't sure that she would like riding pillion with me in control. She went to the local bike-training centre and booked in. In the early evening a week later, she was taken down to a quiet industrial estate where she was introduced to the basic motorcycle controls. She picked it up quickly and soon her confidence flowed. Unfortunately, she hadn't really internalised the coordination of clutch and throttle and half way into one of her circuits she suddenly got things backwards. She wanted to slow down but instead of pulling in the clutch with her left hand and releasing the throttle with her right, she did exactly the opposite. The effect was to make the bike accelerate sharply. There were some respectable cars parked nearby and she headed straight for one of them. As panic replaced reason, there was nothing she could do about the speed of the bike, and self-preservation took over. She managed to swerve and miss a rather nice Jaguar but buzzed straight into the brick wall of one of the factories. She was probably only doing about fifteen miles per hour, but that was still a nasty jolt to a fledging motorcyclist with strong wimpish tendencies.

Of course she came off. The instructor ran over to cut the engine as Cherie hauled herself to her feet. She was quite shaken but the bike was worse. Both front forks were badly bent. The instructor must have assumed it was the end of the lesson, but he was in for a surprise.

She was indignant, 'What do you mean, "We'll try another day"?'

'But I'd have to get the van to bring another bike down from the shop.'

'That's not a problem is it? You said we could get this test done in one go.'

'But you've hurt yourself.'

'I'm fine – go on – hurry up!'

She was definitely no natural, and I'm sure it took her longer to pass her CBT than most, but I was amazed that she saw it through after her collision with the factory wall.

With fondness, I thought about other times we shared as I pedalled along still oblivious to my surroundings. But my main train of thought fell to the sequence of events that sign posted Cherie's illness. One Sunday morning Cherie was complaining about not feeling well. She had mentioned a few weeks earlier that she had passed blood from her backside a few times. She didn't have my hypochondriac tendencies, and she put it down to a pull she must have picked up at the gym. I don't know a great deal about medicine, but I was aware that blood from the back passage was an ominous sign and I had nagged her to get to see her doctor. In the end, she had gone finally and the doctor said that he would refer her to the local hospital. That had been a few weeks ago and we had heard nothing.

Now on this particular Sunday morning, Cherie was feeling decidedly unwell with symptoms that were unusual and perturbing. I became more and more worried and, in the end, I phoned my doctor at his home. It was the first time I had ever done this. Luckily, I know my doctor socially and even though it had been twelve years since we'd been out together I knew he wouldn't mind.

He must have sensed that I was upset, as he said,

'Tony, there's no need to worry. Many things can cause such symptoms. This is off the record but my advice is to take her to accident and emergency in Prince Charles Hospital. You should get to see someone straight away.'

I thanked him and we made ready for the short trip to hospital. On the way, Cherie became progressively more uncomfortable and I felt myself getting more and more worried. I was afraid we would be turned away and told to make an appointment to see our GP, but when we checked into the accident and emergency department, every support was offered. We were taken into a small room off the main corridor where we waited to see a doctor. After a few preliminary checks, the decision was made to take Cherie onto a ward.

'I knew this would bloody happen,' she said, somehow trying to justify her not seeking medical advice earlier. Coincidentally, the hospital had recently won a prestigious award for their programme of bowel cancer treatment so perhaps they were more clued up in Merthyr than elsewhere. On the ward, we waited for the next doctor to come along. By now Cherie was in a gown and the doctor asked her to lie on her side. He used lubricant and gloves and gave Cherie warning that he was 'going inside'. Cherie's face registered the shock as the doctor suddenly entered her back passage. It must have been terrible for her and it lasted for what seemed like ages – and it was - probably half a minute. He didn't say anything to us, but I sensed something was wrong.

Eventually he said what we didn't want to hear, 'Something seems to be there, but you don't need to worry.'

From that point onwards, every time we went to receive news about Cherie's condition, after a few false-hope twists and turns and a variable time lag, it always ended up as bad news. First, we were told it wasn't necessarily a tumour – it could be a polyp – but it was a tumour. Later we were told that it could be removed and the bowel repaired. It would mean a colostomy, but this would only be temporary while the bowel repaired itself. The bowel couldn't – it was too close to the rectum and there was not enough tissue to reconnect at the lower end. Effectively this meant that the colostomy would be permanent. Cherie pushed for the colostomy operation to be performed as soon as possible and the hospital obliged. Good news again - there was no sign of any secondary spread. Then she had to have the main operation that involved removing her rectum and anus completely so she no longer had a bum hole - her back passage now redirected to the stoma (hole) in the side of her tummy.

But, good news again - there was still no sign of any spread of the disease (metastases). However, there was a complication that set in a few weeks after having the main operation. Part of the bowel had become attached to Cherie's body wall (adhesions) and blocked the movement of stools to her new hole. The doctors couldn't be sure what the problem was and they were naturally reluctant to operate again so soon. Cherie had to stay in hospital for three weeks, all the time being fed through a drip, before the decision was finally made to open her up again. Thankfully, the operation did sort out the problem and she was discharged and soon started to gain the weight she had lost. For those three weeks spent in hospital, apart from feeling more ill than she had done at any other time, Cherie was particularly annoyed with the world because she should have been lying on a beach in Tunisia.

To all outward appearances, Cherie made a full recovery and we went back to our daily routines, until one day we arrived home to find a message from the consultant's secretary on our answer phone. He needed to see us both. The consultant's name was Mr Braithwaite, a well-built, good-looking man in his fifties. My first interaction with Mr Braithwaite took place after school one day when I went up to visit Cherie, a few days after she had been admitted on that first Sunday. Cherie was unhappy with one of the procedures she had been subjected to whilst tests were being carried out, and she had asked me to speak to the consultant to see if the same thing could be avoided in future.

'I'm not having that done again!' was how she put it.

Mr. Braithwaite beckoned me into a small room off the ward and I sat down with him, joined by another doctor and a nurse. My main thought was to get Cherie's wish across and I managed to make my point early on in the discussion.

I didn't get to finish, however.

Mr Braithwaite cut in, 'You must realise, Mr. Hill, that your wife is a very sick woman. She has what appears to be a tumour in her bowel, and we will have to operate. We may be able to save the bowel, but she has to have a colostomy. It is possible that the colostomy will be permanent and her rectum will have to be removed.'

I was stunned as I sat listening to his words.

'She could die Mr Hill.'

My objection to the procedure planned for Cherie was now obsolete.

'Do you have any questions?'

I had lots and Mr Braithwaite patiently answered them all then asked me, 'Do you think you will tell your wife what is happening?'

So that's why I had been called into the room alone. The news was so bad they didn't know if Cherie would be able to handle it.

'Yes, I certainly will.' The notion of keeping Cherie in the dark about anything was highly unlikely, and with something as important and fundamental as this, it was unthinkable. I can't remember if I cried but I was badly shaken, and my heart sank even lower as I mentally rehearsed what I was going to say when I returned to Cherie's bedside.

I walked purposefully between the two rows of tubular metal bed ends to where Cherie was lying as she tracked me with her eyes. Sitting beside the bed, I told her directly, word for word, what Mr. Braithwaite had said. A few times she tried to interrupt and ask me what the doctor had said about the unpleasant procedure she wanted me to discuss with him. I cut across her questions just as the consultant had done with me.

Then I held her for a while before taking her hand and looking into to her eyes.

She remained calm and collected as she smiled back at me, 'So that's what Dr Death reckons is it?'

Cherie was referring to Mr Braithwaite's burgeoning reputation as a harbinger of doom and gloom. Then, she picked up on all the positive things that Mr. Braithwaite had said and turned my despair into optimism. As Cherie saw it, there would be an operation to temporarily redirect the stools out of a hole in her abdomen, followed by an operation to cut the tumour from her bowel and stitch the two bits together. Finally, after that had healed, they would re-join her bowel and sew her back up.

She was annoyed that her stomach would be scarred: 'My stretch marks are bad enough already – bloody kids!'

From that day on, we always referred jocularly to Mr. Braithwaite as 'Doctor Death' although naturally, never to his face. Maybe he'd had been right to paint it black, because in the end, it was the worst-case scenario that played out over the following nineteen months.

Friday, the day of the appointment, had arrived, and Cherie and I waited on the third floor of Prince Charles Hospital, in yet another small room, for Mr Braithwaite and the stoma nurse Margaret to join us. We chatted about our misgivings for the five minutes it took for them to come in and settle themselves.

Then came the pleasantries:

'How's things?'

'Fine, thanks.'

'What have you been up to?'

Cherie told Mr Braithwaite about the cancelled trip to Tunisia. (The consultant had in fact been quite helpful, because he had written a letter to the holiday insurance company in which he stated that, in his professional opinion, Cherie had been fit to travel abroad and that her enforced hospital stay had nothing to do with her cancer. The result was that the company gave us a full refund). Cherie went on to tell him about our planned holiday to Bangkok, Singapore and the Maldives.

'Ahh, very good.' He brought the small talk to a conclusion. Then, he started to explain why he had wanted to see us both. The CAT scan results had come back from the processing lab. There were some dark spots showing up on Cherie's liver. Dr Death went on to say that he couldn't be sure what they were and that they needed to go down to the Velindre cancer hospital to be examined and interpreted by a radiologist. Nevertheless, he had an opinion on the matter which was characteristically gloomy.

'They look like metastases – in other words the cancer has spread to your liver.'

I said quizzically, 'But when you operated you thought everything was OK – there was no sign of any spread.'

'We can't always tell just from looking,' came back the inevitable reply.

'What does that mean?' Cherie asked.

'We can't cure it when it's spread to the liver. But we can treat it.' Margaret the stoma nurse nodded in agreement.

'How long have I got?'

'It's hard to say' – another expected reply.

Dr Death and Margaret then exchanged comments with each other:

'Some have lived five years - well one person actually.'

'That's very unusual.'

'Yes, but some survive three years.'

'We've had a few live for three years.'

'It's not that common though – eighteen months is the average survival time after liver metastases have been detected.'

The consultant continued, 'But I must stress, I'm only giving my opinion. I would rather be straight with you: it doesn't look good, but I'm not the radiologist.'

So that was it - after an emotional roller coaster ride, the final piece of bad news.

What is it like to be told you only have a certain amount of time left to live? That has been the subject of many a pub, office or factory floor discussion. Now it had happened to us for real. How did we feel? Numb but not exactly upset – doctors have a knack of telling these things in a way that offers enough hope to keep the spirit alight. There must be a natural human defence mechanism that kicks in too. Five years is a long time, so is three. Even eighteen months into the future is hard to truly comprehend... Then of course, Mr Braithwaite could be wrong – he wasn't a radiologist. But I think we both knew.

I can't remember what happened next, but we must have needed to see the kids in Newport because I remember walking with Cherie across John Frost Square in the city centre, then deliberately falling behind her as she slowly browsed a jewellery shop window. As I gazed at her, characteristically in her element shopping, I had to hold back my tears.

She was just so matter-of-fact about bloody everything. I could see her sitting on the loo changing her colostomy bag with typical speed and efficiency; and, I remembered how, the bag formed a considerable blot on her otherwise flat tummy as, half asleep in the mornings, I ran my hand over her in bed.

Then my thoughts skipped ahead to the day Cherie died. I wasn't there, 'at the moment' – ten past six on Saturday morning – June 23rd – mid-summer. I had said my goodbye the previous day, Friday, at about lunchtime and in private. Cherie had been delirious for a few days already and I wasn't sure how much she was aware of me now. But the drugs were being upped again that afternoon and I had a strong feeling that this would be my last chance to say farewell. I spoke to her gently. I said this might be the last time she would hear my voice.

I told her I loved her and just before I left, I finished with our familiar old fashioned signature, 'Goodbye, Dear.'

My heart was heavy and there was despair in my soul as I trudged the now familiar corridors and stairs, automatically finding my way out of the building and into the car park. Only when I got into the car and closed the world out with the door, did the tears come.

I did see Cherie again, stroked her hair and spoke to her a few times for a while but it wasn't the same. Others were there and she was totally out of it by then. I didn't want to see her after she died. Her mum did. She said that Cherie looked as if she would wake up at any moment.

I thought, 'How many times have I seen Cherie like that ... fast asleep then, shock! Eyes wide open as I wake her, then straight back to sleep leaving her carefully crafted cup of tea to go cold!'

I snapped out of my sad reverie and wiped my eyes as I approached a town – Wooler. Earlier, before leaving the garage I had eaten for breakfast a surprisingly decent roll, but now eight miles into the day's ride, I thought I'd take the opportunity to get out of the heavy rain, rest my bum and get a substantial meal to soak up the hangover. A pallid sausage, broken egg, flaccid undercooked chips, weak coffee and not cheap. I would have been better off with McDonalds if there had been one around.

Back on the road and heading for Coldstream, I wasn't sure if it was the 'otherwordliness' I sometimes experience as a result of a serious lack of sleep and too much booze, or the fact that the cycling was easier. Certainly, the countryside was still pleasant as I skirted the Cheviot Hills, clearly visible and starting to rise just a field away to my left; it was refreshing to be off the busy dual carriageways that I had travelled on for much of the previous two days. My emotions had been purged through my reminiscences and my spirit felt strangely uplifted as I started to compose some poetry about wildlife. I started musing about the life expectancy of a snail crossing the road. It occurred to me that I had seen loads of dead animals on the trip - far more than I ever would have noticed travelling in a car. I also pondered the snail's motives - of all the journeys he could make, why cross the road? Perhaps wet tarmac is a motorway for a gooey snail!

The poem developed in my mind as I put together the first four lines, but I knew that anything else I came up with would be too much for my memory. It didn't stop me though as I mouthed potential stanzas out loud and thought about what I wanted to say.

An hour after leaving Wooler I crossed the Bridge over the River Tweed and stopped to look over the wall and down at the water. Freewheeling off the bridge I passed into Scotland, welcomed by a big blue signpost that read:

Coldstream

First Real Border Toon

The humour tickled me and I debated whether I should take a photo, but in the end I couldn't be bothered. I propped the bike up outside the Coldstream tourist information office and went to see if I could sort out a campsite further on. A very helpful lady gave me a couple of options and, although they were some distance away, I felt confident I would be able to reach them. I picked up £50 from a cash point machine and went into a small café for a cup of coffee with some buttered scones. Apart from being in Scotland (I thought Coldstream was in England), the town surprised me because it was much smaller than I had imagined. Looking for somewhere to eat, I actually cycled clean out of town, thinking there must be more to the place. I had to turn back as I sought out a café. Sitting in a small room, brimming with too many tables and chairs, and poring over my map, I regretted not taking a photo of the Coldstream sign and decided to backtrack to get one. I enjoyed the buttered scone after initially wondering why the hell I had bought it. There hadn't been much choice of savoury snacks and I had just gone with the impulse. I don't generally go for sweets but I ate with relish my substantial snack, as the waitress manoeuvred around the café furniture with her tray of delights and hot drinks, like a novice driver in a crowded car park.

Back on the bike I was aiming to get to a campsite in Carfraemill twenty-five miles away. If that was a bit too far, there was another one in Lauder, five miles closer. The rolling hills of Northumberland gave way to the rolling hills of the Borders of Southern Scotland, with only the sporadic appearance of regiments of trees lining the road to distinguish between the two. I passed over the River Blackadder, learning that a favourite comedy show of mine had a real namesake, before pulling up at a shop in Greenlaw. A girl in her late teens was manning the mini store as I sought out an energy drink and some chocolate. She was very friendly and spoke with a strong Essex accent. She introduced herself as Linda but it sounded more like Leenda. Perhaps it was a mutual need to break our enforced silences, me on my bike and Leenda manning an empty shop in a deserted village that led us into a long chat. Leenda went out of her way to help me. She offered to make me a cup of coffee if I wanted a hot drink, and when I asked her if she sold the really small jars of coffee, she said she would fill a small container for me. I thanked her and declined both offers but accepted a glass of water to help my ibuprofen down.

Leenda had been left in charge of the shop because her father had developed heart disease and her mother had suffered a breakdown trying to renovate the property over the last two years. They had only been trading for six months but now intended to sell up and move, possibly to North Wales. Originally Mum was from Liverpool, and the proximity of North Wales to Merseyside probably made it a natural choice for her, as it has been for so many other well-to-do Scousers. She went on to tell me that the village and the area for that matter, was dead boring for a city teenager like herself.

As we talked, I felt weariness settling in my bones and I realised that Carfraemill was probably going to be too far for me. It would have made the trip for the day up to 56 miles and I was wary of overdoing it as I remembered the grind to Scarborough. Leenda said she was going out that night and I asked her where. She was so easy to talk to I thought it would be good to meet up for a drink, but she was heading in the opposite direction to where I planned to end up so that was that. I decided to abandon Carfraemill and head for Lauder instead saving myself the extra five miles.

Twenty minutes into that last leg of twelve miles, I felt very sore and tired. The weather though, had brightened up to a point where I could stay dry for the first time that day. It wasn't that it had really stopped raining - it was just a lot lighter. I worked it out pseudo-scientifically: the rain-wetting was now being balanced by the breeze-drying generated as a result of my motion. Eventually, it did stop raining; the sun even appeared as late afternoon approached. It illuminated the landscape like well-placed lighting on a painting, bringing out the depth and contrasts in its colours. At the same time, its warmth released a host of fragrances, much as the rain had done when it drenched the seared farmland back in Lincolnshire. It was beautiful. At one point the road swept around the gentle lower slopes of an archetypal 'middle aged' river, that exhibited all the classic meander features, so meticulously drawn and labelled by generations of O Level and subsequently GCSE students. I wished for a zoom lens on my camera but I wasn't about to start hopping over hedges to get closer.

Although Lauder was slightly out of my way, I enjoyed a long 'wheee' down into the valley and pulled up in a large and very well kept campsite. Fortunately, I just beat a coach and the lady managing operations at the site kindly classified me as 'a walker', which meant a charge of four pounds rather than seven. I pitched the tent on a flat piece of ground as the sun continued to shine, and then set out for the toilet block, some distance away, to get a shower and to wash some underwear and socks.

Before setting off, I attached my still wet trainers to a tree branch. The limbs of the trees had invaded the campsite's territory, but now offered me a convenient washing line. As I looked back on my footwear dancing in the wind, I realised that they were lowering the tone of the well-kept site, but was nevertheless confident that no one would want to touch the manky things, let alone steal them.

Spruced up, after a decent shower, I made some phone calls: one to my mum, who filled me in on all the news back home including the fact that Hafina, Cherie's younger daughter, had been admitted to hospital and given an injection to prevent her giving birth prematurely. Communications dealt with, I was soon on my way into town, a distance of about half a mile, where I found a chippy and treated myself to haddock and chips. Having consumed my meal sitting on a low wall in what amounted to a traffic island, I took potluck and entered what seemed to be the busiest pub. Quite a few people were sat at the bar and the room was filled with a fair amount of conversational noise but no music. I sat at a small round table with a pint of Bass, took out my journal and wrote about my day for half an hour, before deciding to get on to paper the 'Creatures' poem I had started to compose earlier whilst on the hoof. As I'd expected, most of it was now forgotten but I remembered the first verse and also the plot. I didn't finish the poem but I made a good start before being approached by a young lad.

'Hi, what you doing?'

I told him about my trip. He seemed very interested, but thankfully didn't prolong the exchange and I was able to get back to my writing. After a second pint, I felt like a change of scenery, so I packed up and set off to explore some of the other drinking holes in Lauder.

At the other end of town, which was in fact only a short walk away, I pushed a heavy door and entered a hotel then thought,

'More atmosphere in a tramp's vest'- one of Yogi's favourite sayings.

It was very quiet with just several people sitting around a fairly big room, softly furnished with fitted carpets and plenty of settees that created the feel of a home from home. I sat at the bar within talking range of a middle-aged man and ordered a drink. Two women, dressed in matching yellow blouses with a pretty flowery pattern and topped off with a mock tie effect, busied themselves behind the bar. I struck up a conversation with the man who told me that he wasn't staying out too late because he had to take his elderly mother back to the Western Isles of Scotland the following morning. As he seemed to know his way around, I asked him about my intended route across Scotland; I was pleased to hear that it wasn't too mountainous after all.

Soon, he offered to take me to his bowls club for a drink but his selling point of it being 'Quieter than here' put me off completely.

I politely declined, still grateful for his friendly gesture – but this was after all, Saturday night. Shortly, he left for the remainder of his night out and I drained my drink and ambled back to the previous pub but it too was now deserted so I made a quick exit. Across the road I found a much busier place.

The young lad I had been talking to earlier once again approached,

'D'you want to come over to Gallashiels with me and the boys?' He pointed towards the door.

'We've got a minibus. D'you know the girls well outnumber the boys there!' His eyes sparkled and his face beamed with his high expectation already fuelled with plenty of booze.

I was quite flattered that this youngster should invite along an old crusty like me and I must admit I was tempted, thinking that there would probably be a bit more craic there than here. However, after my excesses in Powburn the night before I took the sensible option. Also, I was pretty sure I would have felt out of place with a bunch of completely rat-arsed, sap-rising young lads trying to pick off half-drunk teenage girls in Gallashiels. All the same, I thought interesting how age and class get blurred in smaller communities. The same happens in the school where I teach – pupils, years apart in age seem to get on very well. In a large comprehensive school, it's easy to forget that the kids are from ex-mining villages that are very small and close knit. Everyone knows everyone and there may often be a dearth of same-age peers to knock around with. It was only a theory, but perhaps it explained why my new teenage acquaintances befriended me so easily.

As the lads answered the call of the minibus horn, the pub emptied slowly, like a half-finished glass of wine reluctantly being poured to waste. I was left in comparative peace and started to read over what I had written in my log earlier. It was surprising how much time had elapsed and I noticed that it was gone 11 o'clock. I sheepishly asked the barman if I could have another drink, half expecting a refusal but he willingly obliged. I had been ready to head for home, but I thought I might as well write up my journal in the comfort of the pub, with the bar to rest on and good light, rather than struggle to write back in the tent.

However, after a matter of only ten minutes, like the tide coming into a small cove, the pub began to fill up again. Where everyone came from I don't know, but almost immediately, the bar area was full of people, most of them standing. By now, half-pickled myself and being accidentally jostled and poked by the gathering throng, it was almost impossible to carry on writing. A man introduced himself as John and started to talk to me about rugby as soon as he picked up on my Welsh accent. Of course, there is a strong affinity between the Celtic nations when it comes to rugby and I was only now discovering that the Border Region of Scotland was the real heart of the Scottish game. John was very serious about rugby, and he talked to me at length about the ills brought about by the introduction of professionalism to the game. His lament had been provoked by the Lions defeat in the Antipodes earlier in the day – it was all news to me. John went on to expose an interesting theory on why British teams were getting beaten all the time.

'We lost all our big men in the war you see.' It made me laugh - it was so ridiculous.

I asked him, 'Are you getting confused with the police force? You used to have to be five foot ten to get in, but you don't any more.'

I continued, 'And what do you mean tall men in the war - what about the stout British Tommy, bravely scrapping away in the trenches and on the beaches? A lot of them hardly made five foot let alone six.'

John countered, 'Yeah but the bigger men would have been easier to hit!'

'I bet no research has ever been done on the tallness of casualties in the war?'

All these points developed as John and I sparred.

I offered the genetic theory as an alternative explanation for the tallness of the All Blacks and the Australians, 'New World countries have taller people because they've been subject to more racial mixing. When it comes to passing on characteristics to offspring the 'tallness' gene is dominant over the recessive 'shortness' gene, so more racial mixing means taller people - look at the Yanks!' My argument may have held more water but it didn't make us laugh as much as John's war theory.

His taxi arrived to take him home, but he insisted on buying me a drink before he went. I was sorry to say goodbye – it had been a very funny quarter of an hour.

The next minute another young bloke, rather rotund, introduced himself with the unorthodox greeting, 'Guess my weight.'

It was enough to start a conversation with a new drunken companion.

He told me his story: 'You know, playing rugby in the borders is your passport to academic success. If you're good at rugby you get extra support from your teachers, employers – basically everyone in the community.'

He continued, 'I've always been a bit of a leper in these parts you know.'

'Why is that?'

'Can you believe – I loved to play football! That's the reason!' He sounded amazed at his own revelation.

From his account, he sounded like a good midfield player. He felt that lots of talented footballers were lost to rugby in the area, simply because they were not 'allowed' to play football. I told him about a boy from my schooldays whose nickname was Gabby. We used to play football on the school yard every day before school began, every morning and afternoon break time, and every lunch time. There was no organisation involved. Anybody who supported northern teams such as Man Utd or Leeds played on one side; all those who supported southern teams like Chelsea or Arsenal played on the other. The ball was never a proper football but a tennis ball. Gabby could perform amazing ball tricks with the tennis ball (reminiscent of the legendary Pele with an orange) and he could run a hundred metres in just over ten seconds, all the more remarkable as he was a big lad. But he was siphoned from football to play rugby. We had a number of good pitches but all were marked out for playing rugby and the school had rugby teams for each year group but not a single football side. We could never play football 'officially'.

It was akin to the Welsh language not being permitted in early twentieth century school playgrounds. Eventually, in Form VI, we managed, with the help of a young PE teacher, to get some football fixtures arranged, but the team was a laughing stock because permission to play football rather than rugby never stretched as far as providing us with football markings on the pitch or football goal posts. Penalties were taken from an imaginary spot that had to be paced out and goal keepers were all at sea if the ball was chipped ridiculously high over their heads but under the rugby cross bar. Clearly, the fledgling footballers in the Borders had the same problem as those in South Wales.

By this time, all the lads from the Gallashiels escape party had returned – it seemed as if they had only just gone. I lost my footballer companion in the confusion, but was soon approached by a girl who I later found out to be thirty years old and called Bev. She seemed interested in me, perhaps because I was a stranger or maybe because she could see my journal on the bar. She didn't look too unlike Carol Smiley and had what might be considered a Scot's look about her with good teeth and a slightly square jaw line. She had definitely had quite a few drinks and came over as a real live wire. One of her passions was side car racing – she was the one in the side-car and she loved the speed. As we chatted, already having persuaded me to buy her a drink, she tried the same trick again.

Over the hubbub she called the barman, '

Gregg! Gin and tonic, vodka and orange and a pint ... what you drinking?'

'Pint of bitter, thanks.'

Not looking at me, she held out her hand expecting to feel the rustle of a note. I wasn't biting.

'Your round.'

'What?'

'Your round!' I had to shout.

Once was acceptable, but I wasn't having any of it the second time. She didn't seem to mind – perhaps she thought, 'Fair cop'. She quizzed me about the writing paraphernalia she could see on the bar in front of me, and asked if she could read some. I didn't mind and she spent a surprising amount of time leafing through random pages.

She handed it back to me and said, 'I like it – it's good – you should write a book.' It was a boost for me to receive another dose of encouragement from a total stranger.

We carried on chatting and she told me how she was getting married later in the year, and then she embarked upon a little matchmaking for me with her friend. The friend was young, only twenty -five, but very affable. After a while, I made what I suppose must have been a clumsy pass and she frustratingly dithered at about an eighty percent acceptance level. It sounded promising but was still 20% less than a 'Yes' and a miss is as good as a million miles in courtship dances like this.

'I'll wait outside for five minutes – if you don't show up I'll take it as a 'No'.' Well past half past three in the morning, I waited for the promised five minutes, wondering what the hell I was playing at. Partly relieved as well as being a little disappointed, I wandered off when she didn't show up. By now I was very drunk and I had lost my bearings. As usual, I had failed to notice any landmarks when I had entered Lauder on my way up. I meandered down to the end of the town where I imagined I had come in, but could see no sign of the footpath to the campsite. I looked over a wall thinking I should be able to see the site nestling in the hollow, but all I could make out were the contrasts, grey to black between field and forest. Confused, I turned around and headed back into Lauder. I thought that I must have come into the town from nearer the centre, so I backtracked, looking carefully for the dim path that would take me to my bed. I couldn't find it and now began to get a bit frustrated – I didn't want to be wandering around any more and it must have been nearly four o'clock by now – I was completely spent.

Now at the end of town where I had shared the company of the bowls club man in the hotel, I felt certain that the campsite was in the opposite direction, so there was nothing for it but to go back and retrace my original route out of the pub again. But the result was the same. I half stumbled – half walked out of the built up area for the second time, completely bamboozled and amazed at my own stupidity. It was no good - I'd have to turn back into town again – I must have missed something. As I grudgingly started back, I saw two figures approaching in the distance. They were propping each other up. It was Bev and her friend from the pub. As they got closer, I noticed a third person – a young bloke, probably not twenty. I greeted them with a certain amount of relief and asked them where the campsite was. As they offered to show me, I didn't realise that there was hanky panky in the air. The younger girl I had failed to persuade just half an hour before sidled up to me and locked arms. Bev and the youngster dropped gradually further and further behind as we started to leave the built up area and head out of the town.

Predictably, I had ventured this way twice before in the last half hour. If I had persisted and gone another twenty yards I would have seen the path to my left that lead down to the campsite.

I admonished myself,

'What a stupid git!'

As we ambled in the semi-darkness, I could now clearly make out land marks I had noticed on the way up - a piece of machinery, a couple of gates to open, a bus. As we picked our way along an uneven pathway, I chatted with my companion but the trail had gone cold. The fire of banter and laughter that we had enjoyed back at the pub, was replaced with a rather awkward conversation, more like a chat up at the start of an evening out, before the booze has had a chance to loosen tongues, relax inhibitions and send morals to the back of the cupboard under the stairs.

By the time we got back to the campsite the night was losing the battle to the day. Bev and her new man were way behind us as a result of indulging in some heavy snogging. I waited for them so they wouldn't lose us – that was a laugh coming from me. I was also concerned about the noise we were likely to cause. I hadn't formulated any sort of plan although I had wondered what sort of activity could possibly take place given the size of my one-man tent. Colour was filling up the world and as we half stumbled over mown grass and homed in on my tent, our destination gradually became clear to my 'girlfriend'.

'Is that it?'

'Yes,' I replied helpfully.

She must have forgotten what I'd told her in the pub earlier about my mission. Surely she didn't expect a family frame tent with two bedrooms and a dining room? It turned out that she expected much more - a caravan, in fact. Where they got that idea from I don't know, but my girlfriend was sorely disappointed. Bev, true to character was fine, and decided to make the best of it. Being used to dragging her backside out of a side-car at high speed I guessed this wasn't a big deal for her. She rolled into the tent and made herself comfortable before saying,

'Where's the booze then?' Of course there wasn't any.

'Let's get the coffee on then.'

Now, in all its grand splendour, I could see the folly of it, and I shook my head in disbelief as I looked upon the scene in front of me. Bev, ridiculously optimistic and upbeat, lying on her back in the tent, left no room for anyone or anything else. My woman on her feet and chirping on about there being no caravan – the youngster quiet, the same as he had been since I met him on the road.

'Where are we going to go?' said my girlfriend.

I gave a straight answer,

'There isn't anywhere'

'Well, I'm not bloody staying here in a poxy little tent.'

'What wise words,' I thought.

'I don't bloody blame you,' I said and started to giggle. She was not amused.

Bev and the lad were easily persuaded to give up too and the dim flame of romance was snuffed with the briefest of hugs and a brush of cheeks before the trio wandered off in the direction they had come. No party after all. I carried on giggling to myself as I got ready for bed and was asleep in seconds.

The Ride:

Powburn to Lauder (Scottish Borders)
Distance: 46 miles

Lauder to Inverkeithing

Sunday, July 15th

Having had such a late night, I naturally slept in. Eventually, I was awoken by bright sunshine but dithered in my sleeping bag for a long time, trying to muster up the energy and enthusiasm to get going. By the time I did get into the sitting position, the sun had gone and heavy rain began to fall on the tent. If only I had got going sooner, I could have packed up in the dry. As it was, I now had to start organising things in the cramped confines of the tent's interior. I went over to the shower block to get a shave and freshen up and it was twelve thirty by the time I pedalled off the site. Guilt guided my plan for the day – no breaks except to pick up drinks and snacks.

The going was slow for the first ten miles largely because I had to climb the south-facing slope of the Southern Uplands. I worked out that this part of the range might be called the Soutre Hills and I had to walk, walk, walk up three miles of them. Having said that, the gradient was not too steep as I climbed towards the summits of Turf Law and Dun Law: on either side of the main A68 heading for Edinburgh, they modestly capped the ridge at 380 and 394 metres respectively. It reminded me of the A470 back home, and the steady climb over the Brecon Beacons southwards towards Merthyr. Most main roads are pretty well graded and I was glad that I was on one now. Also, since it was Sunday I didn't have to contend with the heavy traffic and trucks that I imagined would fill the route most other days of the week.

I wasn't as introspective as I had been the day before, at least early on, and I enjoyed taking in the landscape. Most of the hillsides were used for pasture but there were many blocks of trees, obviously planted by the forestry industry in the regimented fashion that has since become outdated. The edges of each block were so straight they looked as if they had been drawn with a ruler and they probably had. From my distant perspective, each patch looked about four times taller than it was wide, and resembled a Mohican hair-cut – the forest being hair, the pasture bald head. Some clumps were perched perfectly on the skyline, adding still more to the comic effect.

As I slowly scaled the flank of the Southern Uplands by foot, I thought back upon the events of the previous night. All in all, it had been an entertaining night and I had shared some very funny moments with some of the characters I'd met. Noticing once more the landscape of the Mohican haircuts, I had to laugh out loud again – the lack of sleep and over indulgence the night before having its usual euphoric effect upon me. I calmed down and started to think about Cherie's laughter.

Cherie often used to laugh, but she had one particular laugh that happened less frequently. This would be uncontrollable, tears would roll down her face and she would go into convulsions. And she just couldn't stop; we used to call it 'being in a heap'. Two particular times this had happened came to my mind as I cycled.

The first was the time when we travelled down to Pembrokeshire with my brothers. We stopped off at a café on the way just outside St Clears, not far from Tenby. There was excitement in the air because my two brothers and I were setting off in the boat that day, bound for Padstow, on the North coast of Cornwall. We were sailing with some other boats in flotilla, but this was the first long trip I had ever made; I had spent weeks preparing the boat, buying gear and provisions, practising my navigation on charts and checking procedures for the boat's radio.

In the café, we chatted about the trip and I just happened to say in all seriousness, 'D'you think we should pick up some bolt-croppers from somewhere? You know if the mast comes down in the middle of the sea it could get tangled up with all the rigging – it could pull us under! We could cut ourselves free with bolt-croppers.'

Cherie had been convinced for some time that I had been going over the top with planning for the trip, and this was too much for her. I don't know how she could possibly laugh at the thought of her loved one on his tiny twenty-three foot craft, struggling to employ bolt-croppers on viciously flapping steel wires in howling winds and towering seas, but she was 'in a heap'. For the rest of the day, and indeed at any future family get-togethers, any mention of the word, 'bolt-croppers', produced exactly the same effect.

The second thing that had this effect on Cherie was a new sitcom on TV called *Coupling*. I've heard it described as the British version of *Friends* but I'm not sure how true that is. We first watched it together after quite a few glasses of wine and it bowled Cherie over. From then on she used to actually nurture her uncontrollable laughing. She would deliberately record the programme, even if she was around to watch it 'live'. The reason was that it made her laugh more when she'd been drinking. While I rode, I could picture her 'in a heap' and hear her laughter. Riding along, I laughed out loud muttering to myself: 'Bolt-croppers.'

Pushing the bike up that long hill, my own laughter was tinged with sadness that tailed seamlessly into crying. My mind stayed with Cherie and wandered on to the subject of paintings. Considering she had had no formal training she loved art. As a young girl she used to catch the bus into Liverpool and spend hours by herself walking around the Tate Gallery. One fine Saturday, fairly early in our relationship, we had been driving around Pembrokeshire in our ambulance. We were on our way to St David's when Cherie noticed a sign for a little studio called 'The Pink Gallery'. Although we had passed the turning, Cherie insisted I stop and reverse so she could take a peek. The artist who owned the place was Peter Daniels (now deceased) and Cherie was very taken by his work. There was one large panting in particular. It was an abstract image with strong colours and she loved it. Unfortunately, it was tagged at five hundred pounds

'You can't afford that on your wages,' I sensibly suggested.

'But I love it – look at that.' She pointed to various features on the canvas. 'And look at those colours!'

Mr Daniels was impressed with her interest and they chatted for some time about the picture then he said, 'You can pay in instalments – over a year if you like – I wouldn't charge you any interest.'

'I can afford that!'

I liked the painting too, but I urged Cherie to think carefully before taking the plunge. After lots of hmming and haa-ing, she was finally persuaded to sleep on it.

I reassured her, 'We can always come back tomorrow - if you still feel the same.'

The next day she found it easier to let the picture go and reason came to bear – she didn't buy it. I felt at the time I had done a good job in dissuading her, but she always regretted not buying that painting.

As the months passed by, she would sometimes say, 'I would have nearly paid for that Peter Daniels painting by now.'

Some years later, we went back to the Pink Gallery and she bought a limited print by the same artist that still hangs on the living room wall. It is also beautiful but was never quite the same as that first abstract she took such a shine to.

How well Cherie did, in fact, manage her modest income; she had a very simple principle – don't get into debt. However, she would buy me thoughtful gifts. Cherie would often buy me a pair of trousers or a shirt that she had seen and liked. Thinking about it, I didn't do enough of that type of thing in return. I wish I had now.

During her illness, when Cherie knew she was going to die, her sister Isobel had been to visit from Australia. After Cherie returned from Cardiff having dropped Isobel off at the train station, she came upstairs and said she had a present for me from Isobel. I looked at a box that was about the size and shape of a box of Matchmakers chocolates. I rattled the parcel and felt its weight but couldn't come up with any plausible guesses as to what might be inside. I opened it up to find a small carefully crafted replica of a Fender Stratocaster guitar. It was perfect in every detail and I knew that it must have cost Isobel a lot of money.

'Silly devil – she didn't have to buy me anything.'

'She wanted to.' I went downstairs and put the model onto the mantelpiece – pride of place. A few moments later Cherie came in and told me to sit down, close my eyes and put my hands out.

'Don't look! Wait.' I nervously waited for what seemed like a long time then a hard, bulky object weighed my arms down onto my lap. I opened my eyes to see a large black guitar case.

'And that's a present from me,' said Cherie.

'But why - it's not my birthday or anything?'

She didn't answer. I opened the case to see a gleaming twelve-string guitar. I had said on a few occasions before how I wished I hadn't, years ago, sold my old twelve-string. But that wasn't the main reason Cherie had bought me such a beautiful and expensive gift. This was something that I would be able to keep long after she was gone and the poignancy did not escape me at the time, though I tried not to show my sorrow.

Lost in my thoughts on the bike I started to think about sex. Maybe it was the near miss I'd had with the girl the night before, but I had already resolved that I wouldn't embark upon a course of forced and sustained abstinence. Cherie had told me sternly that she expected me to mourn, Queen Victoria style, for a period of at least one year, but she was only joking. My pending infidelity was nothing to do with a lack of respect for Cherie. I considered sex to be a natural and pleasurable part of living, so if things happened so be it.

Pedalling in a daydream, thinking of death, sex and guitars, I had a major wobble brought on by the sudden emergence of a dead rabbit that shocked me out of my autopilot-like condition - its eyes wide open and gaping at me from the gutter. Whether it was the fact that I had decided to write a poem about creatures and was consequently noticing them more, or whether there were more casualties around, I don't know, but the dead animals seemed to be speaking out to me now, and popping up all the time. I thought about the various stages of decomposition – a fox on a grassy verge I had seen a few days ago, laid gently to rest but dead nonetheless, and a bloated hedgehog fit to burst.*

'One day I'm going to be pushing the bike up a hill and I'm going to step on one and POP! it's going to explode.' I shuddered at the thought. There was a pair of birds in the middle of the road, partners maybe, who had shared their deaths at a speeding wall of steel and glass that was the front face of a twenty tonne truck. Creatures who died some time ago were also visible – skeletons with just a few feathers clinging on; a vole that looked like a half used Brillo pad, with a semblance of mammalian structure and gooey stuff mixed in. Others were unrecognisable as creatures at all – more like parts of an old rope that had fallen off a lorry, or just a stain that could easily be spilled diesel.

As planned, I didn't stop off anywhere until the eighteen mile mark where I pulled into a garage for a pork pie and an energy drink. After the wet start, the weather had cheered up and the ride was very pleasant. The landscape was attractive and the hue was the strange light that is often seen after rain, the passage of a cold front bringing dark clouds interspersed with clear sky and sunlight. The climb to the top of the ridge earlier had really paid off because the ride down the other side was strung out over a seemingly huge distance with just one or two slight up-hills mixed in. In the soft light I bowled along for miles, passing through Pathhead and Dalkeith, hardly having to pedal at all, taking in the scenery and feeling the rain cooled air around me as I drew ever nearer to Edinburgh.

Despite my late start, I didn't feel pressurised – I was relaxed and strangely at peace. When my bum hurt, I got off and walked. The only thing spoiling my ride was the road surfaces. In places, they were so bad that I had to cycle down the middle of the road to avoid potholes and not just drains, but the huge crater like depressions they sat in. I wondered whether up here in the north, it was the extent of frosts that caused so much damage.

Edinburgh is sited on top of old volcano and there is no river running through its centre, so unusually, I found myself off the bike and walking up to the city centre, rather than coasting down as I had done in other towns. I started to lose my bearings as the road pattern became more confused, so I stopped to ask a taxi driver how I could pick up the main A90 to get me on to the Forth Road Bridge. I took a second left then followed the road all the way. I was glad that I had decided not to bypass Edinburgh city centre on the dual carriageway. It meant I had plenty of time to rest my posterior as every traffic light seemed to be on red. The rain started to pelt again – cold front weather - so I stopped to don my waterproofs.

Coasting down a hill in the deluge I caught a glimpse of the road name - 'Castle View' - and managed to steal a glance over my right shoulder to get a fantastic view from the west of the castle on its crag. Despite the inconvenience and the danger of water damage to my camera, I propped the bike up against some railings and walked the short distance back up the hill to get the obligatory snap. I carried on the A90 with about ten miles to cover before reaching the Forth Road Bridge, but not before stopping in an Esso station for a giant garage Cornish pasty that was awful – as usual.

'Why do I keep choosing to buy these damn things?' was the thought that again occurred to me. The cold grisly filling in its waxy fatty jacket was washed down with yet another energy drink. As I sauntered around the edges of the forecourt eating the rubbish (there was nowhere to sit) I noticed an excellent Michelin road map of the UK. I studied it for some time and derived great satisfaction and pride as I picked out my route from Merthyr, resting my finger on every spot where I had stayed the night. Apart from reliving my route, I was able to pore over the Orkneys and the Shetlands where of course, I was hoping to go. I could see how some of the islands were linked by roads and others required ferries. I thought it would be a very interesting journey – if I managed to get there. I had my doubts though. I had become aware of a slight niggle in my leg (left leg again) that felt like the early stages of a hamstring pull. In effect, I was nursing it as I went along, walking gradients however gentle. I hoped the discomfort was not a prelude to a debilitating pull. I had suffered a number of hamstring pulls in my later years of playing football and each time it had felt like an elastic band snapping in my leg. There would be no way I could continue if it happened to me now.

I got to the Forth Road Bridge in fairly heavy traffic and found it to be rather more impressive than the Humber Bridge. The cycle/pedestrian walkways were separated from the main carriageway by outriggers so there was a gap of about two and a half metres between the traffic and me. Once again, I thought how much more you see cycling compared to driving, as I stopped to look at a marina near Newton on the west side of the bridge. Lots of boats were still laid up despite the fact that it was the middle of summer. It was the usual story and the typical fate of so many boats. Finding the time to use them and, even more so, maintain them is a pressure that often results in the owner giving up and leaving their once pride and joy to rot in a yard.

Who was it that said,

'The two happiest days in a man's life are the day he buys his boat, and the day he sells it?'

On the river itself, I could see the opposite. A white yacht with its stern angled outwards in the modern style was ticking over, its bow into the tide and deliberately making no headway. On it and far below me, Lilliputian figures, were preparing for entry into the marina - criss-crossing over the boat, slipping the fenders on to the guardrails and readying the ropes for tying off onto one of the floating pontoons. It brought back strong memories of the days when I had a boat.

Crossing the Forth Road Bridge then turned into a spiritual experience. The light at what was now half past six, together with the grandeur of the bridge and the panoramic view from its considerable height, created an ethereal aura, possibly enhanced by my fatigue. In the distance to the northwest, the rain could be seen as a smudge of grey falling from dark clouds over Alloa. But elsewhere, there was a lot of blue sky even though there was no sun. Considering I'm a godless non-believer it stirred strange thoughts that surprised me. For some minutes, I felt that Cherie was actually with me. I had an overwhelming sense that she was looking over me and looking after me. I began to cry and paused to accept the emotions. The whole experience was truly awesome and as the intensity diminished, I began to imagine that when you die, you are allowed to hang around for a while to help out your loved ones until you can see they're going to be alright.

I was reminded of a drama from the early nineties called, 'Truly, Madly, Deeply', where a very loved man (Alan Rickman) died and his poor wife couldn't get on with her life because she'd put him on a pedestal of virtue, naturally forgetting his shortcomings, of which he had quite a few. He came back to haunt her – live with her, in fact. Initially she was elated, but then she grew once more to see his weaknesses and eventually he was able to leave her, knowing that she could now carry on. Cherie and I had enjoyed the film, so much so that we watched it again when it was repeated a few years later. Still on the bridge,

I tried to again savour the moment that had just passed; but, as in the film, it wasn't the same the second time around. I took some photos but nothing could capture the intensity of that view, that light and the overwhelming presence of Cherie that I experienced for just a short while, on that early Saturday evening at the beginning of July.

As I raced off the bridge, for the first time ever, I saw a speed limit sign for cyclists – '15 mph', followed by a series of bike speed bumps. I managed to slow down just in time to save myself being thrown off. Just past the bridge was a lay-by where several motor bikers had stopped for a fag and a chat. Realising that I was not a very convincing member of the brotherhood, I nevertheless sidled up and started to talk to them. After the usual, 'Where have you been?' and 'Where are you going?' I was lucky to find out that they were locals. I took the chance to ask them about campsites in the vicinity but they said there were none. Still, there was a small town a few miles down the road called Inverkeithing where there was a good chance I would be able to get bed and breakfast. I set off again, feeling weary and aware that it was starting to get late. Within half an hour, I was in Inverkeithing where I pulled under the arch of a coaching inn and secretly propped my bike up out of sight of the main road.

Entering the pub, I walked into a crowd. The bar was busy, to a depth of one or two across its length and there weren't any free tables. The room was medium sized and dominated by a large high round table, with eight or nine people sat in a circle on high stools. I ordered a pint of Strongbow then stood for a short while assessing the situation – I needed some advice on accommodation. The round table was a hubbub of debate, but I decided to politely intrude and ask about somewhere to stay the night. The group was of mixed age with men and women, but they all welcomed me and diverted all calls to the problem of my lodgings. Paul, thirty-two years old, a balding football player and Celtic supporter, took the lead in the debate, then encouraged by his wife lead me over the road to try out a hotel. The owner there said he was full, so Paul took me on to the Queen's Hotel. The bar there was quite busy too, after all it was a Saturday night. Paul pushed past the front line and went behind the bar. The owner, whose name was Guilless, was a well-built guy with a trimmed beard. Paul put a good word in for me using his clout as the person who took the football team to the Queen's to drink. Reciprocally, the hotel sponsored the team.

Paul came back to the punter's side of the bar to give me the options,

'A tenner without breakfast, fifteen quid with – what do you want to do?'

'Without, please.' I could easily pick up a roll or pasty in the morning for a few bob. I told Guilless I'd be back in ten minutes after I'd finished my drink. But it didn't happen like that. I was enjoying the company of the friendly bunch in the coaching inn too much and couldn't be bothered to check into my hotel and unpack, change, shower, etc. Given that I'd made a late start that morning it would have been time for bed. After a while Paul excused himself and went to banter with some of his team mates, who were sat in the corner. The conversation naturally switched to others on the round table - a couple, Gordon and his wife Brenda, who reminded me a bit of my sister Debbie – similar eyes I thought. We were also joined for a while by a single guy Daniel, who had been a steward on a hospital ship in the Falklands. I thought back to Brett in South Shields and the conversation we'd had about the conflict, but most of all I remembered the intensity of the emotion we both shared. Daniel and I talked about the Falklands for a while but Brenda was in the mood for winding people up. It was tongue in cheek and friendly but delivered with a degree of mock aggression,

'Daniel is a poof's name.' After a number of repetitions, the challenge could not be ignored and Brenda succeeded in breaking up our Falklands discussion.

'Daniel IS a poof's name.' Louder this time. There was some debate on the issue, but it didn't last for long and I didn't really notice that Daniel had understandably slipped away. Brenda must have been in the mood for controversy because she turned her attention to me.

'How come you're doing this crazy trip? Are you some kind of weirdo or what? Some kind of nut? What's wrong with you?' Her Scottish accent seemed to sharpen as her questions became more emphatic.

It went on like this for a short while, and I wondered what to do. As with her assault on Daniel, it looked as if she was not to be ignored. I didn't feel I wanted to reveal the reasons for my trip but in the end I semi-relented, 'I could make you cry.'

'I don't think so, Laddie.'

I repeated the line a number of times, only to meet the same defiant challenge. Gordon and Brenda probed a little. My emotions were starting to surface and I paused. Did I really want to tell her about Cherie?

'You're a weirdo, you are?'

I looked her deliberately in the eye and stressed once more, 'I *could* make you cry.'

'I don't think so.'

So I told her – and Brenda did cry - a lot. In fact, she disappeared for quite a while making genuine apologies when she did eventually return. I felt a bit guilty, but she really did ask for it. While Brenda was away, I chatted to

Gordon. Among other things, it turned out that he was an Orangeman.

My knowledge of Orangemen was scant but I knew that they dressed in bowler hats, wore orange sashes and, from my point of view at least, seemed to cause an awful lot of bother in Northern Ireland at certain times of the year. I confessed my ignorance to Gordon, and also my surprise that he should make the annual pilgrimage to Northern Ireland all the way from Scotland. We spent a long time discussing the issue with Gordon doing most of the talking and me putting the occasional question to him. He said a lot of the violence was triggered by the National Front, who travelled to the event much like hooligans to an away football match looking for a fight.

'These thugs use their mobile phones to orchestrate things. Their communications are as good as the police – they can cause havoc but still stay one step ahead of the law. They never get caught.' Gordon went on, 'As usual, it's just a small minority that cause the violence.'

I asked, 'Why d'you go every year especially when there's nearly always trouble?'

'Tradition,' he said emphatically. 'Three hundred years of tradition. How would you feel if someone came up to you and said that you weren't allowed to tell your kids that Father Christmas was coming? Or you weren't able to make bonfires and set off fireworks on November 5th? It's part of our heritage and we're not giving it up for anyone.'

Gordon had the bit between his teeth, 'You know Catholics in Belfast are actually buying up property along the traditional marching route - so they can launch complaints as 'concerned residents' and have the march stopped through the courts.' Gordon's convictions were clearly deep seated and cherished so I didn't upset him by telling him that given all the grief it caused, I still wasn't convinced the annual parade was a good idea.

By this time, I was seriously considering a rest day. I was booked into a hotel, I had done five days on the trot and my one leg was signalling trouble. I spoke my thoughts aloud and Gordon and Brenda immediately offered to put me up and cook me an evening meal. That clinched it, rest day tomorrow.

It was Gordon who had been responsible for me staying in the pub so long. At least initially he was a quiet chap. Whilst I had been chatting to Paul and some of the others, he'd hardly said a word. I'd finished my second pint of Strongbow and was about to leave to check into the hotel when Gordon, who was at the bar, shouted across to tell me he'd bought me another. Of course, once I'd glugged that I felt I had to buy him one back, and so it went on in the time-honoured fashion. Gordon and Brenda hadn't intended to stay long either. In fact, Gordon had been drinking lager shandy but he soon changed to straight lager as the round became established. It meant they had to leave the car and order a taxi when the time finally came to go. Before they left, we made arrangements to meet at the same place the following evening at half past six. They would then take me back to their place. Handshakes and kisses, we said our goodbyes and I thanked them again for their friendship and generosity, 'See you tomorrow!' What a nice couple.

It was twenty to eleven and I was now left alone at the once bustling round table. My bum was numb from the day's riding and also from sitting on the raised barstool for some hours. The booze hadn't dissolved the ache in my knee either, and I was relieved I would be taking the next day off. I finished the dregs from my glass then went outside and down the now darkened alley, suddenly concerned for the security of my bike and belongings.

'Yes – still there, thank God'. I wheeled it the short distance across the square to the Queens and Guilless allowed me to park it under the stairs. Then, I humped the rucksack up to the first floor and down a corridor to my room. I could have unpacked or gone to bed or both, but the drink had made me lively so I decided to pop into the hotel bar. There was only Guilless, the owner and his manager there, but they were very convivial and we had a good time for a couple of hours, telling stories and exchanging gags.

We got into a wacky exchange over what the two Scots claimed was a local saying, 'Yahooresurr'. They were both in a heap, their laughter so infectious I joined in as well. Not the sharpest needle in the box at the best of times, I couldn't figure out if they were taking the micky or being genuine.

'It means welcome - sort of hello, but in a friendly way. It's only used here in Fife. You'll not hear it anywhere else.' They were very convincing, like Patrick Campbell or Frank Muir in a session of 'Call my Bluff'.

But to me, 'Yahooresurr' had a worrying resemblance to, 'You're a whore, Sir', and I had no intention of using it as a greeting in Fife or anywhere else.

'Sorry guys, I just don't believe you!' They laughed all the more.

As the banter bubbled along, 'Yahooresurr!' kept making its way into the conversation and was always followed by more hysteria and tears from the three of us.

Each time my pint got below a quarter full, Guilless would take it off me and fill it back up again - he didn't want money. Feeling the weight of countless pints of cider and beer in my stomach, I asked him for a 'wee one' at one point, but he just ignored me. He must have had a reason, but by now I was too dazed to care. It was one or two o'clock by the time I eventually went up to my room, dirty, dishevelled and disorganised – no charging of my phone, no washing of clothes, no drying of tent, no shower. With all my clothes on I crashed to bed. Not a wise use of my night of luxury in a real bedroom in a proper hotel.

The Ride:

Lauder to Inverkeithing (just over the Forth Road Bridge)

Distance: 40 miles

Creatures *

Studying wild creatures, on my bike for miles,
Pedalling from Merthyr, up to the Shetland Isles.
Not that I'm an expert, those books I've never read,
But one thing is for certain most were positively dead.

Sprinkled quite haphazardly I see them all the time
Sometimes on the roadway, but usually in a line,
Along the gutter, by the curb or nestling on a drain
Some are fresh and some are bones, but all dead just the same

Some they look so peaceful, like a fox I saw asleep,
Never to wake up again, who said that life is cheap?
And they always take me unawares they take me by surprise
Like the rigor mortis rabbit with his scary open eyes
As I pedalled into Edinburgh in the pouring rain
Some were quite a mess and some were just a stain

Why do they take upon themselves the trip of seven yards?
It puts their tiny lives to risk just like a game of cards
I did feel sorry for a snail who'd set off in the sun
His chances of success, I rated nil and none

For some the odds are better if they do not freeze in lights
Or if they're blessed with feathers and can fly to greater heights

Mind you most of the casualties were birds they must be dim
Or were they flattened feasting on some previous victim?

For all the creatures on the road a dance with destiny
And for us it's just the same our fate a mystery
Why do we do the things we do and should we think it out
But would we find an answer, what is it all about?

Rest Day

Monday, July 16th

I got up at quarter to ten and started writing up my journal over a couple of cups of coffee, not really appreciating the novelty of having the water, kettle and hotel sachets of instant coffee at my fingertips. I had managed to negotiate a bit of an extension for checking out, so I took advantage of the long, deep, aquamarine bath. I shaved afterwards and found I couldn't resist the shower so I had one of them too. Back in the room, I carried on with the journal for a while longer. It was just gone noon by the time I'd packed up and I popped in to see Guilless.

'Have you got anywhere I could leave my rucksack?' I explained that I was staying an extra night with friends. Guilless obliged, and I set off to visit a bike shop I had spotted on my way into the town the night before. I thought it might be a good idea for someone to look over my machine and see if anything was about to snap off or give out. The shop was very busy though; so, after waiting in vain for five minutes for someone to see to me, I left, deciding to rely on my dubious but nevertheless favourite philosophy of,

'If it's not broke, don't fix it.'

I went into the pub I'd been drinking in the night before and asked the girl serving if it would be alright for me to tie my bike up around the back in the same spot as before. That done, I picked up two filled rolls from Greggs, and went to eat them in the glorious sunshine in a little planted park I found as I ambled along looking for somewhere to sit away from the road. The park tiered away affording a magnificent view to the south and east. I sat on a bench and gazed down at the Firth of Forth and across to Edinburgh, where I could just make out the characteristically angular form of the castle in the far distance. The fort was perched on its volcanic plug turret, and I could make out the ramp-like tail made up of debris dumped during the last ice age ten thousand years ago. It's a classic landform called 'crag and tail' which features in many of the geography textbooks I've used over the years. For the tail to be where it was, dumped in the area to the lee of the castle on its resistant plug, I worked out that the ice must have been moving from west to east.

After breakfast, I went back to the Queens and sat in the bar again writing up my journal over a cup of coffee. It felt strange because I wasn't thinking in the same way that I would have, had I been on the bike. Having fallen behind with the journal as a result of the revelry the night before, I was now reliving Sunday and the thoughts and events of the day before, rather than generating new ones - Monday. It must have taken me at least two hours getting the journal up to date. When I had finished I went off to do some shopping. I needed Vaseline for my chapped lips, more ibuprofen, more paracetamol, and I felt that vitamins would be a good idea – oh yes – and postcards. I was lucky there was a chemist open, because most other shops were closed. I asked a passer-by what was going on and she told me that it was a workers' holiday of some sort. Fortunately, I managed to get everything except the postcards.

After my shopping spree, I returned to the little park and settled myself on to a bench to write to my son Richard. It was his graduation in a couple of days' time and I wanted to congratulate him and let him know how proud I was. I naturally felt guilty that I wouldn't be there in person, but I couldn't have put off the bike ride. My mum was standing in for me – in fact going with my ex-wife, and I knew it would be a memorable day for her so that made me feel a bit better about my self-enforced absence. I asked a mother who was sat on the next bench, to take a photo of me writing the letter, and thought Richard might appreciate it when I got back. I returned to the chemist where earlier I 'd enjoyed some banter with the staff, and managed to scrounge a single envelope – I was concerned to get the letter away promptly and of course, there were no shops open to buy envelopes. Perhaps I was a bit cheeky but they didn't seem to mind. On the way out, I stopped to chat with a couple that were taking in the sun as they sat on a low wall by the side of their motorbike. They were half way to Inverness on a Triumph Triple and they had left Leicestershire that morning.

'How's it been?' I asked.

'Suspension's a bit hard,' the guy complained. He told me how he had been over to the Western Isles in the past, and I described the trip Cherie and I had taken to Aberdeen on our Kawasaki GT 750. Despite being the middle of August, the main feature of the trip had been the cold Scottish air and the bucketing rain. Even when the rain stopped we had to keep our waterproofs on just to fend off the chill. I thought the bikers might like somewhere more peaceful to eat their lunch so I told them about the secret little park up the road. I noticed a chippy nearby so I went and had a 'sit down fish and chips'. Not a meal in the sense of 'going out for a meal', but a bit posher than eating it out of a newspaper in the street. As I sat at the small round Formica topped table, the noisy jabber of others close by made me wish I had taken my food to the park too.

I still had a few hours to kill before meeting up with Gordon at six thirty, and the weather was so beautiful I decided to go for a walk down to the Firth of Forth. I crossed a bridge over a small river on my way which reminded me of the Taf back in Merthyr; I stopped to look at the sad collection of debris that littered its channel – cans, bottles, a cupboard and the ubiquitous supermarket trolley.

As I ambled on down the hill, I could see the tips of the two Forth bridges peeping from behind a low hill; I stopped to take a photo. As I continued, my thoughts went back to those of the day before: I should have surprised Cherie more with treats. Then I argued with myself. It would have been difficult because she was so fussy. For years she had wanted a new handbag, but every time she thought to look for one she couldn't make up her mind. I promised to buy her a dressing gown one Christmas, but always when we went into a shop to look for one, she couldn't find anything that fitted the bill. She used to drive me nuts in the supermarket where she would deliberate - for minutes - over which piece of mature Cheddar was best, or which carton of mushrooms was ever so slightly superior to the others. To maintain my sanity, I usually had to split from her and disappear into the music section for a while, or go on some menial errand to collect coffee or milk. I even grew fond of at looking at kitchen utensils.

I figured, 'If Cherie has trouble finding what she wants (and she would never buy something that "would do"), what chance have I got?'

Then I thought, maybe I could have taken her out for impromptu meals more, but sometimes we did do that. Looking back, it was natural enough to believe that I could have done more, but I knew in my heart that our lives were full and that Cherie was happy.

Unlike my last rest day in Scarborough, I didn't feel lonely and my mood was simply one of quiet reverie. But, I also thought of loneliness as a germ that might grow with time. It was hard to imagine what it might be like once I returned home. I carried on walking through a park and watched a woman throwing a Frisbee for her dog, occasionally looking back to see if I could see the elevated spot where I'd sat on the bench to write my letter. The scent of freshly mown grass took me back to my childhood as I spotted a few kids messing around on their bikes in a skate park. One girl, who seemed to be on her own, was teetering down one of the ramps in bare feet. Further along was a group of teenage boys noisily drinking from cans on a small grassy bank overlooking a small inlet off the main Firth. As is often the case, they were minding their own business but, all the same, seemed mildly threatening. An overweight jogger passed by me with her dog but had to stop to retrieve her retriever as he came to make friends with me - he seemed more interested in going my way than following his panting mistress.

Down at the water's edge it was not very pretty. The area looked as if it had been important in the past, but now there were just remnants of old dockside with more bits and pieces of rubbish dumped in the firth. I milled about a disused jetty for a while. Looking down from the concrete precipice onto the rocks below I could see the tide was out and the estuary looked dirty. There were the remains of a car chassis – three wheels and a pile of rusted metal with a discarded bright orange bicycle frame perched on top for good measure. For a while I sat on a projecting piece of concrete, dangling my legs over the edge and looking across the wide river, the two Forth bridges now completely hidden by the low hill. I noticed that the sun had disappeared, and started to feel the chill of the breeze as cold from the concrete penetrated my pants. It was time to make my way back up to the town where I could phone Nicole to find out how Hafina and the baby-to-be were. I also needed to pick up my rucksack from the Queen's and get to the pub early – I didn't want to miss Gordon.

I was settled in the pub with a pint of Guinness by ten past six. The eyes of the locals were upon me as I humped my rucksack to a place where people wouldn't trip over it. After half an hour, I could see Gordon was a bit late and I wondered whether to order another Guinness. I was sure I could persuade him to have at least one drink before taking me back for dinner, so I thought it wouldn't matter if he was to walk through the door just as I ordered. I bought a cigar too - to help the drink last longer and give me something to do. Still no sign of Gordon – he was more than half an hour late now.

Doubtful thoughts were seeping into my mind: 'How long shall I wait? I'll have to book back into the Queens if he doesn't show up - if they still have room. Will I get it for the same price again? What if I can't get in anywhere?'

I couldn't believe that Gordon and Brenda would have changed their minds. I felt there must have been some sort of problem or perhaps we'd got our wires crossed. After all, by the end of the night when the arrangements had been made we were all pretty drunk.

Sitting there waiting reminded me of Min Dale, a past colleague of mine. I used to share a lift with her from a half way point between Pontypool and Merthyr. The rendezvous was a pub car park. We were always both punctual and we shared happy banter on our commutes, despite a considerable age gap of nearly forty years. On one particular day in the late '70s, snow had fallen on the mountain road I had to cross to reach Min. My route was blocked and I had to return the way I had come and make a huge detour. I eventually approached the rendezvous point an hour and a half late and wondered if it was even worth checking whether Min was still waiting for me. I decided to make sure and to my amazement she was. Not that I could see her. The small confines of her tiny mini clubman, windows shut to keep out the cold, were thick with the smoke of countless cigarettes and her thermos cup sat steaming on the dash. At first I marvelled at her patience then realised that not being in school might have something to do with it.

So it was that I waited for Gordon. To pass the time, I decided to write a poem about my piles but by five past eight, I concluded that he wasn't going to show up. I felt that if they had changed their minds, they still should have got a message to me – I would have understood. I rued the fact that I had booked out of The Queens because I could have enjoyed a day of luxury - sorted out all my washing, watched the telly for a bit, had another bath ... I also needn't have sat in the pub for two hours, spending money.

Fortunately, I did manage to book back into The Queens at the same rate as before and treated myself to a bath. I avoided drinking coffee, and resolved definitely to get an early night for once. All the same, I felt that a brief visit to the bar for a nightcap could only improve the quality of my sleep; in any case, I was thirsty from my soak in the bath.

True to my word, I only had a single pint as I talked to a man about ten years older than me, who had been stationed in the Shetlands when he had been in the forces. He spoke very highly of the place and the people and said that once I got there, I might not want to leave. The girl serving behind the bar joined the conversation, telling us that her father came from Shetland. She'd been up to the Shetlands for a wedding recently and all her friends had told her she was nuts – what with the distance and the weather. But it turned out that while the rest of the UK was getting blasted with wind and rain, Shetland was bathed in glorious sunshine. She did say that the cost of living there was expensive though, with most goods having to be brought in from the mainland.

I must have been tired because I gallantly refused to enter into a friendly argument with the Shetland forces man, who kept saying in a loud voice, 'Welsh Git!' to another Scottish guy in the bar.

It reminded me of the way my Dad used to take the micky sometimes, and it would definitely have got under the skin of some of my friends back home. But I was not to be provoked, even by light-hearted banter, and I bade goodnight to the small party. Back in the room I watched a chat show for a while. Parkinson was talking to Tracy Ullman and Denise Williams, but it didn't last for long and I got my early night after all.

Rest Day

Inverkeithing to Inver

Tuesday, July 17th

I had been aware of a smell in my room but hadn't bothered to investigate. As I started to sort myself out, I came across the culprits. I'd washed a pair of 'white' socks two days before but not had a chance to dry them. I'd hit upon the idea of pinning them under the bungees on the back of the bike, thereby allowing them to dry and air (in fact, doing neither) as they fluttered naturally in the breeze behind me. The pouring rain in and around Edinburgh had certainly put paid to that grand idea, but I had completely forgotten about them, strapped forlornly to the outside of the rucksack, like Captain Ahab on the wounded Moby Dick.

I had to do something about them so I washed them there and then. That left me with no clean socks so I put the wet ones on, thinking, 'They'll be soaking soon anyway – at least they're clean now.' I had temporarily mislaid the ones I had been wearing and lost four other pairs somewhere along the way. When I thought about it, I hadn't seen them in over a week - they were probably dangling on a branch somewhere in the Midlands.

Having had a shower, I made quite an early start getting away at five past nine. I left without breakfast, satisfied with the free coffee in my room. The weather was cloudy with a bit of rain, but not enough to don my waterproofs as I stopped for a final look at Inverkeithing and took a photo. After just a mile I had to get off and walk towards Kelty, uphill nearly all the way. It didn't bother me too much, but in the first one and half hours I only covered ten miles.

Walking got me wondering about my reasons for doing the trip, and at last I felt I'd worked it out. Yes, it was for me – to get away - a challenge - time to think. And, I decided I was *not* doing it for Cherie – she was dead. How could I be doing it for her? Yet, maybe I was doing it for her memory?

'Memories are all I've got' seemed a cliché, but true; I felt comforted that I was recording them in my journal. I realised that the more memories I could store, the better I would be able to remember her and our life together. Memories can fade and even vanish so now was the time to save them - while Cherie's sun still shone bright.

Satisfied with this line of reasoning, I plodded on up the hill, leaning forwards on the handlebars, so that my body weight assisted my legs in pushing the bike. Being in the hotel that morning meant I had seen the news - the Conservative leadership race had been narrowed to two; Concorde was having tyre trials at Brize Norton; the police had filled an armed man full of bullets, and the guy's gun turned out a replica that doubled up as a cigarette lighter – and the weather forecast - awful weather was about to hit Britain again. The good news was that it didn't look as if it was going hit Scotland until that night.

I thought it would be great if I could get the tent up before it started raining. It had been two nights and two days since I had packed it away wet in Lauder, and I was a little afraid that it might have started to get mildew. So many times in the past, I had borrowed mildew affected tents, or worse, caused them through not bothering to dry them out after use. Although my tent had cost me £250, I hadn't regretted the expenditure. It was so easy to put up and take down, it hadn't leaked a drop of water and it was unbelievably lightweight and compact. I didn't want to wreck it now on its first outing.

As the long hill seemed finally to be levelling off, I remembered catching sight of some writing on the wall of one of my tyres a few days earlier. The tyre pressure recommended was in excess of forty pounds per square inch and I had an idea that I was only inflating to about thirty using my bike pump. As I passed an old fashioned looking garage, its grimy workshop abutting a forecourt with rusting, down in the dumps petrol pumps, I thought I'd check the air pressure in my tyres. Sure enough, they were just hovering above the thirty pounds per square inch, so I inflated them the extra ten pounds - front and back. One dust cap was missing and I bantered with the mechanics in the workshop to let me have one. They put up a joking fight but relented in the end, refusing to accept money from me when I offered to pay - who said Scots were tight.

As I set off again, I wondered at my own stupidity. I had cycled all the way from Merthyr and a quarter of the way through Scotland on under- inflated tyres. And, I could feel the difference. Over the two weeks I had been cycling, the extra drag caused by those under inflated tyres must have been an added drain on my energy, and more critically, must have put extra stress upon my ailing knees.

Now cycling along was exhilarating. The air was cool but neatly balanced by the body heat I was generating. There were surpluses and deficits in the temperature budget though – walking up the hills I broke into a light, warm sweat. Downhill, the moisture on me turned cold and I could feel a chill between my shoulder blades as I freewheeled on a back road towards Glenfarg. I had decided to leave the main road because on the map, it appeared to be a short cut. In fact, there were three routes all going the same way, but one of these was the M90 and pedal bikes are not allowed on the motorway. Almost alongside the M90 ran the old main road, now a lot quieter with the bulk of the through traffic siphoned off. The route I had chosen was little more than a country lane and, as I had expected, was a lot hillier. It turned out to be a good choice, however, despite the extra effort involved. The alternative routes were clearly visible, easily picked out from my high vantage point, graded and gently curving into the distance as if drawn on a map.

For four or five miles I enjoyed some wonderful scenery – tranquil, green, clear conditions – and total peace. Until the encounter with a brick lorry. First, I registered a vague rumble that grew louder as the truck approached from behind. It wasn't moving much faster than I, but inexorably, it drew closer and the racket it made crescendoed as it overtook me. As the road started to rise, the struggling brick lorry began to labour even more and its speed dropped to a point where I eventually undertook it walking by on the inside. Thankfully, as I pushed the bike over a small humpback bridge, our slow speed tango was interrupted by the brow, which effectively cut out the din from the truck's engine. Freewheeling down the hill on the other side, I hazarded a wobbly glance backwards, half expecting to see the damn thing still chasing me like some monstrous dinosaur – from five hundred yards I could make out two headlight eyes, a big grill mouth and a windscreen forehead - its torso and its tail hidden from view behind its big head. Being alone and left to my thoughts for so long, tended to trip my imagination. The brick truck encounter had lasted for quite a while and I found it quite scary. With relief, I realised that the creature must have turned off or stopped the other side of the bridge.

I was left once again to my solitude, the other routes heavy with silent traffic, still coming into view from time to time. I stopped to take a photo in the opposite direction, westward. There was a group of cows, all lying down and I remembered the old wives' tale. Was it a sign of the bad weather that had been forecast on the TV that morning? Gale force winds had been mentioned and I wondered whether they had been evident in embryo form the day before, as I strolled along the banks of the Firth of Forth, looking towards Edinburgh and feeling the keen breeze on my face. It looked bad - the wind was set to swing around to hit me from the north, head on, probably on Thursday – in two days' time.

'My old enemy from Whitby come to do battle again, eh?' In fact, the south-east wind that had been blowing all morning was gently helping me along. Flats were turned into gentle down-hills where I didn't have to pedal, and slight inclines were transformed into flats. It was a pity that it was not set to last.

I started thinking about the chat show interview with Tracy Ullman that I had watched on TV the night before. She was now forty-one and apart from making an extended joke out of 'vaginal dryness', her Americanised accent over playing the first syllable, she mainly talked about the Americans' obsession with their backsides. Apparently, whole aisles of their pharmacies are dedicated to bums. Stool softeners were one popular product and I wondered, if they eat curries in the States – 'a spicy Indian is always pretty effective in softening my stools,' I thought.

'I bet the Americans have their rear ends checked out far more than we do – Cherie would still be alive if we'd been more like them. My piles would have been quickly sorted out too.' Having said that, my haemorrhoid did finally seem to be retiring back into its lair. I wasn't convinced that the steroid cream was anything to do with it because I had stopped using it over a week before. I suspected that piles probably had a life span and that mine had come to its end.*

I freewheeled down a long hill to a quiet crossroads that was Glenfarg. There was a small general store-come-post office, where I bought two aerial photo postcards of the village. I wrote and posted them there and then, one to my stepson, MR, and one to a friend from school, Anne Blake. As I dated the post cards, my memory was jogged - it was MR's birthday - and I made a mental note to ring him later.

The road to Perth was the best 'wheee!' I had experienced since starting the trip, better even than the ride off the Southern Uplands towards Edinburgh two days before. I hadn't realised just how high I had climbed during the morning; I rolled down the hill, assisted by the wind, for what must have been four miles. Even on the plain south of Perth, a gentle slope with the wind behind me saw me clocking up eighteen miles per hour as I drew to within a mile of the city. Earlier, at about 11 o'clock, I'd sat down for a hot pasty and a cup of coffee in Kinross near Loch Leven. I noticed then that the wind strength must have been at least force four because the lake surface was ruffled with white horses. Like that time in the Lake District with Cherie, being painfully aware of a wind that's against you is one thing but a following wind goes largely unperceived.

Perth was very busy traffic-wise and also in the pedestrianised sections through which I wheeled the bike, looking for 'Tourist Information' signs. I eventually tracked the office down and the typically helpful staff confirmed there was a campsite near Dunkeld, ten to twelve miles away. I picked up a Boost bar and a bottle of Lucozade from a filling station just out of the town centre and hung around to see what would happen to the rain that had a started a few minutes earlier. As it came to nothing,

I set off in a street that had been narrowed to one lane by road works, deliberately sticking to the wrong side of some traffic cones to reduce the chances of getting squashed.

I found the main A9 and headed northwards – a very busy dual carriageway with no hard shoulder, the like of which I had not seen since Geordie-land. It wasn't very pleasant having to cope again with massive juggernauts but at least there was a short lived draught that sucked me along for a few seconds, each time one passed by. Thankfully, four miles later there was a cycle path that followed the route of the old main road now superseded by the dual carriageway. Naturally, I took the quieter and safer option and made good time, arriving at the campsite just after three o'clock.

This had probably been the easiest day's cycling yet. It could have been that some stronger ibuprofen helped - I doubted whether the soluble vitamin C I'd taken was responsible. Maybe it had been the rest day in Inverkeithing, but at my time of life my body would have needed more than one day to heal from the rigours of the journey so far; the favourable wind was the most likely cause of my good progress. However, despite my general sense of well-being, my bum was still feeling very sore.

I checked in and quickly set up camp before brewing up a coffee on the Trangia. I sat outside in the sunshine overlooking a tributary of the River Tay which flowed smoothly along one side of the site. Graham Rees came into my mind. A friend who I had met playing squash years ago, he was the first person I'd seen as I stepped out of Dennis' car at the crematorium. I made a mental note to ring him when I got back home and thank him for his support. A large crowd had gathered for Cherie's funeral, and I'd been surprised to see so many colleagues from my previous school there - it was nearly twenty years since I'd left. With hundreds in attendance, it was impossible to notice everyone. Perhaps I'm being unfair, and I know people had come to support me, but for some of these older Merthyrites, funerals were something of a social occasion and they would turn up almost as professional mourners, to bid farewell to somebody they hardly knew. Personally, if I possibly can, I avoid funerals.

Thinking of Graham triggered memories of playing football. Although some of us were already ageing badly, a ragtag group used to gather on a Thursday night and play a six, seven or eight aside game on half a pitch. I often came home injured, and I always ached from tackles, pulled muscles, twisted ankles or knees cut to shreds on 'Astroturf' - falling on it was like sliding on a cheese grater.

Cherie's usual reaction, bless her, was never: 'Well if you insist on doing these stupid things', or 'What do you expect at your age?'

She would just say, 'Go and have a shower, Dear – dinner will be ready by the time you come out', or 'Go and have a bath and I'll bring you up a beer.'

I never ate before playing even though we didn't kick off until half past six. Food slowed me down and it certainly didn't sit comfortably in my stomach as I ran around chasing my tail. Cherie always respected my interests and hobbies and never stood in the way of me pursuing them. It comforted me to know I had done the same for her … suddenly I missed her.

I thought about peoples' reactions whenever I told them of Cherie's death, not close friends or family, but acquaintances. On hearing the news, few would ask any further questions about how I was managing or if I were alright. Nor would they ask how she had died.

Were they respecting my privacy? Were they afraid of upsetting me? I realise it's hard to know what to say especially if the news is dropped on you without warning.

Some people can't talk because they are scared stiff of dying themselves - they know it's going to get them sooner or later. Being afraid to mention death is like a toddler hiding behind his hands in the belief that because he can't see you, you can't see him. But death sees everybody. I doubted whether hiding could help anyone truly come to terms with their own mortality. I may not believe in God, but I can see that religion addresses death in a way that secular society cannot. Again, it made me feel sorry for the Scotsman back in the bar at Scarborough, whose wife endured nine years with cancer and neither of them ever mentioned it to each other; their predicament was an extreme case of failure to confront the D word.

A feeling of weariness came over me and I lay on my mat for my customary nap. Twenty minutes later I was up and wondering how I could dry my socks. It didn't occur to me to buy some new ones, but at least I had realised they needed a wash. After a bit of thought, I had the idea of leaving open the inner door of the tent but closing up the outer flysheet. This meant I could hang the wrung-out socks inside and hopefully, the increased air circulation would dry them out. I had showered that morning so I decided not to bother again; I resolved to make sure I did the next day whilst I had the facilities. Next day, I was heading over the mountains where campsite facilities could not be guaranteed.

I strolled an agreeable mile to the town of Dunkeld through a forest of coniferous saplings, the pink of rosebay willow herb decorating the verges of the pathway. It was getting gloomy, partly because of the hour, but also on account of the gathering clouds. I began to think of Dr Death, Cherie's consultant at Prince Charles Hospital and the day he said to Cherie that she would need to have a BIG bum operation.

He asked her, 'When do you want to come in for it?'

'Tomorrow?' she enquired – typically direct and pragmatic. And she got it. Mr. Braithwaite made a few phone calls and it was sorted. The fact that Cherie had a serious illness and was tragically young to have it, may have explained the medical staff's willingness to fit things around her wishes, but I had the strong feeling that all the doctors really respected her.

'And so did everyone else,' I fondly reflected.

I had a wander through the main street but it didn't take long. It seemed to be very touristy and most of the shops sold leather and woollen goods; it was very quaint – even a façade sign which simply advertised a 'Plumber and Central Heating Specialist' looked oldie- worldie. The place was quieter than might have been expected of a tourist town, but the chip shop-come-café, with only six tables, was fairly busy as I ordered a Scotch pie with chips. It wasn't particularly impressive – sausage meat in I can't remember what.

I noticed the pictures on the walls were of fantasy scenes. Cherie never liked those types of paintings, but she loved the books of writers like Terry Pratchet who wrote scores of 'other-world' tales.

I would have liked a window seat so I could have seen out into the street, but they were all taken. Sitting at a nearby table, I noticed a John Lennon look-a-like and his identical wife, both with pony tails, round glasses and ageing hippy outfits sitting opposite each other; it must have been like looking in a mirror. They were kindly regarding a bratty five year old who was trying to grab someone's attention after he had fallen over. He'd made someone laugh and now felt compelled to carry on with a repertoire of new acts.

The sauce blurped out of its plastic squeezey bottle sounding like a fart and insufficiently pebble-dashed my

Scotch pie causing a few to look up at me and grin. I washed down my meal with a pint of strong locally brewed beer with a typically pretentious real ale name that I instantly forgot; I then ambled down to a small convenience store to buy some chocolate for breakfast in the morning. I needed to take the ibuprofen with food and chocolate would have to do. As I wandered down the street looking for a pub with a bit of life, I accidentally passed wind and didn't realise until some kids passed me on skateboards, all blaming each other for the smell and all denying it. They never suspected me! I carried on mooching around and decided to postpone taking money out of the hole in the wall until I could see how much I had left at the end of the night. There were heritage trail plaques everywhere and though I read a few of them, I wasn't really interested.

Then I noticed an art exhibition that was still open. There was a time when I wouldn't have dreamt of going into such a place, but I'd got into the habit with Cherie, who was always on the look-out for something. There were a large number of paintings on show and I must have been in there for half an hour. I found myself looking for pictures Cherie would have liked – bright splashes of colour and not too well defined -abstract was her favourite. With interior decoration she was the same - magnolia was a four-letter word.

Several ladies were manning the deserted gallery, drinking tea and gossiping and I joined them for a short while.

'See anything you like?' one of them queried.

'There's some nice work here but nothing really for me.' Meaning Cherie. Most of the time, Cherie was quite disparaging of local artists; I had assumed that locals had produced the work I had been looking at, but that wasn't the case – they had, in fact, come from all over the country. But there was still nothing for Cherie.

I wasn't too bothered about pubs that night but thought I'd drop in for a nightcap as it was still quite early. There was no one in the 'local' looking pub I chose, but I had an interesting chat with a great grandmother barmaid, before the clientele was tripled by two old men, both wearing dandy hats rather like fishermen, but not so as I soon discovered. They introduced themselves proudly as Alex and Alex. They were a double act from Australia.

They were very funny guys, especially one who came from Perth, though he was quite cantankerous and rude. His cigarette lighter was a naked woman with flashing boobs and knickers.

We bantered on for half an hour and then they left. I had one more drink and headed back to the campsite. By now it was dark and the return journey through the sapling wood was heavily shadowed and monochromatic. I felt pangs of hunger and I remembered the chocolate bar. I couldn't resist, but I did manage to restrict myself to just half of it, suddenly feeling sorry for the lining of my stomach the next morning after swallowing the erosive ibuprofen tablets. Back at the tent I settled down to update my journal. Seated in the entrance, flap open to the night with my headlamp illuminating the pages, I took a break from writing and spoke out loud in a tone of exasperation, 'Jesus, this journal is taking me ages now. I hope it's not going to end up as a load of bollocks.'

As I settled down to sleep, I thought back to the birthday phone call I had made to MR earlier. Over the years our relationship had certainly been through ups and downs, but a couple of times during the conversation he had asked how I was. He would never know how much that meant to me and I felt sure we would get on fine in the future.

The Ride:

Inverkeithing to Inver (near Dunkeld)
Distance: 46 miles

*You'd think that pedalling with the piles would put me on the rack
But in truth there was no pain, the sod just hid up in my crack.
And for all the cream and ointment off the doctor and the shelf
As soon as I stopped using them, it vanished by itself.

Inver to Newtonmore

Wednesday, July 18th

That morning, the weather was beautiful with bright warm sunshine illuminating the grassy campsite field and surrounding trees. Sitting in my tent, flap open and drinking my day break coffee, I was gazing across at the river glistening in the sunshine and watching the canoeists readying their craft, when a small robin landed on the guy string to my left about a foot from my face. He didn't stay long, but it seemed to me that he had lingered more than was natural. I don't believe in reincarnation, but he struck me as a 'benevolence' of some kind, and not for the first time, I had a strong spiritual feeling that Cherie was looking after me.

I got away at nine-thirty after a brief chat with the canoeists who had paddled down from Fort William and were on their way to Dundee. Once more, I set off initially on the wrong road. I didn't fancy a one mile back-track to Dunkeld in order to pick up the cycle track, so despite the fact that the map was not very clear, I decided to head north up a mystery lane. I checked my compass after walking up a steep hill for half a mile and saw that I was on the wrong heading. I should have back-tracked after all – at least it would have been flat. I still couldn't face the detour though, so I pedalled on to the busy A9 and decided to pick up the cycle track further on. Twenty minutes later, I pulled off the main road, relieved to be away from the noise and danger of the traffic.

The cycle track was not bad but it did take me 'around the houses' on a few occasions. It was frustrating because although I had good views, I was forever twisting this way and that, all the while being able to the see the A9 slicing through the countryside in a straight line - exactly where I wanted to go. A bloke in the pub the night before, had told me that a fortune had been spent on building the cycle track so, first as a cyclist and second as an environmental educator, I did feel a certain obligation to use it. I thought of a maxim I had first heard when training to be a teacher:

'It's not the getting there that's important; it's the quality of the ride'.

And it was pleasurable pedalling in the sunshine along the flat to slightly rising route, through pasture and woodland and from time to time picking up the distinct scent of wild mint as it alternated with that of pine from the conifers. I noticed a sign:

PITLOCHRY – PERTH, NATIONAL CYCLE ROUTE 77

DUNKELD TO BALLINLUIG SECTION

Opening spring 2001

These works are being undertaken by

Perth and Kinross Countryside Trust.

Part financed by the European Communities

Agricultural Guidance and Guarantee Fund

'It's interesting to know who's paying for these things,' I thought. In the distance I could hear the drone of traffic from the A9 below and the occasional rumble of the Perth to Inverness express train. The railway followed the road; in fact, running along one side of the campsite in Inver, the trains momentarily disturbed my sleep during the night.

Pitlochry took me a lot longer to reach than if I'd used the A9, assuming I would have survived the experience. The cycle path took the route of the old A9 in places and was deserted most of the time. This meant I could meander and wobble on the bike as my concentration waned and my mind rolled in sync with my wheels. There was another advantage in taking the more winding route along the cycle track. Because the route twisted and turned I was never actually against the wind for very long and the trees and bluffs along the route also served as windbreaks. As well as that, there was peace and quiet from the noise of the traffic; for a change, I was also getting to see creatures that were alive. There were plenty of rabbits playing in the fields and on the banks and a fair amount of bird life. At one point, a bird I didn't recognise (no surprise there - black on top and white underneath with a yellow/orange beak) was yelling in short monotonous bursts at its errant offspring who was half walking, half jumping up the old A9 about ten yards ahead of me. The mother kept circling, trying to get him on to the grassy bank that sloped off steeply to my left. Junior was squawking in identical fashion to his mother, but seemed singularly reluctant to leave the open tarmac and head into what must have looked, to the tiny fellow, like a forest of grass. This went on for some five minutes until a narrow track appeared on the left and Junior took the opportunity to finally head towards relative safety.

Pitlochry was very touristy and crowded to the extent that I had to keep stepping on to the road to dodge strolling clusters of window shoppers, ice cream lickers and amateur photographers. I had parked the bike against the wall of a busy restaurant, but I felt uneasy about its safety as I searched in vain for a supermarket where I hoped to pick up a cheap breakfast. I called into a Tourist Information and learned that were no campsites at my intended destination for the day some thirty miles further north.

'It's a very uninhabited area,' said the lady, who was otherwise very helpful. A sense of foreboding concerning the Grampian Mountains had been growing inside me over the past few days. I knew I had to cross them and I now had the feeling that today was going to be The Biggie. The Tourist Information woman's comment only added to my apprehension. I sent post cards to Hafina and to Cliff and Pauline, friends of mine whom I knew had visited Pitlochry a number of times on golfing outings. I wrote that, for the first time, I could be roughing it on the mountain that night. It didn't really bother me *too* much - the tent went up very easily and I believed the patter of the shop assistant who had sold it to me in Gloucester, 'This tent is expensive, but it is state of the art and designed for severe mountain weather.' Parting with that £250 on the Saturday before leaving Merthyr now bought me a certain peace of mind.

Anticipating a night next to nature and away from civilisation, I bought in supplies – two pasties, one sausage roll and two jumbo Mars bars (for energy I told myself). I also filled my flask with water and was surprised at how heavy it was, before deciding that it was important for me to have a reasonable meal before setting off into the wilderness. I found a place where I could sit down but still keep an eye on the bike and ordered a baked potato with Thai curry, mayonnaise and coffee. It was eleven o'clock by now and this was my breakfast, a reasonable meal if a little overpriced.

So ... equipped for a night on the hills, I set off with a very real sense of trepidation. However, having left Pitlochry and now with another fifteen miles on the trip meter, and twenty-six since leaving Inver that morning, I still hadn't seen any appreciable hills and I had been going down as much as up so it seemed. The wind was still blowing from the east, helping me to a certain extent, and the weather was holding – beautiful, bright sunshine, good visibility and cool refreshing air. There were still little villages along the way and I stopped at one of them to top up with orange Lucozade.

The slopes did come, but they were still not too bad. As I progressed slowly up the cycle path, I continued to look enviously at the main A9 every time it came into view – a straight, steady gradient - while the cycle track continued to meander all over the place. Even when it ran right next to the A9 the cycle path kept dipping sharply for a distance of fifty yards, as it crossed one of many newly constructed wooden bridges then climbed steeply on the other side. The reason for this roller coaster arrangement was that countless streams crossed under the main road. Of course, provision had been made for this when the A9 had been built, and the road spanned the rivers across a series of short bridges. However, there was no room for the cycle track to squeeze over as well, so the streams had to be traversed by little wooden foot bridges at a much lower level, hence the big dips.

The cycle track also made it difficult for me because its surface was often unconsolidated gravel – red in colour, a bit like a school hockey pitch. I had to freewheel gingerly down the dips in case I lost grip on it. I didn't want to get a nasty graze or, worse still, break something in my body as I fell off. And the gravel surface created extra friction making it hard going even on the flat - and worse going uphill, and by this time, uphill was what I was mostly doing. To make matters worse, the wind started to blow hard against me as the valley funnelled it from the north. My right knee, that had given me some warning signs the day before, started to ache more than my long suffering left knee, and the main crank driving the pedals also began to sporadically creak ominously.

Things were not looking good and I worried,

'I can get the crank fixed in Inverness or Aviemore, even if it means walking most of the way (save for down hills). But my knees?'

Although I had passed the three-quarters stage of my trip the day before, I was aware that I couldn't afford to be complacent. I still had a hell of a long way to go. It was a bit like being in a car that starts to splutter at the end of a long journey. Your brain tells you you're nearly there but it's computing in the language of internal combustion. It doesn't register the fact that 'nearly there - driving' translates as, 'bloody long way to go - walking'. Heading towards the darkening summit of one of the highest passes on my route through Scotland, I was trying to put as little pressure on my legs as possible. If I started to feel what I considered to be too much resistance, I'd change down a gear and let my snail's pace drop still more. If that didn't work, I got off and walked. If the slope was steeper and I could still feel the strain, I walked even slower. Doing the big hours on the road, day after day was punishment enough. I was surprised my legs had lasted as long as they had; I didn't want to push my luck. As I slowly gained altitude, I couldn't see the top of the pass. I didn't know how far I was going to get and I was resigned to the fact that I would have to camp out in the middle of nowhere, with no security and, most likely, no shelter from the wind.

As the long climb continued, I thought about a sign I'd stopped to take a photo of earlier not long after leaving Pitlochry. It read:

> **WARNING**
>
> Drumochter Summit
>
> Cycle track climbs to 457m
>
> Weather conditions deteriorate without warning and can be severe even in summer
>
> No food or shelter for 30km
>
> No snow clearance or gritting on cycle track

At the time I had already cycled 25 miles and I converted the 30km to the more familiar imperial equivalent – 20 miles. Adding the two together meant I would reach food and shelter at 45 miles, which seemed OK; but, I had to take into consideration the fact that I had to get over the Pass of Drumochter. I hadn't been sure about my chances then; hence my current resignation to a night on the mountain.

Apart from the wind, it was turning decidedly colder and the sunshine was now replaced by dark clouds, which spawned the occasional light shower. I thought back to the quandary I had been in over what to do about Cherie's ashes. We had discussed the issue but because neither of us attached much importance to the question, we had never come up with an answer. The undertaker took me through the options. I could have them put into a garden of remembrance at the crematorium, with a small plaque to remind passers-by of a person that was. Alternatively, I could take possession of the ashes and scatter them in what I felt to be the most appropriate manner and place. Most bizarrely, I could cannibalistically have the ashes split.

As the undertaker put it, "You can have the best of both worlds you'll have a headstone to visit but you'll still have ashes to scatter."

My mum had been semi-coerced into this 'splitting of the ashes' strategy when my father died. I don't think Dad would have been the least bit bothered, but the undertaker managed to convince her that loved ones would get comfort from being able to visit 'Him'. Presumably, this would not have been possible if he'd been dropped out of his pot from the top of a mountain in a force eight gale. In hindsight, my mum does regret putting fifty percent of Dad into the graveyard and I've no doubt the undertaker made on the deal. I told myself that it didn't matter two hoots what happened to Cherie's ashes, but in truth it did.

I discounted the plot in the crematorium. Who would want to spend eternity there for God's sake? That left me with having to consider other options. If it had been me, I wouldn't have minded being scattered at sea off one of my mate's boats. But Cherie had never really been keen on the water so I discounted that. The top of a mountain did hold a certain appeal as Cherie and I had done quite a lot of hill walking, but a chat with Cherie's sister, Isobel, gave me two ideas that struck home. Much as Cherie may have liked walking up hills, it was nothing compared to how much she loved her food. And there was one place in our area, that she treasured above all others, The Nant Ddu Lodge on the A470 between Merthyr and Brecon, in the heart of the Brecon Beacons. It wasn't so much the setting of the place, but the quality of the food and the fact that the menu offered dishes that were out of the ordinary. The Nant Ddu Lodge is set in considerable grounds and Isobel thought it would be a good idea to lay Cherie's ashes there. I wondered about the owner's reaction to such a request, but I could imagine Cherie giggling at the prospect of me, and a few others, surreptitiously digging a hole in the corner of the lawn at four o'clock in the morning.

Isobel's other idea was quite simply to bury Cherie's ashes in our garden. It's not much to look at but we had started to turn it into something of a town garden before Cherie had become ill. Once we knew what was happening, the garden project had been thrown on the scrap heap as we began to plan holidays and other more exciting leisure pursuits. But we had created a large raised patio area and built a wall between, ourselves and our neighbour. It had been heavy, backbreaking work but Cherie had done her fair share, mixing the compo while I laid the blocks. Enough groundwork had been done to provide a secluded suntrap where Cherie enjoyed happy hours reading and taking in the rays. When I thought about it, if Cherie would have wanted to be anywhere, it would have been close to me, not thrown to the elements or buried in the countryside away from the bustle of town. And the feeling was mutual. I wanted her close to me. Our home was where she had been happy, and it was the place we had intended to stay; we had no aspirations to move to a better area or a bigger house.

The undertaker had brought Cherie's ashes the Monday after her funeral. He stopped to talk for quarter of an hour, about the funeral mainly, before making his excuses and leaving. A green plastic pot with a screw top, it reminded me of the BDU containers we used when canoeing to keep our gear dry. On it, a simple label was stuck,

CHERIE HILL

It was hard to believe. I took the container out into the garden and found a trowel. I dug a hole in the small patch of earth left after our concreting efforts, and poured the ashes in. I was surprised that there was quite a lot. I knelt down and stared at the grey white ash and the tears silently came. I put my hands into the grave, cupped the ashes within and instinctively raised them up, before slowly allowing the powder to run between my fingers and back into the earth. What could I do? Nothing ... I knelt motionless and lost - time stood still. Eventually, I unfroze and began to use my hands to slowly draw soil back over the hole then made it good with the palms of my hands and my body weight. I went back into the kitchen and sat down at the table, cupped my face in my hands, leaned on my elbows and sobbed my pain out loud.

Although Cherie hadn't considered what to do with her ashes, she had planned her funeral carefully. She wanted it to be a bit different and something that would be remembered. Her main preparation was the casket (I insisted on calling it a 'casket' in preference to a 'coffin') she wanted to make herself. In college, she had been given the option of doing an individual design project, so she thought she would kill two birds with one stone – get a big piece of course work out of the way and acquire a novel coffin in which to get buried.

She worked hard on the casket. It had a ply base with hardboard sides and she wangled, in her own inimitable style, the services of craftsmen at university who helped in cutting and fixing the thing together. But even she was surprised when the cardboard sides warped to create a wave effect that I doubt would have been designed or could have been predicted at the outset. Cherie decorated the borders of the casket with Celtic designs from a book we had picked up at a West Wales cultural centre some months before, on our way back from Snowdon. The lid was also made from ply, and Cherie had done a considerable amount of research on the subject of effigies making special visits to cathedrals as well as on the Internet. Her idea was to make a full body cast of herself from clay or plaster that would lie on top of the casket. She wanted to be wearing a long flowing dress and be holding a glass of red wine in one hand - she hadn't decided what to do with the other hand. The casket itself was lilac in colour and around the four sides was a photo collage that featured herself and family and friends over the course of her life. There were pictures that had been taken just months ago and old black and white faded prints from way back. She had gathered them from albums and our ad hoc collection of photo envelopes full of prints that never made it any further.

I had built a frame for the casket from pieces of three by two timber so it stood three feet off the floor. Nicole, Cherie's eldest daughter, had used some brightly coloured sari material to cover up my bad workmanship so when the lilac casket stood elevated above a curtain of vibrant Indian fabrics, and with the photos around the sides, it would be a feast for the eyes.

Cherie never got to finish the casket. The effigy was never made and she didn't manage to get the collages attached to its sides. However, she did arrange the photos onto laminated sheets and fellow student friends were able to fix them to the casket for her. Cherie knew that the effigy wouldn't get done and we also had doubts as to whether such a heavy piece of work could be supported on a box that was so lightweight. So in the end we had to make do with a lid that was bare except for a single enlarged black and white photo of Cherie as a baby (the same one I carry in my briefcase).

If that was the bad news, the good news was that the top surface would now be flat. Cherie thought that this would make an excellent bar. She had decided that she wanted a wake – she didn't expect to actually be in the casket but she wanted a few hand-picked friends and family to be there. Her main criterion for selection was that they had to be people with whom we had enjoyed at least one alcohol fuelled session. And it was Cherie that stipulated that the casket was to be placed in the middle of the kitchen and used as a bar. So, on the day of the wake as the party warmed up, it was not long before the usual paraphernalia began to accumulate on the casket: cans, half-full bottles, ashtrays, lighters and handbags were strewn over the top together with crumbs, crisp packets, elbows and an increasing number of semi-circular stains. Cherie would have loved it.

So the casket was to be multi-functional, but I now had to check whether it could be used as a working piece of kit at the funeral. I phoned the crematorium and braced myself as the dial tone stopped and the receiver was picked up.

'Hello, my name is Tony Hill - I've got a rather unusual enquiry.' It was a female crematorium employee who answered and a wacky conversation followed.

I continued, 'My wife is very poorly, but when she dies she wants to donate her body to medical science. She's made her own coffin and she wants it to be used for the cremation service even though it would be empty.'

'What's the coffin made of, Sir?' I described the basic construction materials that Cherie had used.

'What paint did she put on it, Sir?'

Now I knew it was lilac, and I thought it might be a satin finish rather than gloss or matt, but that was about it, 'I'm sorry – I really don't know.'

The female voice continued as if conducting a police interview with a suspect, 'Did it have lead in it?'

Again, I had to admit that I didn't have a clue.

She continued, 'We can't use anything with lead in it Sir. It's all to do with environmental health. If it's got lead in the paint, we can't burn it'.

Now, it wasn't going to be possible to do any sort of chemical analysis on the paint, that was for certain, but I made a mental note that the tin might be up in the garage or in college and I could possibly check. It didn't come as a surprise that this obstacle had been put in my way – I had anticipated problems and this was probably just the first hurdle. So I had contingency plans and was prepared to use a different tack.

'The coffin doesn't actually have to be burned,' I explained. 'It can be used for the ceremony and I thought I might be able to pick it up later and take it away.'

'That won't be possible, Sir. There are rules about that. Once a coffin comes here, it can't be taken away again.'

I suddenly had a mental picture of the congregation solemnly filing out the same way that they had filed in twenty minutes before, now understandably with more sniffles and tears. But rather than following the coffin as they had before, the coffin now trailed after them, to be placed back in the estate car of one of my mates before being whisked back to the house. The thought brought a smile to my face and I knew that Cherie would have been all for it – she would have gone along with anything that was a bit out of the ordinary. However, I knew I had to consider other people who might misinterpret the proceedings as a lack of respect. The alternative was almost as farcical. 'The Boys' could slip the casket away out of some side door and clandestinely pack it into a vehicle out of sight of the mourners. In my mind's eye, I saw three of them – an unnoticed side show - one opening the doors and two carrying the lilac coffin, sloping off through the foliage like school boys bunking off school in the afternoon.

I explained to the woman, 'But there isn't going to be a body!'

The woman was shocked, 'What d'you mean, no body?'

Her mind must have been side-tracked by the debate over construction materials and paint. Either that, or she hadn't heard what I had said about Cherie donating her body to medical science at the start of our conversation.

I explained once more, adding at the end, 'So you see, the rules won't really apply in this case.'

Clearly, my request had now exceeded her authority so she asked me to hold while she went off to speak to her boss.

After a while she returned and said, 'It depends on whether there is a funeral scheduled after yours.'

My imagination started to roll again. Now, the assembled mourners for the next funeral stood dumbstruck by the sight of a lilac coffin covered in photos taking up the rear as all the mourners left the building. Snapping out of my thoughts, I realised I had to get logical.

'If I arrange for the service to be the last of the day would it be possible for me to pick the coffin up later?'

She had to refer the query back to the Superintendent again. 'The last service is at 3.30 – you would have to pick it up by quarter past four.'

I was relieved that there seemed to be a way around the problem. If Cherie's body was going for medical research, there should be no problem getting the last slot of the day because I wouldn't be under any time constraint.

But that was only one scenario. Although I had been through all the procedures involved in committing Cherie's body for research, and it had been quite complicated, I wouldn't know whether her body would be accepted until after she died. It basically depended on supply and demand – did they have enough 'material' and was Cherie's sadly diseased shell of use to them if they did.

So, I had to consider what could be done if Cherie's body was going to be present at the crematorium. I pointed this out to the woman. As I thought, it threw up a whole new set of problems.

'Would I still be able to use my wife's casket for the ceremony? The curtain could be drawn for the committal and the coffin could be moved to 'the other side'. Then the body could be removed and cremated and I could pick the coffin up later on.'

I thought, if anything, that Cherie's ashes would be all the more pure for not being mixed in with those of the casket. Off went the woman to confer with The Superintendent again. Why the hell didn't he come and speak to me directly - afterwards, I wished I thought of asking for him to do so.

'No, that won't be possible - staff on 'the other side' are not allowed to handle bodies.'

I stressed that the body would be in a shroud or something similar but it made no difference. Those were the rules.

'Could the undertaker go around and remove the body then?'

'No, Sir - the undertaker is not allowed to go to the other side either.' More rules. Should it have been any surprise that with something as serious as a funeral, a bit of give and take and common sense was not going to be possible? It was certainly very different to the way the hospitals worked. They had been prepared to bend to Cherie's requirements to an extent that had been both impressive and touching.

So that was it. If Cherie's body was accepted for medical research, we could use her casket for the funeral. But if she was going to be present at the ceremony, I was going to have to use a conventional coffin. That threw up another problem – what was I going to do with Cherie's lilac casket. I could use it as a bar at her wake, as she had wanted, but how was I going to dispose of it afterwards.

After some thought, I had hit upon the solution. I could use the casket as a bar for the bash at the end of the funeral as well, then take it out on to the concrete patio we had both grafted so hard to build, and ceremonially burn it.

I still couldn't see the brow of the pass and I decided it was time to take a break. The wind was strong so I needed to find some shelter. There were no trees this high up so my only option was one of the many EU funded wooden bridges that traversed the streams passing underneath the A9. I propped the bike against the handrail on the bridge and prized the Lucozade, Mars bar and paper bag, with the remaining pasty and sausage roll, from under the bungee. Due to a complete lack of space inside the rucksack pockets, I'd pinned my dinner under the two lower tensioned shock cords that held the map, my flask and my sandals. Looking at the pastries, you wouldn't have guessed they had been under low tension. The pasty was now amorphous and melded like Siamese twins with the sausage roll, both now in need of separation from each other. Gentle, surgical fingers could not prevent the spillage of large amounts of flaking pastry and bits of filling – let's not say meat. I felt like a litterbug in the countryside, though to my credit, not a scrap of paper was lost to the wind.

By this time, my fingers were numb with cold and, even though I had donned my waterproofs to act as a windcheater, I had difficulty getting out of the confounded gusts. I slid a few feet down the sides of an eight-foot deep gully that had been cut by the stream. The slope was strewn with rubble, albeit natural - dirt and stones with clumps of green weeds struggling to get a foothold. The river filled the bottom of my little refuge, so I ended up precariously perched on the loose scree. I just couldn't get comfortable. After a minute, finishing off the pasty, it occurred to me that this was not much of a rest. Yes, I was mostly out of the wind, but I could feel the strain on my burdened legs as they tried to keep my weight half way up the slope. I shifted position several times, but with no improvement to the stress and strain on the parts of my body vital to cycling. To add to the discomfort, the sharp gravel was starting to poke into my bum. I jiggled around several times on each occasion, waiting a few seconds to see if the new position was more comfortable. It wasn't, and in a final desperate effort, I dug my heels into the ground and yanked myself closer to the bridge. What a mistake. I had lost my bearings and didn't realise how close I was to the bridge. Vigorously thrusting upwards, I thumped my head hard against the underside of the bridge.

'Argggh!'

'Jesus!'

It hurt. I was badly shocked as I continued to instinctively utter a string of alternative swear words. Slowly, the pain eased off to be replaced by a dull ache and I muttered to myself, 'I can do without this.'

As I sat finishing my meal, at last in relative comfort, I gazed across the gully at the expanse of open moorland that separated me from the distant mountains to the southeast - a meadowy, marshy scene filled with dull greens starved of light by the grey sky. Enjoying the view made me think about all the experiences Cherie and I had shared together, and it occurred to me that this one-off huge trip was not being shared by Cherie or anyone else. I couldn't really say that the people I had met on the way were sharing it, although they had been part of it. Cherie and I would have enjoyed talking about these people. Like the odd couple of men I had met in the pub in Dunkeld the night before – Alex and Alex. Now I wish I had been able to take a photo of them because I knew the mental picture I had formed of them would soon fade into oblivion.

I thought about how long it was now taking me to write up my journal – usually two to two and a half hours, often in the evening, but also the following day before setting off. Although it seemed to me that at least this was one way I would be able to share my lone trip with others at a later date, it didn't make me feel any less lonely now - and it would never be the same as sharing it with Cherie.

Looking into the ripped remnants of the paper bag that had held my pastries, I could see my food was gone – all that remained was a mess of flakes scattered like miniature leaves in an autumnal model village. When I slept on the mountain that night, there wouldn't be any supper or breakfast now – my heart sunk even further.

Back on the bike, the going was slow with the wind now hard in my face. However, at one point, a small bird half hovering, half flying into the wind, seemed to be keeping me company. As with the robin that morning, I imagined I could feel Cherie's presence in the animal, as if it were looking after me.

In places, I started to go downhill but I checked over to my left to watch which way the streams were flowing and I could clearly see they were coming towards me, confirming that I was still generally going upwards. Heading towards yet another bridge-crossed gully, I was surprised to see what looked like a police officer laying his mountain bike, of all things, on its side as he proceeded to clamber up the embankment towards the A9. He was wearing reflective gear and carrying what looked like a radar gun with an aerial, topped with an inverted cone-like contraption. It was like something back street kids would put together for an imaginary game involving aliens. I wasn't sure if the copper was laying a speed trap but, if he was, it seemed rather an SAS way of going about things. I was tempted to yell up at him to satisfy my curiosity, as I watched his tubby bottom finally loll over the top of the bank framed by the day glow green of his jacket - but he looked busy so I thought better of it. It was odd - I didn't think he could have cycled all the way to this remote spot and I couldn't understand why he would need to be on a bike. It would have to remain a mystery.

The thought again crossed my mind that perhaps this was the watershed and now it was going to be downhill all the way. It turned out that I was near the highest point on the A9, and although it wasn't obvious at first, the realisation did dawn upon me after a while. It was a pleasant surprise as I trudged and pedalled over the pass. The gradient, although long, had levelled off sooner than I had expected, even if the saddle I now crossed was fairly unspectacular.

However, I was still not convinced that there weren't other nasty mountains to climb before the day was out, so I stopped to check the map. I estimated there were about ten miles to go. Provided I could find a campsite or bed and breakfast, I optimistically reversed my resigned intention to stay out on the mountain. As I started to descend, I was impressed by the dark, foreboding mountains that rose steeply to my left, and I wondered if these were the ones I had seen from a distance earlier on. I stopped again to pore over the map. On the page, I could see the highest peak in the vicinity was Sgairneach Mhor at 991 metres. I scanned around and picked out the obvious candidate - it was the only one shrouded with grey cloud. I could clearly pick out the skyline and the form of all the other peaks that now surrounded me like witches, but Sgairneach Mhor wouldn't show all. Like a shy lover, wisps of cloud hid the most important and interesting bits. As I resumed, I kept glancing over my left shoulder, risking a fatal wobble on the unconsolidated cycle path, hoping to get a fleeting peek of the hidden summit. Once, the skirts seemed to lift momentarily, but I knew I could wait for an age and not get to see that secretive summit.

The hidden peak triggered a memory of the art gallery I had perused the night before. There had been a picture of a little boy and girl, obviously siblings on account of their eyes. Entitled 'The Secret', the two children, probably eight and ten years old, were smiling in the characteristic way kids do when they know something that you don't. I was surprised to think that I must have taken in more at the gallery than I had thought and I was quietly pleased with myself. Cherie would have been impressed too.

Now, getting assistance from the gradient, I was able to make better progress than I had for hours. At about the forty-mile mark, I stopped at a hotel in Dalwhinnie. By this time I had become quite cold and the barmaid served me a welcoming pot of hot tea into which I spooned an overdose of sugar. The pot made three cups of tea that progressively got stronger – it was exactly what I needed. I talked to a small group of people gathered around the bar and soon learned that they were a mixture of locals and travellers.

'What's the highest mountain in this area?' I was interested to find out if I had read the map correctly.

I continued, 'Why hasn't the cycle path been tarmacked – it's hard going on that gravel stuff.'

One of the locals had his own theory on the latter point, 'Bloody would have been if it had been down south in Luton or Milton Keynes, you can bet.'

I answered, 'But you've got your own parliament now.' This statement provoked some further inconsequential debate and it was clear that there was a consensus amongst the locals that not enough money was being spent on Scotland. The conversation turned to queries about me.

A suggestion came from the man who had been most vociferous in the previous discussion, 'You want to look into getting a bus back to South Wales at the end of your trip. I'm sure if you give them plenty of notice, the bus company would put your bike in the luggage hold for a small fee.'

The idea had certainly not occurred to me, and I said I'd look into it. We also talked about the various cheap train deals that were around and, privately, I settled back on the idea of a train trip back rather than the bus.

The barmaid informed me sympathetically that the nearest campsite was near Ralia, some six miles away. A quick calculation told me that the warning sign I had seen on the way to the Drumochter Summit should have read 30 miles, and not 30 kilometres. It also meant the distance for the trip for the day was going to be about 56 miles – more than I would have planned, but at least I was not going to be pitching my tent on the mountain side in the middle of nowhere. Reluctantly, I left the warmth of the hotel and headed north into the wind again. For the next three miles, it made the going hard and as I battled against the atmosphere, my misery was compounded by a series of old, infrequently placed milestones that counted down the remaining distance to Ralia in painfully small increments.

With about two miles to go to journey's end, and with the wind's strength easing with my lowering altitude, I stopped on the deserted cycle path for a pee. It was now following the route of the old A9 again, and for the time being, the new A9 was out of sight and earshot. The 'road' was straight but was being seriously encroached upon by vegetation on both sides. There was no Mohican style grass strip down its centre, so often seen on little used country lanes, but the edges had long lost their definition as the frayed conduit disappeared from view to its vanishing point. Most of the invading trees were quite young and about fourteen to twenty feet tall. Cats' eyes still ranged down the centre line in various states of decay. Some were pristine and others were intact but discoloured; some had bits missing and the most weathered were empty, frost deepened holes. The road reminded me of one of those sci-fi stories where a catastrophe has hit the world, virtually depopulating it just leaving the artefacts of civilisation to wither. I could see Charlton Heston's jaw drop as he rounded the corner to see the Statue of Liberty in the final scene of 'Planet of the Apes.'

The municipal campsite was actually on the outskirts of Newtonmore, just a little past Ralia. I paid my three pounds, set up camp and went for a much deserved shower, albeit in a cold, draughty unwelcoming concrete block building, more suited to storing forgotten garden implements than to comforting and warming my weary body. But I felt a huge sense of achievement having travelled so far over difficult terrain, and also massive relief that I had not had to rough it. I wandered half a mile into the town and walked into the first pub I came to. I was lucky at about nine o'clock, to catch the last order for food. When the steak and kidney pie arrived, the portion was enormous, as if the chef had decided to get rid of all the food that was left rather than throwing anything out. Although the beans were overdone, it was hot – perfect. I wolfed down the lot telling myself I needed the energy. This was my first evening meal out since leaving Merthyr and I made short work of the transfer from plate to stomach.

In fact, the meal arrived sooner than I expected. I had only just started my second pint of Guinness and was in full flow writing up my journal. After my feast, I continued for some time fuelled further by another Guinness, before deciding to head back to the campsite. I saw no point in staying - except for a youngish couple and a solitary middle-aged man seated at the bar, the pub was empty. Somehow though, as I politely returned my glass to the bar before leaving, I got into a conversation with the single man, Howard. He used to be in the whiskey business and he told me that he had personally been heavily involved with the successful promotion of the 'Famous Grouse' brand some twenty years ago. Apparently, before that time, it was little known. He had now retired from that line of work and was currently on holiday bird watching, on his own and away from his wife who had gone elsewhere. Their arrangement was perfectly amicable and it was something that they did once every year. Not a bad idea I supposed, especially if you had been married for years and were now both retired and at home with each other all the time.

In his capacity as a bird watcher, I asked Howard if he could identify the bird that I had watched trying to tend to its wayward offspring earlier. Surprisingly, from a poor description of its appearance and an even worse one of its song, he proclaimed it be an oystercatcher. We ended up talking for about an hour. I had been starved of human contact that day and perhaps Howard had too, but more than that we seemed to have a natural affinity for each other. Given his previous occupation, we inevitably got onto the subject of whiskey. I was interested to know what the best was. Howard pointed out that it was obviously a matter of taste, but that the single malt 'Highland Park' was his favourite. To prove the point, he bought me one and gave me a brief rundown of how it was made on the Orkney Islands. I bought him one back and we see-sawed quite a few rounds trying other single malts and drawing comparisons with the Highland Park. I wanted to clear up some confusion about how whiskey should be drunk and here I was in the company of a man who had worked for years in the industry.

'I always drink my whiskey neat, Howard, but others drink it with water, ice or dry ginger. My mate Cliff loves his whiskey, but he drinks his with lemonade – what's the best?'

Howard was unequivocal: 'Water, nothing else, only water – the amount can vary to taste, but it should never be more than the volume of the whiskey itself. If you drink it neat, the strength of the alcohol drowns the flavour of the whiskey, so always take some water.'

I took his advice and was convinced that he spoke the truth. This Highland Park with a little water was very nice indeed, even if my judgement was by now getting clouded by the considerable amount of it consumed.

Howard was curious about the little bundle I had safely stashed by my left hand on the bar – he could make out the silver spiral bound notebook through the transparent plastic wallet Hafina had bought me as a birthday present. I told him about the journal and that I planned to write a book when I got home, wondering whether his response would be one of encouragement or nonchalance. He was very interested and coincidently, had written two books himself that he was in the process of trying to get published. The first was all about the whiskey business, so further convincing me of the soundness of his advice. The second was about birds and he had come up with the novel idea of illustrating the book using old postcards. I was very interested by all this and Howard was happy to pass on what he knew about getting a book published. He felt that for the type of book I was planning to write, the best route would be to find an agent and send a synopsis. Apparently, there are lists of such agents in the library.

Far from wanting to leave, I was now in a drinking mood, but my partner had commitments. He had to be up early in the morning for a shooting of the TV programme 'Monarch of the Glen' in which he had managed to get a part as an extra. Before Howard left, we exchanged email addresses and he advised me to look up the Highland Park distillery when I got to Orkney – he said that they gave guided tours of the plant that would help to satisfy my curiosity about whiskey. He also suggested that I spend more time in Orkney than on Shetland and that I look out for him on television next time Monarch of the Glen was on. I left shortly after him and walked up the gentle slope to the campsite.

Back in the tent I thought, 'To hell with the journal', and hit the sack with my watch reading 12.30 a.m. The weather was still dry, but it was quite nippy up there in the Highlands as I cwched up for warmth in my sleeping bag.

The Ride:

Inver to Newtonmore (16 miles south west of Aviemore)

Distance: 56 miles

Newtonmore to Inverness

Thursday, July 19th

I atoned for not writing up the journal by getting stuck into it over a coffee, the sleep still fogging my eyes after a restful night. It was 10.15 by the time I got away under an overcast sky. Although punctuated from time to time by short showers, it was a pleasant ride through woodland and pasture following the old A9, with the new A9 and the railway line occasional companions. Considering I was in the heart of the Highlands, the terrain was surprisingly flat, at least by South Wales' standards; although the mountains were clearly visible in the distance, they must have been at least ten miles away.

As I headed through a remote section of countryside, the 'Planet of the Apes' road flanked by pine trees and a verge of long grass, in my peripheral vision I accidentally caught sight of a dead deer. It was perfectly laid out and set upon the camber of the bank just feet away. I could clearly see the whole animal presented before me like a taxidermist's display. A split second later and I would have missed it. I pedalled on for another ten yards then pulled up. I had never liked the idea of seeing dead bodies; but, I had been thinking and even writing about dead creatures a lot and I thought I should get at least one photo. I clumsily hobby-horsed the bike in reverse and shuddered as I got a better look at the poor creature. It was quite young and must have been recently killed. Like the fox I'd seen before, it could have been asleep were it not for its eyes that were wide open and strikingly blue in colour – they would surely have been plundered by some bird had they been on offer for any significant length of time. I squeamishly stayed astride the bike not wanting to dwell any longer than necessary, but I still had to lean in closer to frame the shot thanks to the wide angled, fixed lens on my camera.

'Zoom lenses certainly have their uses,' I rued. Cycling away and shaking off the death with further sporadic shoulder shudders, the deer faded in my mind as it disappeared in my wake. I found myself starting to get excited about actually finishing the trip. I thought how cycling all the way was going to give me a huge sense of achievement and I began to compose a few limericks that I could include in my journal to mark the start of each remaining day. But I chastised myself.

'There's a long way to go yet – you can't afford to count your chickens! Your legs may be holding up, but you can feel they're very delicate, can't you?'

I could certainly feel the strain from the exertions of the day before - the trip to Newtonmore had been a gruelling one and I had covered a lot of miles. The last time I had completed such a distance was the day I rode to Scarborough. And of course, the terrain was tougher here in Scotland and compounded by the poor surface of the cycle track. Making things worse were the repeated ups and downs as I was forced to cross countless burns flowing under the A9. And, once again, the wind had been against me. With my optimism appropriately dampened by such thoughts, I accepted once more the underlying scepticism that had coloured my approach from day one.

It might have been the sight of the dead deer that made me think about the imminence of death. Was it better to have warning or not? Is a sudden death road traffic accident preferable to a terminal illness? I had been through a number of imminent death false alarms with Cherie, even though she never saw them that way. Even when her eyes had yellowed with the tell-tale jaundice of obvious liver failure, and she had felt so ill that she wanted to die, she didn't believe that she was near the end – and she had been right. We had endured a nightmare twenty-hour journey back from holiday in the Maldives. Cherie was in pain and feeling so sick that the only modicum of comfort she could get was by lying down. The aircraft had no facility for this so we negotiated a place on the floor, wedged between two rows of seats in the first class section of the plane where there happened to be just two free seats. The man sitting in the third seat of the block was not very happy with the arrangement and I had to sit in my original seat some fifteen rows back in economy class, getting up to check on Cherie as often as I could.

Our frustration and worry was made much worse as the plane was rerouted to Manchester, dropping off half the passengers there before coming back to Heathrow several hours later. Many of the passengers were complaining bitterly at the change of schedule. We had booked hotel accommodation that would now probably be defunct – by the time we got there it wouldn't be worth checking in. One aggrieved woman, in particular, went on and on and on at the cabin crew. Sitting just two rows back we could hear every word of her loud, moaning, grating monologue. She thought she had problems, but Cherie just wanted to curl up and die. I was getting more and more upset, but it was clear nothing could be done. An hour or so before touchdown at Heathrow, I walked to the back of the plane, struggling to hold back the tears as my voice quivered to the cabin crew.

'My wife is very ill. She has cancer and it looks like her liver has packed in.' A kindly look of concern came from a female member of the crew.

'Is it possible to phone ahead? We're going to need an ambulance as soon as we land.'

'Yes, Sir, we can certainly arrange that for you.' Some small relief for us, but it was bad news for the other passengers who had to wait for the paramedics to come on to the plane before they could start to disembark. I can't remember if the moaning woman started up again, but that was the least of my worries.

At the hospital in Slough, there wasn't a lot they could do for Cherie, except give her pain killers and anti-sickness drugs, and they advised me to drive her to her own specialist cancer hospital in Cardiff. There, Cherie's history would be known and they could act more effectively. It was a truly awful three-hour drive through the night, as Cherie lay suffering quietly on the back seat of our Ford Focus. Half an hour from Cardiff The toll collector on the Severn Bridge quizzed me about the sticker on the windscreen.

'Are you disabled, Sir?'

'No, it's my wife.'

'Where is your wife?'

'Look! On the back seat! She's very ill and I'm rushing her to hospital in Cardiff.' He must have made out Cherie's form in the darkness and the barrier lifted.

I was convinced that this was the end; I struggled again to get my explanatory words out as I finally took her into Velindre hospital just after daybreak. I stayed a few hours until the doctors arrived and Cherie was taken up on to a ward. I was reassured by kind staff and told to go home and rest. Driving again, my thoughts returned to the imminence of Cherie's death. Even though I knew I was going to have to face this one day, as far as I was concerned it was now upon me. It wasn't until I got back into our house that emotional and physical exhaustion caught up with me and I fell to sleep on a tear soaked pillow. It was a false alarm. I visited Cherie later that day, and although she was still jaundiced and feeling unwell, drugs had brought her pain and sickness largely under control. Not only that, but a scan had revealed that the problem was not the classic liver failure that I had misdiagnosed, but a blocked bile duct that had produced similar symptoms. An endoscopic procedure was used to fit a stent or tube into Cherie's bile duct and within days, her normal colour returned. She was fine again and thankfully allowed to come home. Amazingly, throughout it all, Cherie never believed that the end was approaching.

It was the same a year before, just after Cherie had gone through a big operation to remove her bowel. The procedure had gone well and she was making a characteristically rapid recovery. But then she became very ill and she couldn't eat. At the same time, she couldn't stop being sick, even though there was nothing to bring up. She suffered badly at home for a few days and had numerous doctor visits, before finally being admitted to hospital. I feared the worst but Cherie, as usual, remained upbeat and optimistic. And, she had been right then too. The problem was that part of her bowel had dropped and adhered to her body wall, effectively closing her alimentary canal. An operation to rectify the situation was carried out; and, although Cherie lost a lot of weight, she soon fully recovered.

On both those occasions, I had been devastated and convinced that Cherie was going to die. When the real thing happened, she slipped imperceptibly from just being tired to sleeping most of the time. As soon as she awoke she would be ready for sleep again. Cherie never realised she was nearing the end, and neither did I when it actually happened. It had been just weeks before that Cherie had broken down in the hospital when Mr. Crosby the consultant, had told her that she had less than six months to live. Both of us took that to mean six months and I knew that if Cherie had imagined she would be dead in three weeks, she would have told me.

Mr Crosby had arranged for Cherie to have a procedure called a plexus block. We were working on the assumption that it was the cocktail of drugs that was knocking Cherie out all the time. The plexus block aimed to kill pain receptors in the spine and so negate the need for the drugs. We hoped that the result would be a return to a normal waking state. The operation didn't work but it distracted us both from the fact that Cherie's death was close.

Even when Cherie was admitted to hospital for the final time, I asked the doctor if she was still suffering cold turkey symptoms as a result of having her drug dosages reduced. That was the Tuesday lunchtime and she never managed to regain cogency or proper consciousness again. At dawn the following Saturday, she died. That first night in hospital had been a long one. The following morning, I had been anxious to see the doctor to find out what was going on. The nurses and I had battled to keep Cherie comfortable and calm, but every time she awoke she wanted to sit up and was delirious and agitated, calling for her mum. Eventually, the doctor arrived around midday. When he asked the nurse if there was a room where we could talk I guessed that something important was on its way. As usual, a nurse on her break was kicked out without objection, and dirty cups were quickly tidied. This familiar scenario must have forewarned me, because I wasn't completely shocked when the doctor started.

'The tests have revealed that your wife has a serious infection. However, her liver is also failing; we have to decide whether to treat the infection aggressively or not.'

I understood what the medic-speak meant. The infection could probably be cleared up with big doses of drugs. The alternative was palliative - in other words, control the pain and discomfort but let the infection take its course.

'What will happen if we don't treat the infection?'

'The infection will kill her.'

'How long would that take?'

'A matter of days, maybe less.'

I was stunned – this was indeed the end and it hit me hard. I knew that if all were lost, Cherie would not have wanted to suffer, nor in her current state would she have wanted to draw out her life.

'If we treat the infection aggressively, will she regain proper consciousness – will she be able to talk and understand me?'

I privately thought, 'Will I get my Cherie back, if only for a while?'

'It's hard to say – she might come around, but there can be no guarantees.'

Two considerations came to me and I thought aloud in front of the doctor and a nurse. The first was that Isobel, Cherie's sister from Australia was due to arrive in the country in the next couple of days. I wasn't sure exactly when. I had hurriedly emailed her to tell Cherie had been admitted to hospital and was in a bad way. I knew how important it would be for Isobel to see Cherie. The second thing was Cherie's desperate longing to see her first grandchild - Hafina's baby was due in August, several weeks away.

'If we treat the infection aggressively, how long would it give Cherie?'

'It's impossible to say.'

'Would she live long enough to see her daughter's baby?'

'When is the baby due?'

'The middle of August.'

The doctor grimaced and paused briefly, 'I'm sorry, but there's no chance of that.'

So that was it - the starkest of choices. Treat the infection and Cherie might regain proper consciousness, but not for long; or, just look after the pain and she would die in days, maybe hours.

'Would you like us to leave you for a while, Mr Hill?' the doctor sensed my hurt.

'No, it's OK.' The nurse softly suggested I might like some tea. I think I said yes.

My mind raced for a short while. I knew what Cherie would have wanted. If she couldn't see her daughter's baby she would not have wanted to hang around. Of this I was certain – 100%. I thought about Isobel. I knew how much she loved Cherie and how bad she would feel if Cherie died before she got to see her, but this was Cherie's life and now I had to take control of it and speak for her.

I heard myself decisively saying to the doctor, 'We mustn't treat the infection.'

'Are you sure?'

'Absolutely sure.'

I think the doctor was a little surprised by the speed of my decision and he enquired, 'Would you like to talk it over with anyone - family, relatives?'

He added, 'You can take as much time as you like.'

But I didn't need time. All the late nights that Cherie and I had discussed such a scenario over countless glasses of wine, as if talking about a story in a film or a newspaper that had nothing to do with us. Light hearted and matter-of-fact - what would we do? The answer was always the same.

'It's alright ... thanks. I don't need to talk to anyone. I know what Cherie would have wanted.'

So, the decision was made. I was left alone to soak up the gravity of the situation. I passively allowed the solitude to envelope me and carefully turned thoughts over in my mind. My self-imposed inquisition exposed no chinks – I knew I had made the right decision and I strangely felt a sense of relief that I had, at last, been able to do something for Cherie. Not a powerless attempt to administer drugs that didn't seem to work, nor a clumsy effort to help her get onto the commode for a wee. No sad apologies for inadvertently jolting her electric bed as I tried to adjust it during brief moments when she was awake. This time I had simply carried out my beautiful wife's wishes; although I felt my head and my chest burning with pain as the closeness of her death sank in, I knew that it had been in my hands to bring Cherie's suffering to an end.

I let her go without a fight. We used to talk about fighting cancer, and we were in agreement. It was OK to fight if you had a chance, but when you were told that your illness was terminal, what was the point? I read somewhere that having a terminal illness is like going on a journey. It sounded a load of rubbish, but I could see merit in the analogy. I mentioned it to Cherie once and she instantly sided with the rubbish camp. But Cherie did make that journey – she learned to live with the disease. She understood that she had a limited time, and so she laid plans to live life to the full. This included going on expensive holidays never experienced before and enjoying the luxury of five star hotels in exotic locations such as Bangkok and Singapore. But, we also made a special effort to partake in simple pleasures, such as going more often to the cinema or entertaining friends and family. Cherie gave me cooking lessons and I promised to carry on 'after she had gone' – as if it were all a bit of a joke. It's hard to imagine how else cancer could be managed. Nineteen months may not be long to live, but it's a hell of a long time to wait and brood about the unfairness of a life cut short.

Suddenly, a tangential thought occurred to me, 'I must make a will when I get back home.'

Aviemore was a disappointment although I'm not sure what I had expected. To be fair, I only passed through the main drag of Scotland's most famous ski resort, and the mountains were hidden by low cloud and mist. Nevertheless, only lip service had been paid to the creation of an Alpine village as could be seen in the wooden apex gables of some of the buildings. Under those apexes, the buildings looked characteristically cut-corner seventies or eighties and the whole effect gave Aviemore the distinctive appearance of a struggling British sea-side resort.

I checked the odometer reading for the day so far – fifteen miles, not bad. Stopping in a café, I wrote post cards for Nicole, my eldest stepdaughter and Martin Baker, a school colleague and friend while I waited for a full English breakfast to arrive. Studying the photo on the front of Nicole's postcard, I admired the mountain scenery blanketed in burgundy heather. I had felt Cherie's influence when choosing the card – burgundy was one of her favourite colours. I craned my head forward to read the small print at the bottom of the card: *Slochd Pass*. I wondered whether it lay between Aviemore and Inverness and, much as I could appreciate the scenery, I hoped it didn't. Another pass would mean another day of climbing. I turned to my road map and started poring over it looking for the Slochd Pass. Eventually, I found it and was disappointed to see that it was indeed on my way.

Then I thought, 'I'm still in the Highlands for God's sake. I can't expect it all to be flat.'

My fate in the hand of a tarmac snake, I left Aviemore with a sense of trepidation mixed with resignation. Five miles down the road I stopped at Carrbridge and spent a pleasant quarter of an hour talking to a lady serving in a garage shop. I had pulled in because I could see I needed some oil on my chain. I didn't want to buy a full tin of 'Three in One' and then have to carry it around with me, so I politely described my problem to the woman and she phoned through to the workshops to speak to the mechanics. They cheerfully sorted me out but kept me waiting for quite a while. As I sunk a cold drink and munched on a Topic bar, the lady, who had picked up on my Welsh accent, told me of how she was at the 'Tall Ships' event in West Wales in 1991. If she had by chance gone into the Pembroke Haven Yacht Club, she would have caught a gang of us rather drunk and singing at the tops of our voices. I still remember playing 'Leaving on a jet plane' with the whole room joining in and merrily trying to jam along with anyone who started a song of their own.

'Was Cherie with me then?' I wondered. Yes, definitely – in fact, we were quite well established by 1991.

I thought on about the tall ships. We had planned to jump on Yogi's boat and motor over to get a close look at them as they anchored in the river. But, his boat was for sale and an offer had been made so he wanted to get it out of the water. More importantly, the craic had got going in the yacht club so we just went with the flow, happily distracted and oblivious to the fact that Dave, our mate from Merthyr, had been given special dispensation from his wife to be away for the weekend in order to witness the 'once in a blue moon' spectacle of the tall ships. By the time we got out of the club and managed to scrounge a lift on an unknown boat, they were gone. It was reported later that when Dave's wife asked him what the tall ships had been like, he simply replied, 'Tall'. According to Dave, she was happy enough with the response!

The garage lady told me she had moved from Yorkshire to live in West Wales as her husband had been involved with the oil industry in the 1970s. They had later moved to Aberdeen for the same reason. Whilst visiting friends back in West Wales, she thought the place had gone downhill and, of course, she was right. In the seventies and eighties, the oil industry, like a big Father Christmas, had brought all the associated economic goodies to Milford Haven. But by the nineties, the good folk of West Wales stopped believing, as he moved on to Aberdeen to please a new generation in a new place.

I decided to take the old road up to the pass, even though it was less direct and was marked on the road map in white, with no road number, a sure sign of plenty of ups and downs. Nevertheless, the trip was pleasant enough with good visibility that afforded some marvellous views. After a while, the route changed to cycle path again and started to present the associated difficulties - gates to get through, little ups and downs, and places where it wasn't clear which way to go. I crossed the almost imperceptible crest of the Slochd Summit and stopped to take a photo of the railway line with a sign erected for the benefit of passengers, declaring:

SLOCHD SUMMIT

1,384 feet

I had worked out that the distance to Inverness should be about seventeen miles from this point. Soon, a sign on the cycle track said *24 miles*.

'To hell with that,' I thought. I didn't fancy meandering all the way to Inverness like a twig on a lazy river, so I decided to take my chances on the main road in order to cut down the distance. The A9 was daunting. It wasn't so much that the volume of traffic was great, but more that it was moving fast and included lots of lorries. As I set off, leaving the safety of the cycle track, it wasn't long before I had my come-uppance, experiencing first-hand the rear end of a monster similar to the brick lorry that had given chase to me near Dunkeld. But this one was flying down the hill – its sides were cliffs and it breathed cold air in a sudden rush as it passed me with less than a yard to spare.

'Bastard!' Did he know that there was a cycle path and felt it was his duty to make the point? Or was his twin coming up in the opposite direction giving him no room to manoeuvre? I had hoped that the A9 beyond the Slochd Summit would be downhill all the way, and although I had some good 'wheees', I was a bit deflated to find out there were quite long periods of walking uphill too. At one point, for a brief respite, as I plodded on my pegs up an endless incline, I stopped to look back. I could see the dark imposing angles of the mountains behind me and thought,

'I've just come from there.'

Not for the first time, as I gazed back, I saw myself three hundred yards away, in my waterproofs, pushing my bike towards me. It was a sort of 'out of body' experience and it felt a bit like watching a TV programme or a movie.

The best 'wheee' took me from Daviot to within two miles of Inverness. I was topping thirty miles per hour with a great view across the Moray Firth – the firths really do look magnificent from the elevated vantage points coming out of the mountains. I declined to stop and take a photo, partly because I was in the middle of freewheeling, but mainly because the road had recently been resurfaced with loose chippings. I shouldn't really have let the bike go as I had; at this speed, I sure as hell wasn't going to drop the anchors now – bikes and chippings have never made good bedfellows. It was a disappointment that the hill didn't take me into Inverness itself, and it was another four miles before I reached the campsite on other side of the town. I thanked God that I hadn't opted to take the cycle route.

'I'd still be going now,' I wearily surmised.

By this time, I was feeling very hungry, but I wanted to get to WH Smith before they closed at half past five. I was nearing the end of the notebook I was using for my journal, and I wanted to get an identical book to the one I had bought in Smith's in Merthyr. I just managed to get there before closing time after frantically cycling through the main shopping area, my bike left to chance unlocked against the window. Mission accomplished, I could now see to my hunger. I found a chippy and bought chips with two sausages, before wheeling the bike a short distance so I could sit on the banks of the River Ness to eat. I parked against some railings then climbed through to sit on the grass.

Despite my hunger, I realised I was tiring of chips as my fingers began to accumulate the familiar coating of salty grease. Still, I had a feeling of well-being and as my appetite was slowly satiated I looked across the river with the road bridge to my left and turned over the day's journey. I thought I caught a glimpse of a few baby monsters in the river, but when I tried to look closer I couldn't see anything. If I'd been quicker I would have taken a photo and made a fortune.

Inverness was a busy place, rather like Perth but it appeared to have more tourists. I'd checked out campsites earlier in the Tourist Information Office in Aviemore, so I knew there was one on the west side called Bught Park. It was a municipal site, about a mile out of town and I found it without difficulty. It was big, busy and full of kids, some playing with footballs and others fighting in a pretend war. I pitched the tent and locked up my bike before gathering my stationery to write up the journal. Although nothing came into my field of vision, I quickly noticed someone haring around the site on what sounded like a child-sized motorcycle. I was making a phone call to my brother Chris when it first went past - I could hardly hear what he was saying. As I tried to write, the damn thing kept returning.

'There he bleedin' goes again!'

My annoyance festered quickly as I began to predict the pattern. I could hear it buzzing louder and louder, reaching a crescendo as it passed just feet away ... then dopplered away to silence for half a minute before becoming audible again. Time and time again this went on. How did they get away with it? There were speed bumps and speed limit signs all over the place. Was it some posing teenager on a chicken chaser, or an eight year old with a shit for brains father, reliving his youth through his son? I wrote for three quarters of an hour before my body told me I had to lie down for my evening sleep. The sun was shining in on the tent, and, gratefully, I registered the absence of the budding Schumacher. Kids were still playing football and there was a lot of other miscellaneous campsite noise that might have made it difficult for me to drop off. But it didn't – I was gone in seconds.

It was 9.30 when I set off for the pub. From the map I had picked up at tourist information I could see that there was a footbridge across the River Ness close to the campsite and near to what looked like houses. I reasoned that houses would hopefully also mean a pub; I didn't particularly want to go into town – the distance of a mile was too far after a hard day's pedalling and the plasters on my feet advertised the fact that the Jesus sandals I had bought in Stamford were still not broken in. The threat of pain from the sandals was substituted by the cold because I thought it better not to wear socks. Apart from the unsavoury smell, they would have made the sandals (not the coolest looking of items in any case) look totally geekish. I picked my way through a gathering of trailers assembled in a car park by the river that heralded the coming to town of the fair. I found the footbridge and crossed over it in the three quarters light of the early summer night.

Inadvertently, I stumbled across the Ness Islands that I assumed must be a tourist attraction judging from the plaques dotted all around. The River Ness bifurcates once and then again to create a series of small islands that are pleasantly wooded and crisscrossed with footpaths. Each island is connected to the next by a series of bridges, many of them mini suspension in style, and all of them painted white. I suddenly became aware of my own vulnerability as I noticed I was alone. This would be an ideal place to mug someone for twenty quid or a packet of fags. I was on my metal and, as a couple approached me, arm in arm I imagined them thinking of me as a potential attacker.

As I approached the main river I actually saw the Loch Ness Monster. It looked as if it had just crawled out of the river and was lying on the bank, quite still, between the trees. It stayed still long enough for me to take a photo and I wondered again whether the shot would make me famous. In truth, it stayed still for an inordinately long time - the creature had been carved out of a tree trunk. Now very aware of my vulnerability, I quickened my pace and was relieved to get out of the gloom thrown by the woods as I emerged on to a road. I had arrived at the houses shown on the map but there was no sign of a pub. So I headed towards town for some distance before I eventually reached one. It was a typical local and it was nearly empty. There was a couple playing pool down the far end and a drunk in his thirties. He had long straggly hair and his glass was tipped permanently at an angle to his mouth, as he sleepily ogled the receding liquid. There was also an older man, at least in his sixties, sitting at one end of the bar on a stool. He didn't talk to me and in the hollow atmosphere, I felt no urge to speak either, so I just ordered a half of Guinness and watched a bit of the British Golf Open Championship on the telly.

It didn't take long to finish my half pint of beer and I headed out in the direction of town again. The air was cold and I had to zip my fleece to my neck and bury my hands in my pockets. My bare feet did nothing to help me retain my body heat but at least the plasters seemed to be doing their job as I played in my pocket with two bars of chocolate I had bought in a SPAR just before reaching the pub. It wasn't that I was hungry but I was again planning ahead, to take my tablets with food the next morning as I had done in Dunkeld - a Cadbury breakfast, rather sweet but nonetheless medicinally functional. It was only a matter of minutes before I realised I was at the edge of the town centre, where I met two lads, probably ten or eleven years old, by the bridge at the bottom of the main street. As they approached me they were nonchalantly swinging a black plastic bag.

'Wanna buy some salmon, Mister?'

I politely declined but admired their enterprise, at the same time doubting their chances of clinching a deal at quarter past ten on a Thursday night. The first pub I came to had live music advertised, although no music could be heard coming from inside. There were two bouncers on the door ... security ... and I half expected Jesus in his sandals, two toes plastered up and sporting a grey-blue anachronistic fleece, to get turned away. It wasn't the case though and I entered a long narrow bar that stretched away at right angles to the street. As I aimed for the far end and the toilet sign, I could see two musicians with all their gear set up in front of the window, smoking fags and chatting, clearly on their break.

The place was half full but I managed to find space at the corner of the bar and pulled up a spare stool. Looking across, I had a good view of the duo, as I waited for a rather expensive pint of Guinness. I didn't try to talk to the guy to my right who later turned out to be a contractor from Germany and like me, a stranger to the town. I couldn't be bothered to make the extra effort needed to overcome the deafness on my right side. What was more, the band was limbering up for the second half and I wanted to listen to the music. Once they started up, I had absolutely no chance of communicating with anyone on my right side anyway. The band struck up with some very tasty stuff and I idly dangled my hard working legs free of the stool footrest.

To my right and suspended from the ceiling, was a large TV with News Night featuring coverage of Jeffrey Archer's conviction. I had been vaguely following the ex-politician's demise but this was news to me. With the sound turned off, it was curiously entertaining to ponder the programme's treatment of the story from only the related graphics, captions and featured experts, including fellow politician felon Jonathan Aitkin, who had famously promised to 'cut out the cancer of bent and twisted journalism'. I continued enjoying myself, passively observing the musicians, watching their chord shapes and noticing with disappointment that they made no attempt to sing any harmonies. All the time, the crowd grew in size around me.

I made sure I had a full pint to fall back on before the eleven o'clock guillotine, but there was no need - the show went on until one in the morning. The place now reminded me of the Three Horse Shoes pub in Merthyr, where I first met Cherie back in 1990. There was a preponderance of men but, overall, a real mixed bag of age groups and fashions. As I watched the band, a young man next to me slipped his hand inside the back pocket of his girlfriend's jeans and let it nestle there lovingly. It pained me to think how I was going to miss that degree of intimacy and the tactile presence of Cherie. I felt a surge of emotion but I didn't get upset. I just felt a sense of benevolent envy towards this amorous twosome.

Soon, the place filled up still more and people began to dance, as usual the females first. By now I had sunk quite a few pints of Guinness and its effect of lowering my inhibitions, together with a need for conversation, prompted me to introduce myself to a group of about six women friends who were standing in a circle close by. I chatted for a while until one particular song persuaded my tapping foot to convert to full dance mode, and I went to bop with two of the women in the group who had already taken to the floor. I was enjoying the music and the dance when one bloke, who may have been considerate or insulting - I wasn't sure which - tapped me on the shoulder and repeated until I heard,

'Lose the fleece, sonny.'

I hadn't dressed with the intention of 'pulling' a woman, nor was I kitted out for dancing, but I must have looked a right clown for someone to feel the need to 'tell it to me straight'. There were quite a few continentals in the bar, mainly men, who were energetically gyrating on the dance floor. They clearly loved the music but had no coordination or sense of rhythm. Nevertheless, they carried on with exaggerated exuberance in their distinctively non-British clothes frequently expelling guttural hoots and shouts. One of the women in the dancing group, whom I found the most attractive, bore a striking resemblance to a university friend of mine, Geraldine. Particularly in profile, but her facial expressions, her build, her hairstyle and the way she dressed and moved all reminded me of my old chum. I just had to get a photo of her but it was difficult to get the camera out and line up a shot without looking too conspicuous. I managed one surreptitious quickie in the end. Why I didn't just ask her nicely for permission, I don't know.

At one o'clock, on the dot, all the remaining Cinderella revellers had to go as the security heavies on the door came in to clear the place out in a style that left no latitude for misunderstanding. I even had trouble getting permission to go for a pee before starting my homeward journey. By the time I returned, in what must have been less than a minute, the place was totally empty and nearly all of the chairs were already perched on the tables ready for the cleaners to move in. I went to the spot where I had been sitting to get my fleece but it was gone – maybe the advice to 'lose the fleece' was not such a good one after all. I made a few enquiries with some unsympathetic staff but there was no sign of my warm, fluffy and scrunchable outer layer.

'Shit!'

'Bastards!'

I was so angry. Apart from the fact that I would have to buy a replacement, I really liked my fleece. It would keep a shower at bay, it dried quickly, it could be stuffed in with my sleeping bag and the creases would fall out in minutes, and it was warm. Not only that, although I'm not a lover of fleeces as such, this one was cut quite neatly and what's more, it had been a surprise present from Cherie.

I stood outside on the cold pavement looking up and down forlornly when I spotted one of the continentals from the pub walking up the road towards me with his Duisburg tee shirt on. He was the bearded, middle-aged biker, who, on my deaf side, I had decided not to talk to in the bar earlier. He had been hanging around the same group of women as myself like a vulture, craving the death of an antelope in a vibrantly healthy herd on a feline free plain ... and now he was carrying my blue-grey fleece under one arm. I collared him.

'I thought it was my son's!' He protested his innocence in a German accent. He must have been telling the truth because I had moved in on his son's seat and he did seem to be searching for him up and down the street. Either way, I didn't care – I had my fleece back. Gratefully, I donned it and made my way back to the camp site along the main road.

It was 2.30 a.m. before I finally got back to bed. It had been an interesting night. Yes, I could have saved money; no, I hadn't had much company. Still, I'd been fairly content and relaxed. I'd enjoyed the live music, I'd thought about Cherie, and I now I felt a deep sense of accomplishment in having crossed the highlands. I hadn't known what to expect and I had experienced a sense of foreboding and real misgivings about getting over the mountains under my own steam. Earlier at the bar, I had worked out that I could make John O'Groats in two more days. Now I felt I could take my foot off the gas a bit and just aim to cover the basic forty miles a day.

The Ride:

Newtonmore to Inverness

Distance: 50 miles

Inverness to Dornoch

Friday, July 20th

I didn't leave the campsite until about quarter to eleven. It's not that I slept in, however; I was up at eight thirty writing up the events of the night before in my journal. It took me almost an hour to bring things up to date. I set off in dry weather with the sky bright, but overcast. Within five minutes, I stopped off at a sub post office where I bought some post cards and a filled tuna mayonnaise roll which I ate standing up outside on the pavement.

'Where do you think I can get some methylated spirits?' I asked the woman in the multi-shop post office. 'There's so much 'Out of Town' these days I don't suppose there's a hardware shop in the centre?' She didn't know. I thought about it and decided I would probably get meths in a camping shop and there was bound to be one of those in Inverness. As I pedalled into the town centre, I spotted a sign:

FILMS DEVELOPED IN HALF HOUR

I imagined I could delay for that amount of time so I propped the bike against the shop window and wrestled with the bungees, rueing the fact that I had not thought of putting the exposed film somewhere more accessible.

Eventually, I managed to retrieve the little containers from the rucksack and left them at the processing counter before walking the bike to a cashpoint where I took out £100. It crossed my mind that there may not be many cashpoint machines as I drifted further and further north. I managed to get a suitably small bottle of meths in a camping shop then slowly pushed the bike through the main drag of the city to a spot where a coffee shop had tables laid out, continental style, on the pavement.

Ten yards away, a musician was playing an accordion under the canvas of a small street stage. I ordered a mug of coffee and as I sat listening to an instrument I really like, the sun came out to bathe the whole scene. I watched people crisscrossing by as I sipped on the bitter hot coffee and I felt relaxed and at peace. The guy played all sorts of stuff and 'My Bonnie lies over the Ocean', filled the air as I walked across to the take a photo of him. Politely, I put some money into his box before reluctantly wheeling away my bike in the direction of the photo developing shop.

As I walked through the pedestrianised zone, a song came into my head. Surprisingly, it wasn't one of the tunes the accordionist had been playing, but was an old Beatles song called 'Ask me why?' Why it came to me I don't know. It certainly was never a favourite of mine or anyone else's as far as I know, but it brought me to tears. Unusually, it was the words rather than the melody that seemed to stir me that morning.

I love you – woo-woo-woo-woo, 'cause you tell me things I want to know.

And it's true – woo-woo-woo-woo, and it really only goes to show,

That I know,

That I, I, I, I should never, never, never be blue.

Ask me why, I say I love you,

And I'm always thinking of you.

It was the last two lines that really seemed to get me. I picked up the film and had a quick cursory flick through them all outside the shop, like a young child who can't wait to get home before opening his pop bottle – does everyone do that? I had to fight with the bike again to store them where they wouldn't get wet, then mounted to seek some back roads that would lead me out of Inverness.

I carried on singing, 'Ask me why?' quietly to myself and I pondered why that particular song had popped into my mind. After some deduction, I followed the train of thought to an old school friend of mine called Jeff Watkins. It was Jeff who had introduced me to the Beatles not long after they had split up in the early 1970s. I was about fourteen when I heard the album 'Please, Please Me' which was one that Jeff didn't have. He bought it on my recommendation but, as often happens, didn't think much of it when he got it back home. In those days, it was totally taboo to try taking a record back once it had left the shop. Vinyl was so fragile – scratches appeared from nowhere and even a pristine copy was often prone to jump. Jeff managed it though. He convinced the record shop man in Porthcawl, firstly, that he hadn't played the album and secondly, that the song he really liked, 'Tell Me Why' was not on 'Please, Please Me'. He had made the mistake seeing the title, 'Ask Me Why' on the sleeve. 'Tell Me Why' was on 'A Hard Day's Night'. The coincidence of two similar song titles being on different albums meant Jeff got away with exchanging the album for 'A Hard Day's Night'. In hindsight, the shop owner was probably a good businessman and didn't want to lose a regular customer.

The story had come to mind because of its skirt with dishonesty. Earlier that morning, I had faced a little moral dilemma that tested my honesty. I could have easily left the campsite without paying and I was very tempted to do so. But I had used the shower and been grateful for the pitch and the security it had offered me, so in the end I went to reception, fully loaded up and waited patiently for the lady to get around to dealing with me. As I waited ... and waited... I wondered why I had bothered. The service was poor and it wasn't as if I had to pass reception to get off the site - in fact, it was a detour to get there. But I did pay and as a result was £4.50 the poorer, if slightly richer in conscience.

I questioned myself, 'Just how honest am I?'

I concluded that 'quite honest' was perhaps the best description I could come up with. I'm sure my upbringing had a lot to do with it, but so did getting caught stealing in my early teens. At the time I had been heavily into 'Action Man', the army doll that could be placed in different positions by moving his arms and legs. He was quite a revelation at the time with joints not only in his shoulders and hips but knees, ankles, elbows and wrists as well. There was a whole range of different accessories that could be purchased including guns, ammo, and various types of battle costume. Depending on the cost of the kit, a correlated number of stars were included in the packaging. If a lad collected 21 stars he could send off for another Action Man free of charge. On the day I got caught, I had started puncturing the clear plastic of the package and sneakily removing the stars. I succeeded several times in quick succession and, like a man on a gambling roll, couldn't resist upping the stakes. I left the shop without being apprehended with my mate Glen, and went the short distance up the road to the best toyshop in town, 'Bridges'. Buoyed with success, this bourgeoning felon decided that the small packages containing the miniature outfits, were eminently transportable in themselves:

'Why bother with the stars when I can have the kit as well?'

With the package stuffed out of sight under my jumper, I headed for the street with the unconcerned air of a housewife putting out empty milk bottles. Then my world fell apart as I was collared at the door and led off to a back room. Only then did I see the hole in the toys on the shelf where the staff kept a watchful eye on their young customers. Now I had to put into action the plan I never imagined I would need. Glen had often impressed me with tales of a friend of his who got caught stealing and then gave a false name and address. I did the same, only to discover that Glen, who had been pulled in as well, had told the truth. I broke down in tears and was starkly told that my parents and the police would be informed. Devastation turned to despair. As I left the shop, my trusty pal told me directly that he didn't want to be friends with a thief and pedalled off leaving me without a soul in the world I could turn to.

Distraught, I cycled the three and half miles home, went into the kitchen and woefully collapsed into a huddle on the floor in the corner as I blurted out the sorry tale to my startled mother. I was amazed, relieved and touched by my parents' reaction. No telling off, no shouting, no recriminations. When my dad got home he went to see the owner of the shop and everything was forgotten, except by me – I had learned my lesson. Thank God for well-spoken parents. Yet another crime committed by the middle class which stayed out of the official crime statistics.

Reliving my memories made me think how bizarre our trains of thought are. Under normal circumstances and with a busy life I rarely allowed them to develop. I tend to have a butterfly mentality flitting from one thought to an unconnected next without giving myself time to ponder. But, on the trip with so much time on my own, my mind was being given the chance to follow threads until they petered out. Once I started thinking about Jeff, it brought me around to the subject of death and his phobia of it. His father had died some years before and it had hit Jeff very hard. Like others I've met, he now has a consuming black hole dread of death and his fear extends to anybody, in this case me, who has connections with a dying person. I was so glad that Cherie saw it differently – she didn't fear death – she tamed it.

On the main road cycling out of Inverness I was still upset. Perched on my saddle and waiting at traffic lights I was close to tears with the same song still going through my head, a backdrop to my thoughts.

Ask me why, I say I love you.

And I'm always thinking of you.

I had to endure the busy A9 dual carriageway north out of Inverness with no one-metre hard shoulder to hide. On my precarious two wheels, turning right at one of the busy roundabouts suddenly scared me as trundling, clanking lorries and silently humming cars chopped confusingly past me, to my left and right. When I thought about all the cities I'd passed through, I realised that my hitherto lack of concern and indifference to heavy traffic would all reverse horribly if I were to get knocked off. Fortunately, I have been involved in few traffic accidents in my life, but I remembered how I once slightly misjudged the width of a minibus I was driving, causing the side door handle to buckle into the body of the vehicle as it scraped against a high wall. It was more than a year before I could confidently judge the width of any vehicle I was driving again.

The dual carriageway ended and I had to walk a mile up a long hill that separated the Moray from the Cromarty Firth. It was worth it though, because down the other side, I had one of the longest 'whees' of the whole trip – it must have been three and half miles. Just on the brow before I started to descend, a traditional wedding car passed me from the opposite direction. It looked like a Daimler and was probably built in the 1960s. It typically had two ribbons emanating from its prow making a 'V' with the two top corners of the windscreen. As the sound of its engine faded away, I was directly taken back to the estate car that was used as Cherie's funeral carriage.

She had made it very clear to me that she didn't want a hearse and I duly passed this on to the undertaker. He said it presented no problem and went on to say that the company had a large estate car that could be used instead. I told the funeral director that I wanted some sort of decoration on the car and he suggested strongly that cream bows tied to the door handles might be a good idea. Cherie never liked frilly things so I told him I'd like ribbons set up on the front of the car as if for a wedding. Still he pushed for the cream handles – I had the impression he must have picked up a job lot from a discount store, or more probably these days, from an internet site. Cherie liked bold colours so cream was definitely out. I settled on yellow but I wanted it rich and bright. Cherie had chosen yellow for the upper part of our bedroom wall when she had been decorating earlier that year. So I dragged the slightly bewildered undertaker upstairs to show him exactly what I wanted and, to be fair to him, that's what he delivered on the day.

Then my thoughts returned to school day friends again. One was from Porthcawl where I attended a primary school for six months having moved into Wales from Cheltenham. My father had taken a job with the Steel Company of Wales and had managed to rent a rambling draughty flat in Porthcawl while he and my mother looked for a house to buy. The friend in question lived in a nice interwar suburban semi with large rooms, high ceilings and a characteristic bay window at the front. I had the impression that there was something wrong with his father who seemed very thin, very old, and unattractive and was heavily into smoking, betting and drinking. Suddenly, the family were on the move to a strange new house in another part of town. It was much smaller, boxy and had a strange roof that slanted in awkward directions. I now know that the owner-occupied semi had been replaced with a newly built 1960s council house and I came to the conclusion that my mate's father was probably an alcoholic. The chum himself was a bit of a loner, but he was the only one, in six months, that I really made friends with at the school which was, on the whole, pretty unwelcoming. I was caned brutally across the hand for talking in class and my parents actually went up to the school to complain. This was unusual because I rarely let on to my folks when I had any trouble in school - my dad in particular, would always give me a second turn around the block if he got wind of any misdeeds. Some years later, I found out that the headmaster was eventually sacked for assault and cruelty to his charges.

I went back further to my school days in Cheltenham. I had also moved schools then, this time from the village of Churchdown and an idyllic rural primary school with extensive mown playing fields to an urban Victorian prison of a place in one of the few poor areas of Cheltenham. It was built in two storeys and had a small exercise yard surrounded by a twelve-foot brick wall with a standard 6'6' by 2'6' door guarding the only way out. There I met up with another solitary character whose only friend seemed to be me and vice versa. This friend was the one boy in the school who wore a cap and he was constantly having the mickey taken out of him because of it. Caps might have been mentioned on the school uniform list, but they certainly weren't compulsory. He often couldn't come out to play on the weekends as he had to go off to visit relatives in a place called Rosso-why (Ross-on-Wye).

I wondered why I always seemed to gravitate towards these loner types, and it made me think that moving kids from school to school or area to area was a bad thing. As in the Johnny Cash song, 'A boy named Sue', it might make kids tougher and more adaptable, but at the same time it doesn't allow them to find their level or their place, either academically or socially. I always used to think that moving had been good for me, but more recently, I wondered how much more I might have achieved if I hadn't had to worry about fitting in or struggling with what was going on in lessons. There is some proof for this - I was settled in the same school for all of my secondary education, and although I had failed my Eleven Plus in Porthcawl, I was able to claw my way up over a period of years, through the academic streaming system, to a point where I was able to sit mostly O Levels rather than the worthless CSE's. I'm pretty sure I wouldn't have passed my exams had I been moved again.

Freewheeling now at a comfortable speed, I looked to the hills across the Cromarty Firth before me. Not for the first time, I had an incredible view of another of Scotland's grand inlets - the air temperature soothingly neutral as my momentum created its own wind. Maybe five to ten miles away, I could pick out a wind farm.

My quiet elation and wonderment was curiously upsetting, 'This world is too beautiful to leave behind!'

As I crossed the Cromarty Bridge, I could see that a yacht wouldn't get under it. In any case, there was no sign of any boating activity, just an oil rig probably in for servicing about ten miles to the east. A few miles up the road I called into a tourist facility flagged with the characteristic sign - brown background with white writing. What sort of a place was it? God knows, but it was a modern single storey building, seemingly purpose built for entrapping passing tourists, and it had a lot of multi-media exhibitions that I didn't bother to peruse. I just wanted to rest my bum and have a cup of coffee. I would have ordered some food but it was a bit pricey so I settled for just coffee and waited for it to be poshly delivered to my table. I couldn't get a prime table by the window overlooking the river, but I could still see the firth moving 'en masse' to the right, westward and landward as the tide came in. The atmosphere in that large room was peaceful – almost like a church - hollow footsteps on the wooden floor, people talking in muted tones, instinctively and communally alive to an ambience that was not to be punctured.

I wrote down a few memory joggers. By now I was getting into writing more and more and I knew I couldn't rely on my memory so I decided to keep some paper and a pen handy so I could jot down notes during the day. Up to that point, it had been a strange day. I felt more emotional but it was a feeling from within me and not directly connected with Cherie. Having made up my mind about writing a book I think I was noticing things more. At times, I found myself writing as I pedalled along. No longer was it just thoughts washing through me - I was now expressing them in a concrete and quasi-literary fashion – maybe I should have had a Dictaphone.

Nearly twenty miles out of Inverness I came off the A9 and followed the road into a village called Allness. What a pretty place it was. I didn't think that the stone used to build the place could have been Oolitic limestone (or Bath Stone) but it looked very much like the villages made of that type of rock in the Cotswolds. I had taken the detour, partly out of an interest to see what the place was like, but mainly because I was half way through the day's trip and I wanted something to eat. It was about four o'clock in the afternoon but the sun was still shining strongly as I pulled up outside a chippy and went to order a haddock and chips. I leaned against a wall outside to eat them, happy to have the pressure off my backside. I was just finishing off when a man, who was working behind the counter in the adjacent sweet shop, came out and said in a sharp Scottish accent,

'Excuse me, but I can see you have a pump on your bike. Would you mind if I borrowed it to pump up my boy's football?'

I asked him if he had an adapter but he didn't, so the pump was no good to him. As I ate my dinner, I looked through the sweet shop window. It was hard to see into the shop itself, because the window was full of old fashioned jars of sweets, all labelled up and neatly placed on shelves that filled the shop front. There was an intermittent flow of customers in and out and the friendly shopkeeper who had asked for the use of the pump must have been very busy. I waited for a lull in trading then went in to buy a bottle of Lucozade and some choccy.

Seeing the array of sweets reminded me of Richmal Compton's 'William' books. The books used to belong to my father when he was a boy, so they were old with hardback faded orange covers and bindings struggling to hold the pages together. Just a few simple line drawings were included to enhance the tales. They were unattractive to a kid of my age and I must have been bored the day I picked one up to read. But once I started, I soon developed an affinity with William who, at eleven, was about the same age as me. William was always eating 'Bull's Eyes' and, even though I had read the books some thirty-five years before, I had never come across those particular sweets. I thought that this old fashioned sweet shop would be the ideal place to satisfy my curiosity so I asked the man behind the counter. He was of slender build and probably in his thirties and turned out to be the owner of the shop. It was a family business and he had taken it over from his father. He didn't stock Bull's Eyes and coincidentally, had only heard of them a few weeks earlier when an old woman had asked for them.

He started to ask me about my trip and we had a long chat interrupted at frequent intervals by customers. He had worked in the shop for twenty-two years and he said how much he would love to do something different - like my bike trip. Are men naturally more adventurous than women? It seemed that most of the men I encountered admired the feat I was attempting. The women were more ambivalent. They fell into two camps: the homemaker camp - those who strived for the detached house, prim lawn and a sparkling car or two on the drive - thought I was nuts. Those less materialistic or domestic were more like the men. Having said that, on all the occasions when I revealed my motives for doing the trip, I met with understanding and sympathy rather than derision.

Twelve miles further up the A9 and still in beautiful sunshine, I reached the Dornoch Firth. Fortunately for me, the inlet was spanned by the Dornoch Firth Bridge, which had been built as recently as 1991. In the pub later, I found out that the Queen Mother was due to come up to celebrate the tenth anniversary of its opening in a few weeks. I'm sure it meant more to me that afternoon than it would ever mean to her. It's over half a mile wide and it saved me pedalling a painful detour of twenty-five miles up the valley to Bonar Bridge. I stopped to take a few photos, one of a commemorative plaque that read:

> The Bridge, at 890 m, is one of the longest in Europe to be spanned using the Cast-Push Method

I had no idea what the 'cast–push' method was but it certainly saved me quite a bit of pushing. The scent of coast filled the air as I cycled over the bridge, the breeze stirring the salt with seaweed to produce that characteristic 'tide-out' smell. Just across the bridge was a roundabout where the A949 branched off the A9 for Dornoch. There was a motel and it crossed my mind to stay the night in luxury. I stopped to look at my map and could see that I had covered over 43 miles. But I felt OK and decided to resist the motel and carry on to Dornoch where I hoped there would be a campsite. I pedalled the three miles easily and booked into a campsite on the seafront. The place was windswept with few trees and a preponderance of short dry grass and dune sand. The facilities were good though and I took full advantage of them.

Once I had spruced myself up, it was time to find a drink and a seat and do some writing. The first place I saw was a hotel with a lounge bar so I went in and settled down. I hadn't realised Dornoch was such an important golfing venue until I looked around at the photographs of famous golfers that had played there, sprinkled liberally on all of the walls. I quickly settled down to write my journal, which I did for an hour and a half. On one refill visit to the bar I exchanged quips with a couple of local lads. The sign behind the bar read, 'Happy Hour!' So it was, with Guinness at £1.50 a pint.

'The more you drink, the more you save,' I joked with the lads. They laughed.

'You must watch *Twin Town* with an accent like that.' They were referring to the film depicting life in Swansea where Welsh accents had been encouraged to roam free and the censors had left in the coarse language.

'No need to watch it, I bleedin' live there!' More laughter and a pleasant interlude in my otherwise solitary schedule. By the time I finished writing it was twenty to eleven. I suddenly realised that I might be running out of drinking time, and I hadn't even started. On local advice I left the quiet lounge and went to seek out the liveliest pub in town. I had some trouble finding it, which yet again said a lot for my spatial awareness – Dornoch was only a small place. Increasingly getting worried about missing stop tap, I found the pub just before eleven and wriggled conspicuously to the front of a crowded bar. I needn't have worried – serving was not about to cease. There was a very wooden musician of mediocre abilities playing in one corner. However, he had a reasonable voice, and as he came to the end of his song I instinctively clapped. I was the only one and he commented dryly to me, 'You're not from around here are you?'

I couldn't fail to notice a couple of motor bikers stood nearby. They were both tall blokes in full leathers with customised denim jackets worn outside everything else. In a way they looked a bit daft but in another sense they really looked the part – the sleeves on their denim jackets had been cut off so that the line of their shoulders extended on both sides an inch further than it should have done making them appear even broader. They clearly fancied themselves quite a bit – apparently they walked three miles in their biking garb over the links to get to the pub - I hoped it was worth it for them. I went across and started chatting to them, but they weren't interested in me and the fact that I too was a motor biker cut no ice whatsoever. What did grab their attention was the adulation of a petite woman in her thirties with a longish hairstyle and slit-like but nevertheless benevolent looking eyes, that reminded me of one of the characters in Star Wars, or was it Gremlins. She was drawn to them like a virgin to Count Dracula. In the crowded bar, I leaned against a wall with my pint and watched her flirt outrageously. Her husband was close by, so I don't think it was a serious sexual advance but she invited them both around for dinner the next day.

I drifted to the bar to where I noticed a vacant stool. Perched and glad to rest my legs, I struck up a friendly conversation with a man called Robert Allan McGregor, a joiner with a voice so gravely it made Rod Stewart sound like Julie Andrews. He was clearly drunk and he was getting immense pleasure from reciting his name out loud in his pleasant Scottish accent.

'Robert Allan McGregor! Robert Allan McGregor!'

He insisted that I write it down carefully and he checked my spelling. I discovered at this point that I had swiped someone's bar stool – a lady called Cath who returned, presumably from the loo. I gave her back her stool but stayed by the bar and chatted to her. She said she was about the same age as me but I doubted it – older I thought.

'Still, it is a woman's prerogative to lie about her age,' I thought. After some time, I told her about Cherie. She fell into the, 'You've got guts' rather than the 'You're a nutter' camp. Like the sweetshop owner I had befriended in Allness, Cath seemed to understand. She signalled me into an empty space in front of the singer that served as a dance floor, but we yawed around talking to each other rather than dancing with me cocking my head to hear better. Back at the bar, I exchanged a few more rounds with Robert Allan McGregor and got into a conversation with a barmaid from Aberystwyth, before being invited back to someone else's house for a party. It was an excuse for us to carry on drinking and we were met by a house full of people as we merrily bumbled in through the front door.

By now in a state of considerable inebriation and high spirits, the inevitable happened. I started singing and couldn't resist a crude rendition of a song written by a couple of lads in Dowlais years ago. It runs to the tune of 'You picked a fine time to leave me Lucille' but is renamed, 'My fanny's on top of my head'*.

I just about managed to remember all the words, hoping that pauses would come over as dramatic timing. Bertha went down very well and I had to sing it another twice before the night was out. One local guy was particularly impressed. He was employed as a caddy and although he seemed like a nice enough bloke, I don't think I should have given him my phone number, email address and an invitation to come down and visit me any time he liked.

Yvonne, a lady who I discovered was my host, gave me a beautiful single rose. Poking my drunken nose into it, I was moved by its fragrance and by the kind gesture itself. I promised to keep it. As I got ready to leave, I chatted with Yvonne's father. I left with the caddy (whose name I can't remember) and as a precaution made it clear that I was not gay - I'm not sure how subtle I managed to be. As I remember, I didn't go as far as giving him my address. We tumbled out of the house and hit the fresh air and the daylight simultaneously. I looked at my watch – quarter to five a.m.

The Ride:

Inverness to Dornoch
Distance: 46 miles

*In a bar down in Merthyr
I met this girl Bertha
She'd a sweet little smile on her face,
I was feeling quite gloomy
'Till she came up to me
And invited me back to her place.

When we got to the bedroom
My heart it went boom boom
This was better than drinking in bars,
It was then that she told me,
Really and truly
That she'd just descended from Mars

Well she took off her shimmy
But she's got no jimmy
Just a blank where her clodge ought to be
I must have looked frightened
'Cos she then enlightened
By turning and saying to me

CHORUS

My fanny's on top of my head
No use you lying there waiting on the bed
Climb to the ceiling where the paint started peeling
Dive down like a bird just shot dead
'Cos my fanny's on top of my head.

Well I ran from there screaming
Thinking I'm dreaming
I skidded around the first bend
Bumped into a feller
Whose face was quite Yeller
Who looked down at me and said friend,
Have you seen my Bertha
She's come here to Merthyr
And I want to take her to bed
Well he was from Venus
With a four foot three penis
As I ran, I turned and I said

CHORUS

Her fanny's on top of her head
No use you lying there waiting on the bed
Climb to the ceiling where the paint started peeling
Dive down like a bird just shot dead
'Cos her fanny's on top of her head.

Well I woke in bed sweating
My girlfriend's she's fretting
She reckons I've gone 'round the bend
Between Stella and whisky
And feeling a might frisky
I tried to screw the wrong end
So hark to my story
This ain't Jackanory
I'll remember till my dying day
If you're ever in Merthyr
And a young girl called Bertha
Should come up to you and say friend

CHORUS

My fanny's on top of my head
No use you lying there waiting on the bed
Climb to the ceiling where the paint started peeling
Dive down like a bird just shot dead
'Cos my fanny's on top of head.

Dornoch to Helmsdale

Saturday, July 21st

It just turned half past eleven as I sat in the entrance of my tent, writing up the log from the night before. I looked up to watch two men, their bellies leading the way, purposefully striding towards a shoreline dotted with beach paraphernalia: shoulder bags, towels, wind breaks, buckets and spades, cricket stumps, lonely surfboards, downed kites and runaway balls. There wasn't any wind, or any sunshine for that matter, but it was pleasant – you might call it bright 'cloud-shine'. I started to remember things from the night before. I was talking to Yvonne's father who told me about how he made his living from salmon in the days before fish farming had come to Scotland. It seemed he didn't so much farm the fish as farm the fishermen themselves; he had a special word for it, now lost to me.

A lady sat with her husband outside a caravan opposite my tent called across to ask me if I'd like a cup of tea but I politely declined. This was going to be my latest start yet, even later than Lauder. I wasn't bothered though. Leaving Inverness the day before, I had been a bit of a laggard but had still managed to cover the miles, write my journal, clean up and get to a pub. All the same, it was half past twelve by the time I set off. I decided to take the minor road that followed the firth out of Dornoch, accepting the fact that it would probably be more up and down, but also aware that from now on the A9 was going to be my constant companion almost as far as John O'Groats. It would be good to stay off it at least for a while. So I headed off in purposeful mood straight into the car park by the beach – dead end – spatial awareness meltdown again. I backtracked and passed the famous Dornoch golf clubhouse and could see swarms of what I assumed to be rich Americans riding in their buggies or sitting in the club lounge that overlooked the course.

By now the sun had come out and it was glorious – azure sky and rich blue sea - even the Scottish air was warm. I passed what looked like a disused chapel, the sort that had been starved of money for many years. What startled me were the flowers. I later discovered they were Canterbury Bells and they had taken over the whole of the area in front of the chapel. I freewheeled past on the other side of a four-foot high stone wall and was truly bowled over by the colour. Royal blue I would say. All standing on higher ground above the top of the wall and packed closely together. Being at near eye level I had the concentration of colour you sometimes get when looking at bluebells from a road below. I only had seconds to appreciate them and at the bottom of the hill I regretted not stopping to take a photo. Even after one and a half miles I was still tempted to turn back, but I was already behind schedule – I simply had to get on.

Following the narrow road that took me around the un-bridged Loch Fleet, I had a totally overwhelming experience. Maybe it was the sunshine, not seen for a while, and the blue calm waters of the inlet just feet away, or perhaps it was the scented air – a mixture of countryside and coast. A single car disturbed my peace as it squeezed past me on the narrow road but my feeling of profound tranquillity remained intact. I took a few photos that I knew would inadequately capture the scene. As I pedalled on at a fair pace, I suddenly realised that there was no wind noise, not even that generated by my own motion – it was just completely quiet and peaceful.

'Oh ... my... God ... J e s u s!'

I uttered the expletives aloud, slowly and emphatically. This was really a most wonderful moment. With the blue Loch Fleet to my right and the opposing green fields to my left, I was suddenly struck again by the sadness that seemed to be hiding wherever and whenever I was in awe. I felt myself filling with hurt from the depths of my chest, through my throat and up into my head; I wished Cherie could have been with me to experience it all.

As I came up on to the A9, I crossed the bridge that spanned the narrowing Loch Fleet and dismounted to walk up a long hill. Memories of the night before started to come back to me in a way that is often the case after drinking - like a session of hypnosis on the psychiatrist's couch. Yvonne's partner was a geographer/geologist but he told me he wasn't working in connection with those subjects at the present time. Suddenly, I remembered one guy's comments as I was giving my second rendition of 'My Fanny's on Top of my Head'.

'I don't find it funny,' I heard him say through the melee. As we were leaving at the end of the night/morning, I patted his back, smiled and apologised for singing the song.

'I know it's a bit earthy. Don't beat me up,' I joked.

He turned and scowled, not the reaction I expected in response to my friendly approach. I'm not sure exactly what happened next but I looked him square in the face and I told him directly, 'You've got angry eyes.'

His wife laughed to her friends – she thought it was hilarious.

'He's got angry eyes, he's got angry eyes,' she chanted like a skipping school girl.

'What d'you mean?' the bloke fired at me. I thought he was going to hit me. I didn't back down.

'You *have* got angry eyes,' I emphasised the point. 'You are carrying a load of anger inside you.'

Now I don't know if I was trying to get my head kicked in, but he just quizzically gazed into my eyes, cocked his head slightly and with a furrowed forehead said, 'That's fuckin' amazing ... that's spooky.'

Then he turned and walked off. The aggressive encounter was brief but had been defused by a sixth sense I must only possess when extremely drunk. He seemed convinced that this complete stranger knew more about him than was natural. Maybe it is possible to see through people at times? I wondered if I had sad eyes. They were sometimes - I could often feel them filling up. It had happened the night before when Cath had been talking to me about her relationship.

As I pedalled on, my mind turned to flowers again. The caravan man whose wife had offered me a cup of tea that morning had listened as I described to him the rose I had been given the night before.

'Simple things can give such pleasure,' we agreed.

My thoughts turned to Cherie's flowers outside on the grass after her funeral. I had broken off my round of speaking to as many of the mourners as I could in order to go and look at them. I felt a sense of resignation and regarded them as little to do with us.

Cherie Hill

The card alongside was clear. Seeing her name in writing affected me deeply and I returned to my social commitments in case I lost control. I didn't mind crying but it wasn't the time or place.

The countryside along the eastern edge of Scotland was much as I expected it to be – fairly flat with a few ups and downs. Rabbits were now the main casualties on the road, easily outnumbering their distant feathered cousins. Still, lots of live ones could be seen on the verges and in the hedges and they regularly startled me, as I reciprocally alarmed them causing them to bolt. Sometimes they sounded like a gambler fanning a pack of cards as they shot out from their hiding place in the foliage. At other times they made a sharp, loud noise like kids playing the card game Snap. In the quiet of that sunny afternoon, and lost in my thoughts, it's no wonder that I jumped too.

I had intended to breakfast (2.30 p.m.) at Brora, eighteen miles into the day's journey, but I came to a village called Golspie that was bigger than I had expected. I had covered eleven miles so I could have legitimately stopped, but I had remembered to take my paracetamol and ibuprofen earlier so I wasn't aching at all. I had the sun shining on my back, a gentle breeze in my face and a wholesome feeling of well-being, at least partly attributable to the large amount of grog I had consumed the night before and the insufficient amount of sleep I had managed to get. This feeling of 'otherworldliness' was the same as I had experienced the day after the drinking session in Lauder and my epic 'wheee' off the Southern Uplands.

So, I decided to push on to Brora as originally planned and seemed to cover the miles with little effort and in no time, without any rest breaks other than to take a few photos. In Brora, I had a sit-down meal of sausage, chips and egg. I had been told on at least three separate occasions about the hills I was going to encounter later that day – The Berriedales - so I thought I had better replenish my carbohydrate reserves. It was a big meal and I was given lots of coffee. I wrote post cards to Hafina and Viv as a group of drunken football fans jostled by. Brora were playing Dundee in a testimonial match. They were all very good-humoured though and they bumbled past my loaded bike without mishap, deliberate or accidental.

'It's a shame all football fans can't behave in the same way,' I thought and I remembered a song called 'Football Hooligan' that I wrote not long after the Heysel Stadium disaster where thirty-nine innocent fans were killed as a result of crowd trouble*. English clubs were banned from European competitions for five years and Liverpool for an extra two.

Waiting for my order, I came close to tears as I listened to music playing on the sound system – 'I will always love you' beautifully sung by Whitney Houston.

'Not here,' I told myself and I bottled it up, not quite in time to stop my eyes brimming. Back on the bike, I thought about my boozing and late nights. I started to feel tired in a sleepy rather than a muscular way.

'Why do I do these things?' I asked myself. I had come across an unexpected campsite just before reaching Dornoch, where I might have stopped for the night. But I thought it looked boring and I was quite willing to pedal the extra six miles, sore bum and all, to Dornoch itself where I hoped there would be more chance of a bit of fun. I began to think about work and going back to see everyone in the staff room. I thought I should at least say a brief thank you for the support and love given to Cherie and myself. Although I had thought of my friends and colleagues from work on the trip, so far I hadn't given work a second thought. 'I'll have plenty of time to get back into work mode in September because I'll be on my own ... on my own... on my own.'

I carried on from Brora along the coast road, sea still blue to my right and mountains to my left. I stopped to take a paracetamol and put the camera on to 'timed' for only my second self-portrait of the trip.

It wasn't long before I reached Helmsdale. This was the start of the nasty bit and it was already quarter past five. I called into a garage for Lucozade and choccy, but the man working there said he only sold petrol and antifreeze, which he served personally – no self-service – a real old fashioned petrol station. I told the man of my intentions.

'Jesus, are you kidding!' He didn't fill me with confidence.

I pointed and asked, 'Any idea where the next campsite is travelling that way?'

'Thurso, I think.'

That was no good to me – it was on the north Scottish coast and way out of range.

'I might have to rough it,' I said.

'You'll have a job in the heather.'

'Hmmm,' I pondered. Daunted, I backtracked to the main village street that went off at a right angle to the A9. What a quandary. It was twenty miles to the next place and I'd already come thirty miles. What's more, I'd been warned about the terrain:

'You'll just get into third in a car *if you're lucky.*'

Worse still, due to my late start, time was now getting on. I felt alright but I must have been tired. I stood outside a pub/hotel with a sign outside,

Bed & Breakfast £18

Friendly Atmosphere

Bikers Welcome

'Hey, I'm a biker!'

What to do? I had only completed twenty-nine and a half miles. I had never covered less than forty before and nearly always I had done more.

'To hell with it,' I thought. 'I'll go and get some soup and bread and if I get knackered, I'll pitch the tent in the heather. Is this supposed to be an adventure or not?'

'No grog if you do that, Billy Boy.' Another downside presented itself. I noticed a SPAR sign a little way down the road and ambled down to get some soup and bread.

'Where am I going to put bread?'

I picked up the soup and some Lucozade then got talking to a man and woman behind the counter. I explained to them why I was aimlessly padding around their shop with soup and Lucozade in my hands. Their message could have been a recording of the conversation at the garage, except it was more graphic and scarier.

The man described the roads: 'They're cliffs!'

I thought back to my O Level geography lessons – so much for the east coast of Scotland being flat.

'What to do?'

The man pressed home his point, 'You'll be fresh in the morning; you'll need to be – cliffs they are!'

'Hmmm,' was the only response I could muster.

'I'd stay here if I was you,' the wife chipped in.

Again, I thought, 'But I've only gone twenty-nine and a half miles,' the arguments now going round and around. I'll have to do fifty plus tomorrow to get to John O'Groats and that would include the scaling of the cliffs. What to do?

'Does it matter if I don't reach Johnny tomorrow? Is there any point in getting there late – especially if there are no campsites there? What to do?'

Finally, I made my decision: 'That's it. I'm staying here.'

I checked into the hotel to discover that there was karaoke that night. My thoughts rambled on in disjointed fashion.

'Maybe it wasn't such a good idea to stay here after all.' I didn't particularly like karaoke and as it started to limber up downstairs, it was clear it was going to be loud.

'I'm going to find it difficult to get on with my journal down there. And I need to get some food. And I told Viv in my post card that I should make John O'Groats tomorrow but I don't think I'm going to make it now. Serves me right for counting my chickens.'

I had some wonderful chips, if you can be a connoisseur of such things, from a chippy a few doors down the terraced street from the SPAR I'd been in earlier. I took the option to have curry sauce as well and ate my meal outside on the pavement, sheltering from heavy rain under a small canopy above someone's front door. The porch did a reasonable job except it allowed the occasional big blob to get through. One plopped right into my curry sauce. Two or three others landed on my head with the force of thrown coins. As I stood there on that grey terraced street, most of the buildings were houses but there were a few services including the chip shop and the SPAR. I watched an overweight teenager, probably approaching his twenties, riding around on a bike that looked far too small for him. His legs went bandy as they bent in response to the rise of the pedals and he meandered up and down the street occasionally stopping for a rest in the downpour. He wasn't wearing a coat of any sort and he must have been soaked. He was there for the whole of the time I stood eating my chips and I came to the conclusion that he must have had something wrong with him. It also occurred to me that if the man and woman in the SPAR had had an ulterior motive in persuading me to stay in Helmsdale, it hadn't worked for them, because I ended up buying nothing from their shop.

I dropped my empty cartons in the chip shop bin as I headed back to the hotel pleased with myself for having had such a satisfying meal at a knock down price (I could have opted to have my second proper evening meal of the trip at the hotel). Back in the room I started examining my sorry stock of clothes. When it comes to wearing dirty clothes or housework for that matter, everyone has their own threshold. Some thresholds are very high; my mother for example, must have the most spic and span house in the world, but for others it's much lower. Looking at my clothes I realised that I had fallen beneath my cleanliness threshold. Sniffing successively the four pairs of underpants in stock, I tried to work out which were the least high but there wasn't much in it. Being in a hotel I felt I should be able to do something about the situation. I had tried at the campsite the night before but there had been no drying facilities. So I washed my vitals – cycling top, both remaining pairs of socks, and three pairs of underpants, then hung them around the open window to dry as I had done in Stamford, now weeks ago, relieved that the rain had stopped giving them a sporting chance of drying before the morning.

I had a long bath, and for the first time since I was a kid, ran the cold water for a while before getting out in order to cool down. Back in my room I discovered that it was chucking it down with rain again. There was no way that my clothes were going to dry now so I went down to reception and begged for the use of a tumble drier. An obliging woman gave me a black bag and I went back to the room to get the articles. Quickly, I washed through my cycling pants – I hadn't before because I couldn't take the risk of them not being dry by the morning. I had run out of washing powder though, so I used one of the complimentary hotel mini soaps. That seemed to work OK so, forgetting two socks that hung like a pair of mediaeval criminals from the gallows, I took the wet clothing down to reception.

'What room number?' I wondered whether she was going to charge me – the place was hardly the five-star Shangri-la Hotel in Bangkok where Cherie and I had paid for laundry service. But it didn't matter - it would be worth it to have a full set of clean, dry clothes again. I got ready to go out, then passing the karaoke room that by now was in full swing, I left the hotel and crossed the road to a pub on the opposite corner. The rain was still pummelling the pavement and road and unbelievably, the teenager was still out in it on his little bike – definitely nuts.

Inside, the single square shaped room with a bar on one side, was more or less full. The only spare table, essential for me to get on with my writing, was at the other side of the room to the bar and bang in front of a musician who was playing the accordion. He had four or five pints of beer lined up on top his amplifier, no doubt contributions from grateful punters, the average age of which must have been in excess of fifty five. I set myself up for writing and went to order my first pint of Guinness. As I began to write, I sensed I had become part of the show, as this stranger to the village was in everybody's line of sight as they watched the accordion player. It was enjoyable writing and sipping my Guinness to the tunes knocked out with some panache by the musician. Occasionally I would stop to listen and I always applauded when I noticed a tune had just finished. As I relived my day on paper the music punctuated my experiences. Whilst writing about the mediocre musician and my dance with Cath the night before, I joined in with others to clap the accordionist – he was certainly far more accomplished and, admirably, was totally live with no recorded backing. As I wrote about my breakfast in Brora, he played a western theme. I called across to ask what it was.

'Theme for Young Lovers – The Shadows,' he shouted back. Whilst writing about the tide-out smell just before Dornoch, he played his instrumental version of the 'Skye Boat Song'. It was beautifully arranged and well performed and it brought me to tears. My journal reached the discussion with the man and woman in the SPAR shop as the accordionist played and sang 'Dirty Old Town'. I must also have heard Rod Stewart singing it recently and I felt I would like to add it to my own repertoire. I had almost brought the log up to date when a woman approached me from the bar. She might have fancied me but more likely, she had been overcome by curiosity. By this time I had been sitting plop in front of the musician for a few hours, talking to nobody but writing studiously, drinking steadily what was by now five pints of Guinness, and stopping from time to time to clap. Helmsdale is a small place and I suppose a stranger in the midst of a community where everyone knows everyone was always likely to raise a certain amount of curiosity – my odd behaviour must have made me a stranger-than-your-average stranger.

I politely side-tracked the woman's questions by saying that I had nearly finished and that I would come over to chat shortly. It took me another ten minutes and I was glad to pack my book and pen into the plastic pouch for the time being. As I went to stand up, the accordionist, who was by now clearly inebriated, invited singers from the floor to join him.

'I'll sing a song in a minute,' I said to him as I left my seat. But first I wanted to get a fresh pint and go and talk to the woman as promised. Her name was Stella and she was with her friend Linda and two men, both called Clive, and all very friendly people. Stella asked what I was planning to sing.

'I think I'll do "Where do you go to my lovely?" by Peter Sarsted. It's got an accordion part in it, but I've never had the chance to sing with one so it should be good.'

After a little more discussion, I started to get to know the group and that's what probably gave me a rather silly idea – I could sing 'My Fanny's on Top of my Head'.

'I know a song I could sing,' I announced mysteriously. 'The trouble is it's a bit risqué. Do you think I should do it?'

'You should be all right but ask the gaffer, he's stood right behind you.'

I put it to the landlord and voiced my concerns that the lyrics were a bit close to the bone, especially considering the rather elderly make-up of his clientele.

His raspy response allayed my fears, 'You'll nay offend these fuckers - sing what you like!'

I went over to the accordionist and checked that he knew the tune to 'You Picked a Fine Time Leave me Lucille'. He did and he set off with gusto. I had to stop him because he was going far too fast. He started again. All eyes were on me now as the song innocently opened up and the story started to unfold.

The naughty bits arrived, '... she took off her shimmy but she got no Jimmy, just a blank where her clodge ought to be ...'

I didn't want to look too closely at my audience, so I just fixed my eyes on thin air. Still, I could make out jaws dropping and eyes popping.

When I got to the chorus, 'My fanny's on top of my head', peels of laughter erupted and I symbiotically responded raising the volume, increasing my inflection and proceeded to make accompanying gestures with my hands and arms. The song reached its climactic finale and the whole place filled with rapturous applause – at last I had made it as a pop star! The crowd demanded that I sing some more so I did a couple of standard songs before graciously stepping down for the accordionist to take over once more. With a roomful of eyes following me, I sheepishly walked back to the bar to meet my public. Many came over to talk to me and I had to promise to send a recording of the song to the pub when I got home.

Getting back to the little group I had talked to before, I found out that one Clive was in the oil business in South Vietnam.

'They're like sponges,' he said. 'They soak up everything you tell them. But Africans ... I'm not racist but when it comes to learning, they either can't be bothered or they're more interested in seeing what their mates are up to.'

I was interested in what Clive had to say including a conversation we got into about Bangkok and Singapore. I told him about Cherie when he asked me if I was married. He had assumed that my wife couldn't have been very happy with me going away on a bike trip for a month. Like so many people I had told, he was moved by the truth. And I had been moved by the 'Skye Boat Song' earlier and now had the chance to speak to a third Clive who was in fact the accordionist. By day he was a town planner and he was also Linda's partner. I was impressed with his playing and I had noticed that some of his chords were different to the ones I use in my guitar arrangement of the same tune. We discussed his chords - a seventh was very effective where I played a full major, as was his choice of a major E a few bars in, where I normally played E minor. Clive went on to explain to me how the bass section on his accordion worked.

'Give me live music any day,' I said, a reference to the karaoke that was probably still going on over the road. Another joined us, an ex-grocer who was now practising his hobby professionally, working as a gardener at the nearby Skelbo Castle. Looking at the map later on, I realised I must have passed it earlier in the day just as I experienced my emotional blitz rounding Loch Fleet. It was also the place that Madonna had chosen to get married. The ex-grocer, who now presumably had first-hand knowledge, thought she was 'a bit of a dog'. He also requested a recording of 'My Fanny's on Top of my Head'.

I re-joined Stella and co. and she informed me of an interesting 'fact': 'There are loads of attractive women on Orkney but all the blokes are ugly!' Presumably, some genetic aberration that happened hundreds of generations ago must have been responsible for putting a curse on all the new-born males born since.

'I have listened to some top theories on this trip but that's the best so far!' I smiled. Talking to Stella I concluded that she must have been married a few times.

As she was leaving, she laughed, 'I got half every time! I don't need to worry about money any more!'

I reckoned she must have been a bit of a girl but I had the feeling she was at least partly joking. Oilman husband

Clive, whom I warmed to very much, said that they had been married twenty years.

I joked,

'I've lost half each time!'

But inside me it rang hollow because it wasn't true. It was time for bed, although I would have carried on had it not been stop tap. I wasn't too worried about not making Johnny the next day now. Stella had told me that they'd all be in the pub– twenty miles up the road and just past all the mountainous bits - the next day for lunch. I thought it would be good to meet up with them again – it had been good fun.

Back at the hotel, the karaoke was winding up and people were getting kicked out. Up in my room, however, a lot of noise was still filtering through, so I decided to take my coffee, a poor substitute for beer, downstairs and see what was going on. Of course, I could have turned in but I decided there would be plenty of time for that when I got back to Wales. Downstairs was a disappointment, so I returned to my room and brought my journal up to date. I didn't finish until two o'clock and I signed off with thoughts about drinking. I was determined that when I got back home, I would not hit the bottle, the wine box or the pub unless there was an occasion. An 'occasion' as opposed to a 'good reason' because I realised that there would always be a good reason if I was looking for an excuse for a drink. The trip so far, was not really setting a good precedent for the frugal drinking days ahead.

As I lay in bed I thought about the measly twenty-nine and a half miles I'd covered and consoled myself. I had been a naughty boy getting up late that morning, but it meant that by the time I did set off, the sun was out (it had been cloudy when I was packing the tent). If I had started earlier I would never have seen those beautiful flowers in the chapel grounds sparkling in the glorious sunshine. And, it would only have been a second rate cloud-shine that illuminated the magnificence of Loch Fleet - 'Clunny' or 'soudy', as Cherie called that half-way house weather condition in the Far East and the Maldives.

I set the alarm because I wanted to get away early. Not for the first time, I decided to forego the social gathering with my new friends at the pub the next day and strike out for John O'Groats instead.

The Ride:

Dornoch to Helmsdale
Distance: 29.5 miles

*Every Friday night I make my way down to the ground
Whether we're away or home you know I'm always found
In the pub where friends will be I'll gather with them all
To lay the plans for Saturday, We're going to have a ball.

CHORUS

United we drink our beer
United we have no fear
United we'll beat the ban
I'm a football hooligan.

From the terraces it's great to watch the opposition
First we jeer and taunt a bit then fight for their position
Last weekend at Liverpool we trapped a group of ten
Six we knocked unconscious and there's one won't see again.

CHORUS

Now the match is over and there's something new to do
Scratching cars, slashing tyres we'll put windows through
Aggravate old codgers, well they shouldn't be alive
Grab their things and get away, before The Bill arrive.

CHORUS

On the train at twelve o'clock I hate to be alone
I hate my job, my mum and dad, hate everything at home
They all think I'm respectable their well-trained little pup
I hate the smell of whiskey, now I'm going to throw up

CHORUS

Once I was a hooligan ten years have since gone by
Today I've got a wife and kids and I often wonder why
The government, society my parents made me be
That cruel malicious drunkard or perhaps it was just me

REFRAIN
United we drank our beer
United we had no fear
United we beat the ban
But I was not a football fan

Helmsdale to Kirkwall

Sunday, July 22nd

This was the day I made a couple of important discoveries, granted a little bit late in the trip and on, hopefully, my last day on mainland Britain. I was up at eight o'clock and had time to start packing and doing my ablutions before breakfast. The trouble was my clothes were downstairs somewhere having been put in a tumble drier. I decided I would put the clothes in last rather than first for a change. These days, so my Basic Outdoor Leadership course had taught me, good practice was to put the heavy things in the top of the rucksack with the lighter stuff at the bottom. This supposedly put less stress on the back and this is what I had been doing. However, I was seriously corrupting the design brief of this particular piece of equipment because I was not carrying the rucksack vertically. It was being laid horizontally and pinned down with shock cords to the back rack – itself on the threshold of adequacy for the fifty pounds load. As I found out once I started to pedal, the result of packing the rucksack with the heavy stuff at the bottom was that the weight was pushed closer to my bum and the centre of gravity of the bike, making it much more stable.

My second discovery involved simpler physics. I had been using plastic bags to keep items separate even though these things had their own bags anyway – pillow, sleeping mat, bath bag and so on. I decided to dispense with them cutting down on unnecessary weight and bulk. I also threw out two glass spice jars, one now empty of washing powder but still quite heavy, the other full of slowly escaping washing up liquid that I had never used, never having cooked.

Breakfast was as greasy as could be imagined. The four large mushrooms, upside down like Sabbuteo players, were filled with oil. I ploughed through most of it but had to give up in the end. Since I had started with Frosties and toast and also polished off a large pot of coffee, I felt that I had eaten enough to set me up for the day. I picked up my clothes, settled the bill and was away at ten o'clock on the dot, very much wondering how bad the much hyped terrain of the Berriedale Brae was really going to be.

The slopes turned out to be long and steep, but there were downhill sections mixed in to provide some relief. I just took my time, walking very slowly where the gradient demanded and taking the opportunity to cast my eyes over the panoramic scenery. I thought about breakfast – I had been the only person in the room, surrounded by laid up tables and empty chairs. I had felt tears welling up and was lonely as I imagined Cherie sat opposite me chatting.

Then it occurred to me that she would have probably still been in bed. She would have given instructions to bring her up a cup of tea in bed before allowing me to get on with my breakfast. Or more likely, I would have used the room kettle and made her tea before I went down. I could see her so clearly performing her little tea ritual. It consisted mainly of just going back to sleep. But on a good day, she would emerge temporarily from slumber, reach out her left arm and cautiously dip her finger into the cup. The tea needed to get down to warm, rather than hot, to be at its optimum temperature. If it needed more time, she just dropped off again. I was never sure of the success rate of this process, but 50% might have been overly optimistic. I often returned to find the tea untouched and cold. Every morning, I took her tea in bed before I left for work, even if I was late. I would put the cup by the bedside and kiss her goodbye. It didn't matter to me, that more often than not the tea would remain untouched. She liked to have it there, so I did it. As I thought back on it, I could see that it was one of those simple little things that I did for her because I loved her, and she knew I did.

The weather was ideal to start with as I pushed the bike along, my body now well used to having to throw itself forward in order to make progress up the hill, whilst at the same time leaning sideways to counteract the weight of the bike and keep my balance. It was quite cool with no wind and cloudy but dry. Half an hour into the Berriedales it started to rain. I put on my waterproofs but soon dropped the hood, as it was getting too hot. The Berriedales were really two major climbs with a very big 'whee' in the middle a bit like a giant dromedary. Coming down the hill, I slowed to ask a cyclist who had stopped if he was OK.

'Just fucking knackered,' came the humorous reply. I released the brakes and flew on down, the bike feeling a lot more stable since my early morning alterations. I felt pretty good – my knees and my bum were fine for a change. I had gone through the tablet ritual before setting out – ibuprofen first then paracetamol an hour later, but of course, I hadn't been in the saddle that much – mostly I had been pushing. It took me two hours to come through the hills. The sun came out and I became aware, that for the first time on the whole trip, the wind was now fully behind me. It didn't seem very strong, but when my speed dropped and the wind caused by my own motion disappeared from my face, I could feel it gently pushing me along from behind. I was glad I wasn't pedalling the other way.

I stopped and hopped over a crash barrier to take a leak at the top of a steep embankment. Whilst shaking off the drops, and trying to keep my balance in long grass at the top of a serious incline, I was set upon by a large swarm of flies. It was just like a cartoon where some unfortunate bear is attacked by bees. I tried to swat them but my flailing arms were useless. What was worse was that I now had to push the bike up a long hill. The sun beat down, and with sweat on my brow, they were everywhere. I could feel them in my hair, on my face, and crawling over my hands, up my arms and down my neck. I lost my temper.

'Fucking, stinking, dirty bastards!' I cursed them all - the only remedy to hand that might make me feel slightly better.

It was five long minutes of every expletive I could bellow, before I reached the brow of the hill and was able to escape them. It had been a most regrettable pee and I rued my decision to stop for one.

I began to think about what I was going to do when I got back home, and I resolved to keep as much variety in my life as possible. Being surrounded by golf the day before made me wonder whether I should take it up. Would a new activity, rather than returning to old ones, be a better option? But I wasn't sure if I fancied golf. I hadn't done much windsurfing in recent years, but I had been out on the water one afternoon in the Maldives, and it had whetted my appetite – I thought I might take it up again. In the hotel room, the Scottish Tourist Board brochure featured four images on its cover and one of them was a windsurfer. I wondered why it was such a popular activity in terms of being featured on so many promotional materials. Very few people do it, watch it or take any interest in it at all. Perhaps it is a metaphor for excitement in the same way that castles are for heritage or golf is for - well - golf.

'Variety is the spice of life.' The cliché popped into my head as the following wind picked up and I started covering a lot of ground. I thought how absolutely true so many of these sayings were - clichés, of course, but still a simple shorthand way of saying something quite profound.

My mind ambled on, 'If I were to invent a saying, what would be the opposite of "Variety is the spice of life"? "Routine is the harbinger of boredom", maybe. "Boredom is the thief of time",' I continued, stealing the tail from the procrastination adage. I liked it though because I felt it rang true – on any occasion where routine is broken, a weekend away perhaps, time lasts so much longer and everything that happens is that much more memorable.

'It seems like we've been away for ages,' Cherie and I would agree as we travelled back the ninety miles from Pembrokeshire, only having gone at lunch time the previous day. Whatever the maxim, I resolved once more to live as varied a life as I could. I have always believed 'Live for today and hang tomorrow' and in that respect I was not going to change.

Looking at my trip meter, I confidently predicted reaching John O'Groats as I sailed on, often at fifteen to twenty mph, even on the flat! It was wonderful. Shooting down the hill towards the bridge at Dunbeath, I topped 41 mph - I couldn't believe it. I had to grip the handlebars with clenched fists to keep control, not that it would have done me any good if something had gone wrong. Childishly again, I was paying too much attention to my instrumentation with the odometer now reading 799 miles, wanting to see it change to 800. 800 was my magic mathematical construct and it was what I had been using since my first week on the trip.

'180 miles – only 20 miles off 200. 200 – quarter of the way there.' Later it was, '400 miles – half way there – Yeaaaaaaaay!' I was slightly disappointed that the clock didn't transform to 800 until halfway up the hill on the other side, pushing rather than coasting. But all the same, I was making fantastic progress and I seemed to be able to just keep going. Whether it was the fact that the day before had been an easy one, at least in terms of miles covered if not amount drunk, or whether I was getting the timing of my tablets right, or whether I was getting fitter, I wasn't sure. Probably though, it was the feeling of achievement I was getting in seeing the miles clock up so fast; that was largely to do with the wind, for once a friend instead of an enemy.

A few miles from Wick, the skies opened and it absolutely pissed down. Monster heavy raindrops hurled down on me and the road, throwing up silver plumes and turning the tarmac to a black lake, its former smoothness transformed to the frenzied surface of a fish farm pond at feeding time. Inside ten seconds my right foot was 100% wet. In fifteen so was my left. Why the delay, I didn't understand, because the road was completely awash. I didn't know much about the phenomenon of aquaplaning but I was afraid that cars were going to lose grip and hit me - I was on a fast, straight road. In fact, I was still travelling at speed myself and I did ponder the physics upon which my own safety relied too. But I pushed on, despite my fears, with water tumbling off every edge – my nose, my chin, the rim of my hood, my elbows and my knees, as well as pooling up temporarily in every crease of my waterproofs. I could sense the change in the feel of my jacket and I knew the rain was getting through. As suddenly as it had started, it stopped and I gratefully pulled up at a local garage for a ten minute stop.

Shaking myself like a dog coming out of the sea I plodded inside to buy chocolate and some Lucozade to swill down my next dose of tablets. The place appeared to be run by three schoolgirls and I chatted with them for a while before setting off once more for Wick.

A few miles on and the heavy rain started again. The landscape was really quite flat, not exactly fen-like but similar at least from a cycling point of view. The sea was, as it had been for days now, to my right and beyond what seemed to be a continuous cliff line. I wondered whether this coastline was a part of Britain that was rising, because that usually produces cliffs. Other parts of the country are sinking and that tends to create flood problems. I resolved to check it out when I got home.

I felt I should perhaps get myself a decent meal – I didn't know anything about John O'Groats, but I had a suspicion that there may not be much at all in the way of services there. Also, I was now only seventeen miles away from the end of my mainland epic and, so far that day, I had made really good time. I didn't need to push myself too hard. I got to Wick inside four hours with just the one stop in the garage, not including the pee stop with the flies. What excellent going!

'Was it the greasy breakfast?' I wondered? With the raindrops still bouncing all around me I parked up outside a chippy, surprised to see one open at 2 o'clock on a Sunday.

As I went to order, the woman behind the counter said, 'You made it then!'

Who should it be but Linda, the woman I had been talking to in the pub the night before and partner of the accordionist, Clive. I asked her how she came to be so far from home, but of course, she lived just twenty miles away, equidistant between the chip shop where she worked and the pub in Helmsdale where she sometimes drank. She served me up a massive plateful with chips, two fish, some salad and a big hot mug of coffee. My waterproofs were discarded and left to create puddles under some empty chairs in a forlorn attempt to drip-dry them. I started to eat, not feeling particularly hungry, and with little confidence that I would be able to finish the mountain of food. I was wrong though, and it must have been an indication of just how much energy I had used up since breakfast.

As I went to pay the bill, Linda said, 'I'll get it.'

I was touched by her kind gesture and we chatted for a short while. She surprised me a bit by asking for my address. She said she would write and I wondered whether she had any other motives – probably she was just being friendly. I hadn't consciously given out any signals and in any case, she was with town planning, accordion playing Clive. Perhaps she wanted to make sure I sent a recording of 'My Fanny's on Top of my Head', as I had promised. Naturally I obliged with my address then donned my still saturated waterproofs and said my goodbyes.

As I started to warm up in my wet clothes over the first few miles out of Wick, the rain continued to hammer down. I wiped a drip off the end of my nose and it made me think of Cherie. She used to signal to me that I had a bogie caught in the nook of my nostril at the end of my Roman (I would always say, 'aquiline') nose. Her gesture would be several short touches of her own nose with the back of her fingers.

'Don't use your fingers!' she would say, then fish out a tissue. Where she kept them I don't know, but she could always lay her hands on one at a moment's notice.

'The other one, Dear ... no, it's still there ... gone now!' She would do the same sort of thing while I was eating. Before I met Cherie, I was not in the habit of using a serviette to dab the corners of my mouth.

Then I thought, 'Come to think of it, how can you do that if the serviette is on your lap where it should be? Or, are you supposed to tuck it into your collar like a baby wearing a bib. And if you wipe tomato sauce out of the corners of your mouth, do you then put the serviette back on to your pristine trousers. Or do you tuck it back into your neck, so you look as if you've been accosted by a drunken middle-aged divorcee with too much lippy on a boozy Friday night?'

Whatever, the answer, the result of Cherie's training for dinner was that I now habitually dabbed the corners of my mouth, even when I couldn't sense the existence of any wayward deposits. Naturally, Cherie had her habits too. The main one could best be described as a mild facial grimace that looked like someone with bad eyesight trying to read a sign. Her face would set in this expression for quite long periods often when she was watching television. On a few funny occasions, I told her she was 'doing it' and she tried to hold the expression while she moved to look at herself in mirror but of course, it would have vanished by the time she got there.

It was no big deal but I would tell her, 'Don't squint!' in the manner of a friendly order, and as a way of lightly scoring points for her corrections at the dinner table.

She would reply, 'Sorry, Dear,' making a cursory adjustment to her countenance before quickly settling back to her habitual expression. It upset me thinking about these types of things because they made her seem so real – the irony in this case was that she had perfect eyesight so why the need to squint?

I looked around me – the route was flat with a few small ups and downs, but the road was now drying out. There was a complete contrast: the sky over the sea to my right seemed to have rain in it and the mizzle easily hid the horizon. To my left, though, it was much brighter: no sun, but sizable chinks of clear sky, turquoise rather than blue, tinged by the surrounding grey. There were no longer any hedges; the landscape was now a mixture of open heather moorland and fields given over to pasture and delimited by wire fences. Looking seawards, the cliff line continued and became even more dramatic. For some miles, the half-mile corridor between the A9 and the cliffs had been dotted with a mix of derelict crofts and newly built bungalows but these had now petered out. Instead there were a small number of huge, totally isolated houses standing monolithically and stark atop the sheer drops to the sea. They looked the archetypal haunted house and I wondered what sort of people might live in them.

I soon noticed the water to my right curving around so that it was now in front of me too.

'This was the corner! It must be John O'Groats – just a few miles away now.' I could make out islands and skerries in the distance and I watched them closely as I pedalled towards my goal. As I came over the last brow, I was struck by sea cliffs, which I could see miles away on what must have been the west side of Orkney. Despite only average visibility, I was moved to swear out loud in awe. Freewheeling down the hill, I had to stop at the road sign which read,

John O'Groats.

After marvelling at it for a full minute, I went into the shop a few yards further on. The proprietor, a very friendly old gent, reliably advised me, after consultation with an unseen person in a back room, that I would get a ferry that evening at six o'clock. I could hardly believe it.

'Brilliant, I'm going to actually make Orkney a day earlier than I thought.' That morning, I would never have dreamed I would get to Orkney as I tentatively set off for the infamous Berriedale Braer. And it was still only quarter past four!

I bought some postcards and chatted for a while with the shopkeeper, who very kindly agreed to leave his station to take a couple of photos of me and the bike by the John O'Groats signpost. He really was a most delightful and helpful gentleman. I glided a little further down the hill, still gazing at the distant cliffs on Orkney before pulling into a 1970s style motel. I ordered a coffee at the bar, but was tempted to buy something stronger. A few others were on stools sipping beer and I felt that now of all times, I certainly deserved a real drink to celebrate my achievement.

'John O'Groats ... from Merthyr ... I've done it!' Somehow, I resisted. I discarded my sodden waterproof top, and sat down at a table to write my postcards. After I'd finished, I went to find a post box. The shopkeeper had told me that mail sent from anywhere in John O'Groats was franked with an official John O'Groats stamp before it left the village. So MR and Graham in school would have that honour. I continued down the hill into the village proper and bought my ferry ticket from the booking office. Outside, I briefly chatted to a woman who had come up from Milton Keynes on the train and who was on Day 1 of her holiday and bound for the Orkneys. I thought how it contrasted with my own trip where, at last, I was seeing light at the end of the tunnel.

I wandered around the tiny settlement until renewed torrential rainfall sent me scurrying into a gift shop where I started to read about the incredible cliffs I had seen across the water. I discovered they were a mighty 1200 feet tall and on the island of Hoy – the place where the 'Old Man' is also to be found. As a geography teacher, I don't encourage the kids to use a ruler when drawing landforms. But God must have used a setsquare on those cliffs – straight up they went - at ninety degrees to the sea. I mooched around for a while longer, taking little interest in the array of typical tourist tat on display – key rings, postcards, mugs, scarves and the like, all emblazoned with the words, 'John O'Groats'. I soon got bored and decided I would prefer to wander around in the rain. Thankfully, it had abated to some extent and I was able to drop my hood.

At the other extremity of the country, I had visited Land's End years before; I remembered the signpost there, put up for the benefit of tourists, that gave the direction and distance to the nearest landfall and other places of interest. There was a similar one at John O'Groats. For a while, I thought that the local vandals (don't they get absolutely everywhere) had pulled out some of the wooden pointers from the famous post. It was only when I looked at the nearby photo kiosk - closed, of course, on a Sunday evening - that I could see the photos in the window. There were all sorts of people featured: walkers, bikers, groups, couples, singles and one bloke standing by his car proudly displaying the fact that he had come all the way from Essex in his Ford Escort.

'Big deal,' I thought, '... not even a decent car.' The point I had missed though, was that the photos of all these people had the signpost in the background with the name of their own hometown on it. So the missing pointers were removable by design and not by vandals (don't they get the blame for absolutely everything). Looking across the sea, I spotted the ferry approaching from the direction of Orkney. I collected the bike from where it was propped against a dry stone wall and made my way down to the harbour. A small crowd had already assembled, and as the rain started to hammer down again, a loose queue continued to develop behind me.

I took a couple of photos as the ferry pulled in and was surprised to see it was quite a small craft. Once the incoming passengers had alighted, I wheeled my precarious burden over the gangplank. A burly middle-aged crewman took over and I questioned his judgement in trying to carry my bike, still loaded up, down a narrow steep stairway to the level below. I think he had underestimated the weight because he struggled, just as I would have done. The only assistance I could provide was to helplessly support the weightless front wheel and my heart stopped at one point as the whole lot nearly went over the side. Safely down on the lower level deck, I gratefully took charge and propped the still loaded bike against some seats at an angle of forty-five degrees so it couldn't go anywhere, then went inside to an interior rather like a very wide bus. I didn't seek company as I had done outside the ticket office, but opted to sit on my own by a window. That only lasted a few minutes as I decided I needed a better view, so I went outside and up the stairway again on to the exposed upper deck.

In my still sodden clothes, it was cold in the wind; although, thankfully, the rain had stopped once more. On the way up, I had noticed a warm draught coming from a vent at the foot of the stairway. I went back down to investigate and discovered that the warmth was excess heat being pumped out of the engine room. I sniffed the output to make sure it wasn't exhaust fumes then spent the next half an hour standing under the vent using it as a hot air drier. I rotated myself systematically, periodically raising my arms against the highly placed vents so I could dry the inner part of my sleeves. I must have looked like the nutter on the bus but I gradually dried out and felt a lot more comfortable. Even the case holding my camera, which had been under my waterproof top, had become damp and I was able to dry that too.

The trip to Orkney took about forty-five minutes and I gazed across a grey sea to see mainland Scotland gradually diminishing in the distance. When the ferry pulled in, I did a Cherie and was first in the queue to get off. Any thoughts I had of finding accommodation were dashed immediately. Apart from a porta cabin waiting room and a car park, there was nothing there – it was just a place name on a map – Burwick – but there was no place. I had picked up a leaflet in John O'Groats advertising *wheens* – apparently, these were similar to bunk houses – very basic accommodation but at least with a bed. There was one six miles north of the ferry terminal, for a price of £6.50. I didn't feel like camping after such a long day, so it seemed like a good idea to try to find it.

It took no more than half a minute to suss the situation in Burwick, so I was first to set off up a long gently sloping hill on a straight road about the width of a B road on the mainland. I was soon overtaken by two coaches that had come from the car park, plus a few cars, all of which had picked up foot passengers from the ferry terminal. As there were no other bikes on the boat, I was the only cyclist represented. At the crest of the rise I was struck by a wonderful view over to my left. A rubber sky was lighting up a thin, broad lens of water in the bay some distance away as dark mountains rose up behind (my father showed me once how to draw shafts of light emanating from under a grey sky – the page has to be shaded with pencil completely then, with a ruler, a rubber can be drawn across the page to reveal the 'white light' underneath - since then I've always described such a scene as a 'rubber sky' and passed the tip and the description of it on to my own kids). I stopped to take a photograph but, as usual, I knew the print would never do justice to that wonderful vista.

As I pulled off, I passed a parked car with what looked like a courting couple sitting in the front enjoying the same scenery but with the bonus elixir of young romance to fuel their senses.

'Going to Kirkwall?' the boy shouted out of the window.

'No.'

'I was going to offer you a lift if you were.'

'Thanks!' It would have been so easy but I wanted to cycle. I had turned down offers of lifts before – from Chainy outside Coventry and from the guy with the pick up as I climbed that awful hill out of Whitby against the wind.

I was not going to spoil it all now. Still, what a generous gesture it was from a young couple that would have had some difficulty getting me, my bike and my luggage, into their car.

'Besides,' I thought, 'The wheen is only a few miles away now – Kirkwall can wait until tomorrow – I've done well enough today.' At this point in my journey, I had come up with a definitive theory for the reasons for my trip and I mulled over it again now.

'It's to Cherie's memory.' The guy in South Shields, Brett, was right. I was doing it *for her*.

'Does that make sense? She's gone.'

'She hasn't gone! Not completely. I remember her. She's in me – part of what I am. If I'm doing it for Me, then I'm doing it for Her because we are the same now. She is no longer a different person – we are one.'

I cried and pushed harder on the pedals to the top of the rise. Freewheeling down the other side I vowed I would cycle to the very top of the Shetlands. Before, I hadn't been sure what I would do when I got to Lerwick - maybe stay the night, look around then come home. Now ... there would be no question in my mind on that final journey. The trek across Shetland would be:

For Cherie, My Love.

At last it was clear to me and whatever debates I had had on the subject before were now resolved.

The wind was still helping, pushing me gently forward whether going up, down or on the flat. My progress was as impressive as it had been earlier and that strange early evening light was upon me again. Once more – how peaceful, how tranquil and the hills gently sloped away offering splendid views of the sheltered sea to my left and the rolling fields to my right.

The three-hour break I had effectively had whilst waiting for, and travelling on the ferry, plus Linda's massive fish and chip tea, must have given me extra strength as the miles continued to disappear behind me. Six miles from the ferry terminal there was no sign of the wheen and nobody to ask. I didn't care – fourteen miles to Kirkwall, the capital of Orkney.

'I'll get there.'

There wasn't a tree in sight, just open moorland with heather and fenced enclosed pasture dotted with sheep and a few big black Aberdeen Angus cows. To my left was a water-world with great ponds of seawater, separated by numerous headlands and lit in part by the fading northern sunshine. That time of day – pre-twilight might be the best way of describing it, had been a revelation to me on my ride. I wasn't even aware of its existence before.

As I crossed the causeways of the Churchill Barriers, built, so I had been told on the way up, to protect the eastern approaches to Scapa Flow from U boat attack, and as I climbed or rolled down the intervening hills, something made me think of the cards I was sent after Cherie's death. I had read them all as they had arrived and again just before I threw them in the bin. Several, I kept for posterity because they struck a chord with me. I have always done this – kept one or two things – sometimes a birthday card from one of the kids, sometimes a painting they did in school, sometimes a newspaper cutting. I thought about a card, a valentine card that Cherie had sent to me in our early days of courting. It was by tradition, from an anonymous admirer, and handwritten inside was a Shakespeare sonnet*. I read it and although I knew very little about Shakespeare, I was very moved by the words. I wondered whether I should tell Cherie about the card. It had appeared in my pigeonhole in school and I had sort of assumed that it had come from one of the members of staff, perhaps an English teacher. I decided to tell Cherie and she owned up. Cherie hadn't done at all well when she was in school and I remembered feeling embarrassed that I had not thought of her when I tried to imagine who could have sent the card. As I rode through that wonderfully illuminated land, it occurred to me that her handwritten anonymous sonnet was the most romantic thing ever to have happened to me.

Riding over one of the Churchill Barriers, I saw that a small group of people were gathered for a picnic. We were the only people in the land, it seemed, so I stopped to chat for a short while. The banter cheered me up and I gained extra heart as I passed quickly through one isolated village after another, munching the miles as I had done all day, with the signposts flagging an ever-decreasing mileage to Kirkwall. I reached the capital at nine o'clock with my bum sore again, but otherwise in good shape. After a quick ride around, I walked into a hotel and managed to persuade the youngish man at reception to let me have a single room for £20, rather than £40, admittedly, without breakfast. I had learned from salesman friends that it was always worth trying to get the tariffs down, especially if you're booking in late.

I had politely used the same patter, 'Twenty quid is better than nothing ... and the chances are that you won't let this room tonight now.'

The guy at reception was very helpful and he allowed me to put my bike in a spare staff room before showing me to my room upstairs. It was fairly basic and I was glad that I hadn't paid the full whack (not that I would have anyway) but the room did have an *en suite* shower and toilet, the first time on the trip I had enjoyed such luxury.

I had a quick shower then went down to the bar. It was fairly Spartan with just a few people sitting around and just one man at the bar on a stool. I sat just outside his personal space but soon started talking to him. His name was Dodds who turned out to work for the Highland Park whiskey distillery, just up the road. Of course, Howard had told me about the place back in Newtonmore, but it had completely gone out of my mind. As I talked to Dodds, I asked him the same questions as I had put to Howard. His answers were in complete agreement with Howard's and it seemed to confirm that I had indeed unravelled the secrets of drinking whiskey correctly.

'How should it be drunk, Dodds?'

'With water - never ice, never straight – no more than the same volume as the spirit itself.'

It was like listening to the same record twice. We bought each other a drink then got booted mysteriously out of the bar to the lounge. I soon realised it was because it was past closing time and the lounge was less conspicuous from the street. I had forgotten just how late I had arrived in town. Dodds had gone off to a corner to talk with friends as I came in a few minutes later from the loo, so I stood at the bar for a while before joining in a conversation with two old blokes. They made me laugh with their lightly drunken humour. We bantered for a while until it came out that I had cycled up from South Wales. Gordon, with bottle bottom specs and no front teeth, was an ex-sergeant major. In his own words, he was a bastard but also a cyclist too. Now, at the age of sixty-two, he would habitually cycle twelve miles to the pub for a drink in order not to lose his licence.

He had the same interpretation of the law as I had: 'You can get done for 'Drunk in Charge of a Bicycle', but they can't touch your car licence.'

He was a nice guy, and although I suspected that the twelve miles might have been a bit of an exaggeration, he was very funny. At twelve o'clock we were kicked out of the lounge as well, so I went back up to my room and was asleep in seconds.

The Ride:

Helmsdale to Kirkwall (Orkney Islands)
Distance: 74 miles

*When most I wink, then do mine eyes best see,
For all the day they view things unrespected;
But when I sleep, in dreams they look on thee,
 And darkly bright, are bright in dark directed.
Then thou, whose shadow shadows doth make bright,
How would thy shadow's form form happy show
To the clear day with thy much clearer light,
When to unseeing eyes thy shade shines so!
How would, I say, mine eyes be blessed made
By looking on thee in the living day,
When in dead night thy fair imperfect shade
Through heavy sleep on sightless eyes doth stay?
All days are nights to see till I see thee,
And nights bright days when dreams do show thee me.

Rest Day

Monday, July 23rd

The plan had been to set off for Stromness, the main ferry port on Orkney in the afternoon and head for the Shetland Islands. Depending on the sailing times, I hoped I would be able to have a good lie-in because the hotel staff had kindly allowed me to use the room until three o'clock. However, I found a P&O brochure in a drawer in the room and started leafing through. It was typical of me not to plan and now I could see that I could so nearly have come unstuck. The ferry only sailed to the Shetlands twice a week from Orkney. Luckily, the next crossing was the following day at 2200 hrs. It meant I would have to spend an extra night in Kirkwall but at least I didn't have to get a ferry back to Scotland and then pick up one of the daily sailings to Shetland from Scrabster. At the hotel, I managed to negotiate the half price room rate for a second night and was relieved that by chance, things had worked out all right and that I now had an unscheduled rest day and an opportunity to get to know Orkney better. Coincidentally, this rest day fell exactly three weeks into the trip, a week since my last rest day in Inverkeithing and two weeks since my first rest day in Scarborough - who said, 'I don't like Mondays?'

I wandered along the main street in Kirkwall picking up a mince-filled pasty that had a special Scottish name - a bridey. I dropped some film off for processing then, taking the advice of Craig at hotel reception, strolled on down to the harbour to book some ferry crossings. Despite the warmth from the sun, a competing keen wind was whipping around the harbour and I was glad to get into the sheltered confines of the booking office. The two sailings, from Stromness–Orkney to Lerwick-Shetland and from Lerwick to Aberdeen, were overnight and I paid extra for a shared cabin with a shower for both trips. The other option was a reclining seat and I had experienced trying to sleep on one of those a number of times in the past. I decided that the extra cost for a bit of comfort and peace would be well justified. On my way back through town, I bought some post cards before making my way back to the luxury of my hotel room.

I wrote post cards to friends, Dennis and Margaret, Chris and Dawn, (my brother and his wife), and Nicole (my eldest stepdaughter) and then I phoned British Rail (or whatever they're called now) to check times and availability for my return journey from Aberdeen to Merthyr. It seemed as if I was jumping the gun a bit – after all, I hadn't got to where I was going yet and I couldn't be sure how long I was going to take. Despite my hitherto lack of planning, it now seemed prudent to think about the practicalities of my return journey home. I could no longer make it up as I went along – I had to rely on external transport systems again. It transpired that all bookable seats on the 9.15 from Aberdeen to Crewe had already been taken so I would have to take my chances when the time came.

I also remembered the advice of the man near Newtonmore who had said I might get a National Express coach. I phoned them, but they refused to take the bike unless it was foldable. I still felt it might be an option though – you can often get around these problems face to face in a way that you can't when speaking to a regulation driven jobsworth over a telephone line. It appeared that my planning, such as it was, had come too late. I hadn't forgotten about the idea of trying to get myself on to a tramp steamer but mulling it over I realised that if and when I reached the Shetlands I would just want to get back home as soon as I could. As I considered the problem of not being able to get on the train, another wildcard idea occurred to me. I could perhaps talk to some truckers on the ferry back to Aberdeen – there might be a truck bound for the Midlands or anywhere south for that matter. It was just a thought. Whatever happened I was going to have to leave my options open. It was perhaps fitting that the journey back, although on motorised transport, was going to be as ad hoc as the trip up.

The last few miles into Kirkwall the night before had been pretty triumphant but I had detected an intermittent grinding noise that sounded like the start of wheel bearing trouble from the front of the bike. My attitude to servicing - 'If it's not broke don't fix it' - was my first reaction, but it seemed that there was something, if only in embryonic form, going awry with my machine. Although I was still tempted to ignore the noise given that I no longer had that far to go, wisdom won out in the end. I reasoned that I didn't want to fail at the last hurdle because of a mechanical breakdown.

'Imagine being forty miles out of Lerwick on Shetland, in the middle of nowhere, when the front wheel seizes or falls off. What about having to get a lift back in a truck, then having to get the wheel fixed before starting off all over again?' It wasn't as if I didn't have time on my hands here in Kirkwall, plus I had spotted a bike shop on my way in yesterday – almost certainly they would have repair facilities. In any case, I'd have to get the bearing fixed when I got back home, so I retrieved my bike from the staff room and pedalled off down to the shop. One of the staff told me they were very busy, but when I explained that I had cycled from South Wales and that I had a ferry to catch, they sympathetically said they would fix it for me by the end of the day.

I mooched around town for a while and bought a Cornish pasty. It was surprising how quickly time passed. I had been awake and drinking coffee at eight o'clock that morning. Just doing bits and bobs it was already lunchtime. Now that I had an unexpected extra day, I decided I wouldn't mind going to take a look at those magnificent cliffs I had seen in the distance on the island of Hoy. I was a bit disappointed to find out from Tourist Information that no trips were running on a Monday. I could have jumped on to a service bus but it wouldn't have got me to the cliffs. I toyed with the idea of hiring a motorbike (if they were available) but thought better of it. It would be expensive and I didn't have any motorbike gear. I had also seen the weather forecast predicting the passage of a front and rain later in the day. In any case, I had my doubts as to whether the view of the cliffs would be as good from the land as it had been from the sea.

I settled for a trip around the Highland Park distillery. It was a walk of about a mile up the hill to the plant and when I saw it I realised I had failed to notice it on the way in the night before. Following the brown Tourist Attraction signs, I was surprised to see that the distillery didn't have arrows directing people off the road and into their car park. The place looked quite deserted but, after a few minutes, I managed to find what looked like an employee.

'Where's the visitor centre?' I asked politely. He chuckled.

With his strong accent, the wind and my hearing loss I thought I heard him say, 'This is a cheese making outfit.'

'Pardon?'

I was right. The employee of the cheese production unit put me right on my directions for the distillery and made me feel a bit less foolish by saying that I wasn't the first one to have made the same mistake. Privately, I blamed bad signposting for the error but of course, most visitors to the distillery would be in cars and not walking, so the sign needed to be some distance from the distillery proper. A few hundred yards up the road I soon saw it. It was an imposing building – dark grey and looking, for all the world, like a Victorian lunatic asylum. A tower emerged above the general height of the other buildings, square in section, but with a roof slanting in the manner of an Alpine lodge. From under the eaves of this roof, smoke was puffing out dramatically as if through the nostrils of a dragon. I realised that I had left my camera back at the hotel but the view made a visual impression on me that was as good as a photograph.

I bought a cup of coffee and a Kit Kat at the deserted visitor centre while I waited quarter of an hour for the tour to begin. I didn't think it was appropriate to ask if Dodds, the guy I had met at the bar the night before, was around so I just asked the woman behind the counter if she knew him.

'Not really, I never go into the distillery itself.' Others started to gather in the café and the little congregation chatted privately in muted tones, as if in church waiting for the bride to arrive: a Norwegian couple with their two children, a couple from Glasgow, a lone guy like me and another couple whose home town I missed as the tour guide posed his introductory questions. It was an interesting tour visiting each of the main stages that make up the whiskey making process. I was surprised to find out that Highland Park, having gone to all the trouble of malting their own barley and using their own peat, still brought in barley from mainland Scotland to supplement their own stuff. Apparently, if they didn't, the whiskey would be too earthy and peaty, much like a west coast variety.

Standing up on a high gantry overlooking one of the operations, I felt a tap on my shoulder – it was Dodds. We exchanged friendly grins, shook hands and said our goodbyes on the back of our hellos, both of us knowing that we'd probably never meet again. The audio-visual presentation at the end of the tour was also enjoyable and it provided some excellent footage of Orkney and its history, before getting on to the inevitable subject of whiskey making. It was all the better for the complimentary dram which was provided for us as the film rolled. Mine had long disappeared by the time the presenter raised his glass at the end of the show to raise a toast – 'Schol!' the Orkney equivalent of 'Cheers!'

I pointed myself back in the direction of town and donned my waterproof top as the forecasted rain began to pick. I followed the road down the hill, realising too late, that I should have turned off right at the top. Why do I always make these mistakes? Unlike Cherie, I often failed to take in the visual prompts on my outward leg - she did it naturally. I resolved to make a point of remembering next time I ventured out, but it was unlikely I would be able to change the habit of a lifetime. I didn't think Cherie would have been too interested in the distillery, nor with St Magnus Cathedral in the town for that matter. It had looked impressive as I walked past a number of times earlier in the day, but as yet I hadn't mustered up any enthusiasm to go in. The detour back to the hotel was a minor one and, luckily, it took me past a chippy. It wasn't open until six but at least I knew now where I could get dinner later on. Further down the road was the bike shop so I went to see if my wheel bearing had been fixed. The bike was in the same place I had left it propped against a wall, but now pointing in the opposite direction. I assumed it had been repaired but was told by one of the lads that it hadn't been done.

'Come back at quarter past five – we should be able to look at it by then.'

I suddenly felt forlorn and helpless, like when you drop off your car at the garage after they've told you it's bad news, or when you leave the house key with builders but you're unsure of their credentials. Something tells you that things are not going to work out right. I really needed that bike fixed because I had to get to Stromness for the ferry the next day. It was three o'clock already.

As I walked past Woolworths, I remembered that I had run out of stamps. I planned to send a load of photos or cards (I hadn't decided which yet) from Shetland assuming I could still get there, so I bought thirty-six stamps – another nine quid. Back in my room, I began to write up my journal from the day before. I broke off to go out and pick up the bike. My earlier fears proved unfounded, as it was ready for me – in fact, it had been the last time I'd called in. I sat writing for hours, the usual routine now, recalling yesterday's journey, the people and my thoughts of Cherie. I was determined to finish but my eyes began to herald the closure of my brain and I had to catnap for quarter of an hour.

I woke in time to see an episode of Corrie – the Platt kids, Martin, Sally and the Croppers were off camping - '... not that I watch it' - I always jokingly ended any conversation about The Street with the phrase.

It was half nine by the time I walked out of the hotel. I stopped off at a late shop to buy some cigars and headed off in the rain for the harbour pubs I had spotted earlier when picking up the ferry tickets. They looked promising from the outside – real 'pub' pubs, with quaint facades and a welcoming yellow glow from their leaded windows. But appearances can be deceptive – these taverns could have been zoo compounds where the animals refuse to appear from their lairs, nests, bushes, ponds or holes. There was hardly anyone about – what did I expect on a Monday night? I chose one at random and sat at the bar supping a pint and ritually lighting and relighting a Hamlet cigar (they always go out), puffing out smoke and flicking ash into the ash tray, no sop to a nicotine addiction – just occupational therapy and the satisfaction of creating of an earthy waft. Or was it the subliminal effect of growing up with those classic adverts - Air on a G string and the association of Hamlet cigar smoking with relaxation?

I didn't see the point in staying any longer. Someone had told me that the Albert hotel had a bit of life so I sought it out on the way home. It was pretty empty too; but, I sat at the bar along with several others and ordered a pint of Guinness, which I consumed in tandem with puffs from another Hamlet. There was a bloke reading a book around the corner of the bar and separated from me by a pillar. After five minutes, he put it away and I felt I could strike up a conversation without intruding.

'*Men of Men* – is it good? I started it once myself but never got to the end.' I had noticed the Wilbur Smith book from its cover earlier. We got into a conversation about the author and some of his other books that we had both read. The man was a former bank employee now turned insurance man called Douglas. He used to live in former Rhodesia and left at about the time the Ian Smith government fell in the seventies. His African connection was one of the reasons why he was reading Wilbur Smith and he told me that Smith's Egyptian sagas were very good. I said I'd give them a go but this time, start at the beginning of the trilogy and not in the middle, as I was prone to do.

The conversation turned somehow to whiskey – I probably mentioned that I had been around the Highland Park distillery that afternoon. Douglas introduced me to several single malts as we took it in turns to buy. Highland Park was not a favourite of his and I think he wanted to introduce me to others. He had been planning to turn in because he had business in the morning but we ended up drinking whiskey and chatting for another hour and a half. Before he left at midnight, he told me that when I reached Lerwick on the Shetlands I was to go into the bank and look up an acquaintance of his. He told me the man's name and said that when he appeared I was to say:

'Hello Four Eyes!'

He assured me that his mate would love the joke, so I agreed. It was midnight when Douglas finally went and I was refused another drink by the bar staff. I reluctantly left too and set off for my hotel with my mind wandering. After all that whisky I was pretty drunk but nevertheless in a very reflective mood - my thoughts strung together easily and, perhaps influenced by my philosophy studies at university, everything suddenly made sense. It was like a spiritual awakening – all strands were pulled together - my life, my tribulations and the future. I was taken aback by the intensity of it all and I told myself that I would have to write it down back at the hotel room. But something happened – either I forgot to write, or I just lost it – all of it. I seem to remember hoping that it would come back to me. Either way the experience turned out to be as ephemeral as a desert flower. The whiskey that so effectively spawned the revelation, just as surely destroyed it. I ended the night watching the last bit of a documentary on Terry Dene, pop idol of the fifties and sixties. I might have had a coffee. I don't remember. Guinness and whiskey had done their work.

Rest Day

Kirkwall to Lerwick

Tuesday, July 24th

I woke up at seven but went back to sleep until half eight. For the second day in a row I enjoyed the luxury of making coffee in a room and watching breakfast news on the TV. The main item was an attack on Colombo airport in Sri Lanka. I decided the first priority was to write up the journal – I knew if I didn't stick at it I would quickly fall behind. It was 11.45 by the time I finished and started to sort out my ablutions. Whilst shaving, I thought about what day of the trip I was on – Day 22. I would reach Shetland on Day 23 - Cherie died on the 23rd of June. It also occurred to me that 23 was roughly the number of days that Cherie fell really ill before the end. A symmetry in time – 23 days to ride and 23 days to die 23 days into the month.

It was quite busy as I walked down the main street and past the cathedral. I picked up my film from the chemist - £5.99 and, unlike Walter's in Merthyr, no free film. So I had to buy a film – another fiver more or less. I thought it would be interesting to see if I had lost any weight on the trip so I looked around the pharmacy for some scales. A member of staff said Boots was the only place in town that had any. I found Boots and unearthed the scales in a forgotten recess at the back of the shop. It couldn't be a normal set of scales could it? It was one of those computerised things that, for an outlay of twenty-five pence, gave you a read out and told you whether you were right for your height and build. The result was a weight loss of half a stone putting me at 11st 6lbs. I thought that was surprising considering I had been on greasy spoon breakfasts, chippy suppers and a minimum of five pints a day for the last three weeks. It must have been an indication of just how many calories I had been burning up with the cycling. Anyway, as usual the machine told me I was still overweight - I needed to lose another stone, which would have put me at ten and a half. I hadn't been that weight since I was sixteen – if I lost that amount of weight now I'd look like a man who'd been lost in the jungle for a year. It did occur to me that I should weigh the rucksack as well. I knew it was heavy but I was curious to know just how heavy – it must have been approaching fifty pounds or so. Perhaps I would lug it down later – maybe not. My immediate thoughts turned to the need for a late breakfast.

A long queue filed into the bakery so I carried on down to the chippy, hoping to get a pasty but the place was not yet open. In fact, my appetite was still asleep so I wasn't too bothered and decided to keep on going down to the harbour for a general mooch about. I hadn't properly taken it in the day before when I had gone to pick up the tickets. The weather was beautiful and although a fair breeze still shaved the edges off the warmth, the sunshine illuminated the harbour vitalising the colours and enhancing their contrasts - just half a dozen yachts, a big motor cruiser from the south coast, the lifeboat and a collection of fishing boats of various sizes floating peacefully in dark blue water under a light blue sky with the low green treeless Orkney Hills as a backdrop. Gazing at the scene, I still fancied the idea of sailing home but as I dwelled on the prospect, pragmatism regained the upper hand.

'Too long,' I thought, as I took my time to frame a photo of the harbour (one that I later enlarged and framed to put on a wall in my spare bedroom). There was no hurry because the ferry didn't sail from Stromness until the evening so I didn't have to rush to cover the seventeen miles to the port. Sauntering back up from the harbour, the chippy was still closed despite having all the appearances of being open. A young man stood busying himself behind the high chip shop counter.

'Twelve o'clock,' he mouthed to me from the other side of the shop window.

I ambled back up through town to find that the bakery queue had now disappeared so I had a pasty and a bridey, both warmed up (in fact, too warmed up) by the young girl serving. I sat on a wooden seat outside St Magnus Cathedral to eat my brunch in the wind and the sunshine. I thought back to the previous night, sitting in the bar near the harbour on a barstool. The place had hardly any customers and to all intents and purposes, I was alone. I remembered thinking about loneliness again and was aware that I hadn't really felt lonely that often. I supposed that there had been plenty of things to think about, but it occurred to me that maybe I had got used to sitting alone in a bar during the twenty odd years I played in pubs. During much of that time I played as a solo artist and I was well used to arriving alone, sitting alone before starting and again at half time. Twenty years was perhaps an exaggeration – I played with my mate Cliff for quite a few of those. And when I met Cherie, she nearly always came with me; although, understandably, even she waned and lost the enthusiasm to accompany me in later years. It was a shame she had no musical talent whatsoever – we might have made a decent duo.

My greasy brunch gone, I went into the cathedral as I had promised I would. Either I wasn't in the mood or it just did nothing for me. It was probably a bit of both, but I had seen more inspiring cathedral interiors - not that St Magnus wasn't impressive. The day before, I had thought that I might go and settle on a pew and meditate for a while, but with the relative gloom inside the nave and scores of people from a host of nationalities milling about, the bright sunshine outside was more of a lure and I satisfied myself with just a quick wander around. As with the distillery, Cherie would not have had much interest either and I could hear her response to a suggestion to go and look around at the vaults, buttresses, flying buttresses and all the rest of it:

'No Dear - I can't be bothered!'

Back in the hotel room, I finished writing up the journal from the day before, and as I started to pack, I remembered that I hadn't annotated the latest batch of photographs. I needed to do it sooner rather than later, so despite the fact I had promised the cleaner, on her second unannounced entry, that I would only be half an hour, I spent an extra fifteen minutes on the job. Packing took quite a while as I continued to experiment with different loading options. I finally checked out and loaded up the bike – promptly setting off in the wrong direction again – how could I? The usual story – if only I had paused to THINK. I soon realised my mistake and found my way on to the right road. It wasn't too difficult - this was hardly rush hour in central London. I stopped after only half a mile at a garage. I had taken my ibuprofen but not any paracetamol, so I bought a lemon Lucozade and used it to wash down my bum relief tablets. Only seventeen miles to Stromness – small fry, but I had learned the difference that the tablets could make. Half a mile on and I stopped to look back down the hill. I could make out the harbour and the town, now smaller from my vantage point, but it was the blue of the sea that struck me the most. As I pedalled on, my mind began to wander in a way that it didn't seem to do on a rest day. It must have been because there were fewer distractions on the bike and I could just switch off. I couldn't get a postcard, walk this way or that – cross a road or go into a shop – only pedal and daydream.

Pedalling more or less against the breeze, but making steady progress, the thought hit me that Cherie was no more. NO MORE. Everything she had been was gone – certainly as far as she was concerned. Her looks, her body, her thoughts, laughs, voice – everything. Gone. She was now just a memory in the minds of those she once knew. The more they knew her, the more she was there. But when those people were themselves gone, what would be left then? A name on an official register - a name that was born, that got married then divorced, then got married again, then died on the 23rd June, 2001.

I thought, 'This is what awaits us all.' I questioned whether I should have had a gravestone erected somewhere, but only briefly. Some stranger may happen to look upon its inscription in years or even generations to come. What would it mean to them?

CHERIE HILL

Beloved wife of Tony,

Devoted mother of

Nicole, Hafina and Morgan Rhys

Followed by a verse, what would it mean to that stranger? Perhaps something trivial such as, 'Same name as me' or, 'Unusual – Cherie', or 'Same age as me now.'

I felt I would rather Cherie disappeared with me, her loved ones and her friends, than be reduced to a passing whimsical thought cast in stone. NO MORE. I thought how lucky we all are to occupy our slot in time. We're not there, then we are, then we're gone again. We shouldn't complain when we reach the end of our slot. Yes, Cherie was only forty-one and although the average is longer, for many it is shorter. I was thankful for the eleven years I shared with her.

At about nine miles into the day's trip, a lucky coincidence befell me. I passed through a hamlet/village called Finstown on the southern edge of a sheltered reach of water called Wide Firth. There was a small car park and a sign indicating the presence of a tourist information plaque. The sun was shining, my bum was slightly pained and mildly protesting, but other than that, everything was fine. I wasn't pushed for time, so I thought I would pull in to look at the plaque and give my backside a rest. It didn't tell me much, although the map showed me the location of the ferry terminal in Stromness (not that it would have been difficult to find in such a small place – even for me). The lucky coincidence was that I just happened to look over the bolt on my back rack. I had checked it, with increasing infrequency, since the motor spares man in Guisborough had told me the locking washer would do the trick. And it had, until now. But somehow the bolt had become almost completely unscrewed and as in Scarborough, if it had come undone at speed, the arm of the rack would have fouled the back wheel, sticking into the spokes and God knows what. I tightened the screw with my inadequate multi-screwdriver that I had surprisingly located fairly quickly in a side pocket of my rucksack.

As I pedalled on, somewhat relieved at my near miss, I had a recurrence of the pleasant and benevolent thought that Cherie was hanging around for a while to look after me. The idea had first come to me pushing my bike over the Forth Road Bridge in that ethereal light of early evening.

My mind ran on:

'What if Cherie was up there and we could meet up again when my turn came?' A common belief I know. The train of thought developed.

'What if you could meet only your own loved ones in eternity – or what if you were just able to pick one. Cherie would pick me – I know.' My mind turned to the following day. Day twenty-three. I had more or less made up my mind that I would camp rough at the far end of Unst, the most northerly point of Shetland and the British Isles. I had given up the idea of throwing my bike off a lonely cliff top in a supreme gesture of triumph and anger. Apart from the pollution element, I had become very attached to my trusty steed. Not only that, if I chucked this one, I would have to buy another. I also felt that I now wanted to keep this particular bike forever. When I eventually got a new one, I would still maintain it as a backup. But I still thought I needed a grand gesture to mark the end of my quest.

'What about throwing my severely worn and scruffy 4x4 ex-squash trainers into the sea?' They had been my saviour on this trip. Now, for the first time, they were strapped onto the outside of the rucksack, swapping places with the Jesus sandals I had bought in Stamford. Today, with the good weather and still with a plaster in place, I felt fairly confident I could use the sandals for walking and cycling ... so the trainers were at last becoming expendable. I had inserted a pair of no longer white sports socks into each trainer in case my confidence in the sandals turned out to be ill founded. The idea grew. I would throw the right one for me and the sock could go too ... the extra weight would make it go further. The left would be for Cherie. She was always on my left. She walked, sat and slept on my left and she rarely forgot about my deaf right side. However, I did feel a little guilty about polluting such a remote and I imagined, beautiful coastline, by such a frivolous act. But then again, I didn't really think it was a frivolous act – it was very important to me.

The germ of another idea emerged. I could picture my lone tent, either a safe distance from a cliff top overlooking the vast northern sea, or above the storm line of a beach watching the white surf crashing in, and I could see me in there in total isolation, left completely to my own thoughts.

'Highland Park whiskey – I could buy a bottle, get a glass and polish off the lot in a huge solitary toast to my Cherie.' It was settled – the cycle up to the north of Shetland, the location of my journey's end, and the rituals. My ultimate destination would find me, on my own with my memories and perhaps on a heightened emotional plane – courtesy of Highland Park.

Dropping down into Stromness, I coasted past the ferry terminal that I had seen on the tourist map in Finstown. I wheeled up the main drag and bought two postcards – one for Hafina and one for Yogi. In a café, I ordered a baked potato with tuna and mayonnaise and, for once, was a good boy resisting the chips. Again, I copied Cherie as I mixed hot with cold - the hot potato with the cold coleslaw, lettuce, tuna and tomato. It was all washed down with a big mug of hot coffee - very enjoyable. I wandered around looking for a pub and found one opposite the ferry terminal. Locking the bike to some railings, I adjusted all the straps on my rucksack and turned it, for the first time on the trip, back into a rucksack proper that I could carry on my back. In the pub, I rummaged through my rucksack to find a normal set of clothes, and then slipped off to the toilet, still dressed like a geeky cyclist but soon to return in my new costume like Superman.

I finished off a pint of Guinness and repacked my rucksack, and then left the pub, now walking with the bike left locked to the railings, to see if I could buy a bottle of Highland Park whiskey. It wasn't difficult finding the required brand on its home territory so I accomplished my mission quickly. However, I still needed to acquire a glass. I didn't want to buy four so I gave up looking and returned to 'The Ferry' pub to write up the day's journal and kill some time – it was hours before the ferry sailed so I needed to watch my drinking. By ten to eight I had drunk three pints of Guinness, which was reasonably slow by my standards - I had started at quarter past five – good boy. I went to the bar to order another pint of rather expensive Guinness.

The barman asked, 'Anything else, Sir?'

'Actually, yes,' I replied, after a pause that allowed a thought into my head. 'I've got a bit of a strange request.' I told him that I was on a cycle trip from South Wales and I described my plan to drink some Highland Park when I got to the end.

'So, I need a whiskey glass. I can't drink Highland Park single malt from a plastic thermos flask cup. I don't mind paying.'

He replied, 'I think I've got just the job downstairs in the cellar. I'll get it while I'm on my break in about twenty minutes. If I forget, remind me!'

The kind barman didn't need a prompt. He brought it to me at my table after just ten minutes, safely cosseted with tissue and packed up in a plastic bag. I thanked him profusely and waited until he had gone before I took a peek, like receiving a birthday present and wanting to avoid the embarrassment of showing your reaction –

surprise, delight, disappointment or worst of all mock delight. It was a plain whiskey glass with an inscription on one side which read: *Classic Malts of Scotland*. Perfect.

I suddenly noticed the time – bugger, I was cutting it fine for the ferry. I hurriedly made my way back to where the bike was locked to the railings, half expecting to have lost the key – what then? The ferry terminal building wasn't obvious either – it had 'Tourist Information' written on it. I made the mistake of thinking I could get straight on to the ship with my ticket. I couldn't. I was directed back to Tourist Information where I eventually found the P & O desk and traded my ticket for a boarding pass. Pushing the bike with the rucksack on my back was easy so that was good news as far as getting around train stations on the way home was concerned. Once on the ferry, I picked up my cabin key from reception and went to change and shower. I was very impressed with the shower, even if it was tucked into a tiny corner of the toilet.

Wandering around the ship, I soon ended up in the bar. I sat on my own with a pint and a cigar for about an hour, happily lost in my own thoughts. I noticed a small group of people sat in a corner not far from me. I couldn't hear what they were saying but they seemed to be friends and they were having a good time chatting, smoking, drinking and laughing. I decided to end my quiet period and invited myself into the group. There were four of them; one chap in his twenties called Brian, was an Open University student studying environmental science who worked part-time as a fisherman. He was with his girlfriend who had a hairdressing business on Unst, Shetland's most northerly island, although she lived on Yell, the island to the south. Clive, in his thirties, worked as an engineer on the ferries, and the fourth, Allan, told me he was a teacher.

'What do you teach?' I asked.

'Everything,' came the reply. I looked at him quizzically.

He elaborated with a slight air of smugness, 'Biology, history, maths, physics, geography, technology, computers, English, religious studies – you name it.'

'So you're a supply teacher?' I quickly interjected.

Allan didn't know that I was a teacher in a comprehensive school and it was easy for me to surmise correctly that he must be on supply - not a subject specialist at all. Maybe he was a failed teacher who had been prised from a permanent post and was now forced to baby-sit in any school where there was a shortage of staff. I could have been wrong but I was mildly pleased to have taken the wind out of his sails a little bit. He was from Keighley and he was moving to the Shetland Islands, disillusioned with life in urban England and all its associated problems. He had a distinctive appearance – quite old, sixty in fact, with long grey hair that was tied into a ponytail. Fairly slim and wearing the jeans and leather waistcoat you might expect to see on a younger man, he was on a reconnaissance trip looking for a house, before bringing his girlfriend up to live with him. It was an unusual situation to say the least – she had never seen the Shetlands and was taking her boyfriend's word that it would be OK. Also, in her early thirties, she was the same age as Allan's daughter.

We chatted for a couple of hours and I soon switched to Highland Park, aware that I didn't want to disturb the person I was sharing a cabin with in the middle of the night as I clambered down for a pee. In addition to being a multi-disciplined teacher, Allan was also an erstwhile clairvoyant. He read tarot cards too and divined for objects other than water (although he did water as well). He told us a string of tales that all proved, conclusively, that the future could be foretold. In addition, he was a counsellor and he helped people through 'Rites of Passage' as he put it – people who were dying or bereaved. Clive, the ferry mechanic, was as sceptical as I, and he pleasantly put Allan through hoops, asking questions and probing for more information with what was my first hearing of a Shetland accent. It was a Scottish accent but discernibly different. We had a good time sitting there in the corner, chatting, exchanging stories and telling jokes. Allan had plenty to say for himself, and Clive and I enjoyed some provocative banter with him as he espoused his magical divining powers.

'Listen to this - here's proof that divining works.' We waited for the story.

'Once I lost a copper bracelet. I knew it was in the house somewhere so I got my divining rods and concentrated ... COPPER, COPPER, COPPER. I went through every room in the house – nothing. Then suddenly, after two hours, I was in my bedroom – bang! The rods moved. I had to pull up the carpet but ... guess what I found under the carpet?' Nobody spoke.

'Not a bracelet, but some old coins ... made of copper. You know what I did wrong?' Nobody answered.

'I concentrated on COPPER instead of COPPER BRACELET.' Silence ... a pause ... for a few long seconds to be abruptly broken by Clive.

'If I looked around my house for two hours I'd find some bleedin' coppers too!'

Everyone fell about laughing; in fairness to Allan, he took it all in good humour.

I came back from the bar and found that the conversation had turned to the subject of dying young. Brian and Clive were describing how three people they knew had all died young – forty-one (the same as Cherie) was the only age given. The first fell off his pushbike riding home from a Hogmanay. He suffered head injuries and his life support machine eventually had to be switched off. The second had a brain tumour and the third discovered he was 'riddled with cancer', surprising the doctors by not responding to treatment at all and dying within weeks. As the subject had come up, I told my companions about Cherie. I was slightly taken aback by their lack of surprise. It seems they had been discussing me earlier as I sat alone. As my thoughts took me off I may well have looked sad at times.

Brian, the penniless student, kindly bought me a drink as last orders were announced.

I entreated, 'No, no! It's my turn, I won't be able to buy you one back!'

'Don't worry – it's OK, we're not into all that shit.'

We carried on chatting and were turfed out at one o'clock.

The Ride:

Kirkwall (Orkney Isles) to Lerwick (Shetland Isles)
Distance: 17 miles (land)

Lerwick to Hermaness

Wednesday, July 25th

Six thirty and the bloke on the premiere bottom bunk had set his alarm. I dozed while he used the broom cupboard bathroom to sort himself out. It felt quite odd to be sharing a room, in itself an intimate experience, with someone I had not spoken to or even seen. I had heard him breathing and later snoring but he was already in bed by the time I had turned in and now he was still a mystery man as he readied himself for the day. I waited until he had gone, then went to tackle my rucksack. It was partly unpacked from the night before, only because the bath bag had been at the very bottom. I now had to rifle through it once more to find clean cycling gear. As the ferry sailed into the port of Lerwick, I satisfied myself with just a coffee, planning to take the advice of the Shetland boys from the night before and picking up a Co-op breakfast on terra firma.

Oddly, I didn't feel any real elation or excitement as I walked off the ferry. I was more concerned with practicalities. How did I get away from the ferry terminal? The cars seemed to be taking a circuitous route following white lines that seemed to go the wrong way. I suddenly noticed a sign,

Foot Passengers

With the rucksack on my back, I pushed the bike through a Perspex-covered tunnel that brought me out onto my first Shetland road. It was about eight o'clock and it was surprisingly busy – Shetland rush hour. My rucksack straps all had to be readjusted so they would fit safely on to the back of the bike. I did experimentally try to cycle off with the rucksack on my back, but as I went to cock my leg over the crossbar I very nearly fell over like some circus clown. So it was back to plan A.

My next concern was: 'Where's the Co-op?'

I sensed that the town centre must be to the left and was relieved to see the superstore just a few hundred yards down the road. Clive, the ferry engine fitter, was in there already, and Allan came in later, but I sat on my own.

'No greater love than the love between two drunks ... was that the saying?' It was strange how, having gelled so well the night before, now in the sober light of day, we were almost strangers. Clive was with his wife and kids and I didn't want to intrude. Allan came in as I sat alone but content – he didn't want to intrude ... he must have read my mind! Even so, we all acknowledged each other with a nod or a smile and that suited me - I was happy to sit by myself and generally think about my day.

The weather was overcast but dry and I backtracked past the ferry terminal as directed by the road sign,

North Isles

'That's for me.' Perhaps reaching John O'Groats was *the* big achievement and this was now the icing on the cake. I just didn't feel jubilant now. There was a huge hill out of Lerwick towards the north. It went on for miles and the first part was really steep.

As I walked, taking care to ease the pace, I remembered my vow to get to the top ... *For Cherie*, and I spoke to her silently, 'Today is for you, Dear ... <u>*definitely*</u> for you ... I have wondered so many times why I have done this trip but today is for you.'

At one point, I suspected that I had come the wrong way. It wouldn't have been the first time. I knew the wind was southerly and now it was hitting me in my left ear – I was heading west. I checked the compass and it was confirmed. Stopping and keeping one hand on the brake, I twisted around awkwardly to check the map pinned under the bungees behind me and was relieved to see a section of about three miles where the road looped around before heading off north, so I hadn't made a mistake after all. The sky began to get brighter and I could make out an embryonic shadow in front of me, confirming that my heading was now northerly once more. The landscape was hilly, perhaps mountainous, would be more accurate, but mountainous in the South Wales, rather than the Alpine sense - there were no sharp edges or bare rocks. The cloak was a blanket of heather underlain by peat, which alternated with polygons of pastureland. It was not as green as Orkney but the relief was much stronger.

I stopped at the beginning of what I didn't know then was another really long hill. A sign had caught my eye:

Shetland Golf Club

I took a photo looking across a deep inlet with clusters of fish farms, and I made sure that I had the Shetland Golf Club sign in the foreground.

'It proves I've been here!'

I had been a bit disappointed that there had not been a 'Welcome to Shetland' sign as I came off the ferry. I had thought that I might get a friendly looking passer-by with time to spare, to shoot a whole roll of film of me and the bike by the sign. I could then get them developed at a one-hour processing shop and use the prints as postcards. It was not to be though – there was no signpost.

I nonchalantly thumbed the button on the bike computer to see the number of miles travelled so far. It read 899. As I pedalled slowly up the everlasting incline at 6 mph, I once more impishly watched the digital display to see the 900 come up … and watched … and watched, a steep bank rising to my left and a metal crash barrier guarding the steep fall to the inlet, both only visible in my peripheral vision as I concentrated on the LED, only occasionally chancing a look at the road ahead.

'Shouldn't it be the other way around - watch the road ahead and look at the computer from time to time?' The inlet to my right was not named on my map, which had changed scale for the Shetlands and now gave less detail.

'Bit prejudicial against the Shetland Islanders,' I mused. Nevertheless, to the northwest was another inlet called Dales Voe that was becoming ever more impressive with my increasing altitude and the strengthening sunshine. But still I looked at the trip counter. I felt so guilty about missing the views that I stopped a number of times and crossed the road to take in the vista and photograph it, knowing that the trip meter couldn't flick on if the bike was stationary. A long gash of water, maybe a quarter of a mile wide, stretched ahead of me then turned right, out into the open sea where semi-lens islands looked like a family of green hippos' backs in the distance. The road was not a solid grey tarmac, but a conglomerate of different colours that started to make my eyes go funny as it seemingly sped beneath my fixed gaze on the computer – still reading 899.

I realised, 'At 6 mph this could take some time.' But the longer it went on, the more determined I was not to miss it. And I didn't.

Of course it was a bit of an anti-climax, but I still clenched my fist and growled triumphantly, 'Yesssssss!'

Near the top of the hill a few bunches of flowers had been laid on the bank to my left. I was tempted to stop to read the cards but in the end just pedalled past.

Whoever had recently died at that spot never got the chance to say, 'Goodbye', 'I love you', or, 'I want so and so to have this and so and so to have that', or, 'I want my funeral to be ...'

'Be grateful for small mercies,' I thought.

As I looked around me, I noticed lots of small cliff-like features, just two feet or so high, cut into the ground and disrupting the smooth contours of the slopes. They might have been the result of the small landslides that create terracettes, but that didn't make sense. I soon realised that they were the work of peat cutters. This was confirmed later, when I saw the peat laid out in neat little piles waiting to be collected. A bit further again and the peat had been put into plastic bags scattered conveniently ten steps apart, ready for collection. I wondered whether the rights to cut peat had to be bought and decided I would have to look it up.

As I pedalled across Shetland's biggest island, called Mainland, I repeatedly encountered long climbs followed by equally long 'wheees'. For only the second time on the trip, the wind was behind me and giving me a lot of help. Most of the hills I could pedal up and when I got off to walk it was to give my bum, rather than my muscles, a rest. I have to say, the place was quite bleak with just the occasional settlement, and there were only a few places where I could stop off to get even basic supplies like chocolate, Lucozade and pasties. All the same, the expanses of water – bays and lochs, were mightily impressive, just like on Orkney but not so pretty – more rugged. It was twenty-eight miles to the ferry that would take me over to the island of Yell - the half way point for the day's ride. I had left Lerwick at about nine and I actually got to the Yell ferry at one o'clock.

A couple of miles before that I happened upon a rare shop – wow! I wasn't going to miss the opportunity. I bought two bottles of Lucozade, one for now and one for later, two bars of chocolate and a strange pie that contained baked beans under a layer of mash topped with melted cheese. I wasn't hungry but I felt I should line my stomach as much as possible, knowing I would be hitting the Highland Park whiskey later on. It was quite windy and I realised how much help I must have been getting. I needed to find a place in the lee of the breeze but the shop was small, not much more than a port-a-cabin. I was grateful when a young girl came out of the shop and untied her dog (more a rat on a rope) from a drainpipe that was occupying the spot with the best shelter from the wind. I quickly took up the prime spot and my appetite kicked in with the first mouthful.

I enjoyed the mish-mash meal then wind assisted, headed down the gradient towards Toft to catch the boat across to Yell. As I bowled down the hill with the expanse of the sea to my right and swinging in front of me as I changed course, I could see the channel separating Mainland from Yell. It wasn't that wide a channel and half way across, I could make out the shape of a small ferry. As I watched it I could see it inexorably closing on my island. I wasn't sure if I could make out the terminal but I put on a spurt, not wanting to have to wait to catch the next shuttle. Although the ferry beat me to the terminal, I still had plenty of time to embark.

I pushed my bike over the metal drawbridge and spoke to the deck hand, 'Where do I put it?'

'Stick it anywhere ... stick it there.'

So I did – propped against a metal wall at the bottom of a stairway that led to the upper deck. A man came to collect the fare and I was quite surprised how cheap it was from a tourist's perspective – only £1.30. I was sure the locals that used the boat every day wouldn't agree. They might say it should be subsidised by the government – is it their fault that they live on a remote island? On the car deck I talked to a motor biker for a while. Of all things, his Suzuki GSX 1100 was loaded with building supplies he had picked up in Lerwick. It seemed a strange mode of transport for carrying such things but I could identify with his desire to ride rather than drive.

The weather by now was beautiful and the sea was blue-blue. It took me a minute or so to explore the boat and I wondered where everyone was. There were at least six cars on the ferry but no people except for one elderly man who was in the 'lounge'. This wasn't a room but more a small passage with a few seats that, at least, was undercover and protected from the elements. I went back outside and looked down upon the cars below.

'Silly bugger!' I admonished myself. All the missing people were in their cars, reading papers, smoking fags or presumably, listening to the radio. I found a spot out of the chill wind and enjoyed the crossing until the motor biker signalled to me from the car deck then shouted up to tell me that my bike had fallen over. The boat had made quite a sharp turn as it manoeuvred itself to come in to land stern first. It was then that my bike must have toppled. I made my way down the steel stairway to sort it out. The motor biker had kindly propped the bike back up but the rucksack was hanging off the side suspended by its shock cords. I tried to manhandle the load back into position but it was just too heavy. I had to release all the elastics and start to load back up from scratch.

I set off north again, across the second island of the three I hoped to cross during the day. The road took the west side of Yell and after a climb it offered me beautiful views across the sea to my left. I could see the flames burning in the sky as the tall towers of the Sullom Voe oil refinery broke the line of hills behind me on Mainland. The watery world looked beautiful in the sunshine - a mat of calm blue gently disturbed by small islands here and there. Some of these were connected to western Yell by man-made causeways that I assumed must have been built to provide access to the pastures there. I passed a lone garage on my right that had me puzzled for a while. It was a single householder's garage but there was no house. Then I figured it out. There was a house some way down the slope towards the sea to my left but it had no drive or track. Presumably, in the winter it would be hard enough to keep the main road open, let alone a track down a fairly steep hill. What was the point in having your car near your house if you couldn't get to the road?

Yell was not as rugged as Mainland; but, as far as the roads were concerned, it was – interminable, but pedallable up, and freewheelable down. I had been told there was a café on Yell near the ferry crossing to Unst and I was looking forward to finding it. After seventeen miles crossing the island I was relieved to see it. I was quite surprised that it was a sizeable place with plenty of seats and tables, not an architectural masterpiece of modern art, nor a quaint converted croft – just a fairly modern functional unit. Two women worked there and one served me up a rectangle of pizza that might have been more at home in a set of Lego. Fortunately, the two cups of coffee

I had to accompany it were much better. Fuelled up, I went outside to wait for the ferry in the now glorious sunshine of mid-afternoon. Clambering down to the water's edge to get out of the wind, I set the camera to self-time and took a photo of myself.

Crossing Bluemull Sound, no more than half a mile, from Gutcher on Yell to Belmont on Unst, and with an estimated ten miles to go, I felt that journey's end was in sight. I made sure to steady the bike as we came in to land and crossed the threshold on to Unst – the beginning of the end. Pedalling ever-nearer towards my northerly goal, the weather remained uncharacteristically beautiful colouring the bays, inlets and lochs dark blue. The bright sun caused my pedalling silhouette to dance before me and I could see my shoulders and hips moving rhythmically from side to side on the tarmac ahead.

I had been told in the café that there was a post office in Baltasound, just a few miles away from where I wanted to finish up. I sought it out and found that not only was there a post office, but also a fully stocked and licensed shop. I had unsuccessfully tried to buy cigars at the café earlier. I had also hoped to get a couple of beers. Although I had my full bottle of Highland Park, I really wanted to puff a few cigars and I needed beer to counter the rasping effect of the cigars on my throat. The shop at Baltasound was able to supply all my needs – what luck! I also picked up twenty postcards from the post office and tried, unsuccessfully to get bulk discount from the ladies behind the counter – my jaunty failure allayed by the inevitable banter. I was already carrying bottled water that I had picked up at the café, so with the two of those, plus choccy, bread, Lucozade, a full flask of water and two tins of beer, the weight on my bike was appreciably increased and as I cycled off I felt even more unstable than usual. In fact, it had taken me ages to attach all the new peripherals – there were bits hanging off everywhere and the whole lot slewed from side to side as I cycled along, wobbling, clanking and sloshing in time like an overburdened Mexican mule.

Up the hill from Baltasound I came to a bus maintenance depot to inquire about bus times back to Lerwick the next day. There was bad news though.

'You won't be able to take your bike on the bus.'

The man in the overalls continued, 'The bus might be pretty empty when you get on here in Unst but by the time you get near Lerwick it'll be packed.'

Three others joined in a full scale debate on the subject. In the end, one of the older hands cut across the others, 'You'll be OK to take your bike – I'm on tomorrow morning.'

I assumed that once I was on the bus with my bike, no one was going to kick me off. Brilliant!

'What time do the buses run?'

'There's only one – 7.40.' I made a provisional arrangement with the driver to meet at 7.40 at the bottom of the hill.

As I pedalled along what I hoped would be the last leg of my epic journey, I turned west and came into the wind. The road became single track with passing places here and there – one car passed, typically just as I had stopped for a pee in a hedge. As I wheeled the bike to the top of a steep section, a long blue inlet came into view – this was Burrafirth and it stretched for about four miles to the north and flanked my ultimate goal – the peninsula of Hermaness the most northerly point of Shetland, indeed Britain. I carried on around as the road started to climb on to the Hermaness headland. Waiting for the ferry back on Yell, I had read an information board telling of the six hundred foot cliffs of the Herma Ness nature reserve. So I knew I might have a climb in store because I was now at little more than sea level. I looked across the deep blue voe and marvelled at the crescent of deserted sand that heralded its transition to land. A quarter of a mile on and the road ended completely in a car park. Up ahead, I could see walkers returning down a steep footpath to their cars. I asked a middle aged lady hiker about the route ahead.

'It's a three quarters of an hour walk to the headland, and it's a tapestry of heather.'

I looked around the car park – where could I lock up the bike? I wasn't going to be able to push it, over laden as it was, across this rough terrain. I noticed a semi-rusted lorry trailer that looked as if it hadn't been used for some time. Perhaps I could hide the bike up behind the trailer on the bank.

'What a strange place to be conscious of crime.' Back in South Wales, it is the most remote of places that have become prime targets for small-time criminals. They know that cars are going to be left for hours and that their chances of being caught are very slim. Maybe here was the same? I told the lady hiker of my intentions to camp.

'It's *very* soft underfoot,' she said.

That did it. I had reached the end of the road, slightly prematurely perhaps, but I had come far enough.

As I had climbed the last quarter of a mile to this spot, and as I had marvelled at the deserted sandy beach at the end of the Burrafirth gash I had also noticed that behind the beach was a flat valley bottom, about five hundred yards wide with a small river, just two yards wide meandering across it. I had considered camping on the beach, and from my high vantage point above the bay, I had tried to pick out a route to it. The wind was still blowing hard from the south and out along the inlet towards the North Pole. It was in my face as I retraced my route away from the car park and southward. I decided that the beach would probably be too windy but, as I descended back towards the flood plain, I could see the ideal place for a spot I was to name, *'North Camp'*.

It was a hundred yards from the single-track road and on the flood plain facing north. It was also road-side of the river – had I decided on the beach I'd have get across it. Better still, there was a two metre high embankment that would act as a natural windbreak. I descended back down to the flood plain, freewheeling with the brakes on hard. At the bottom of the hill, I dismounted and pushed the bike with its heavy clanking load to North Camp. The ground behind the embankment was perfectly flat, and although the grass was long by campsite standards, the tent would have no problem flattening it down. There were a few cow pats dotted around, seemingly dry, but I sensed that an unsuspecting foot in would surely find moisture.

As I put the tent up I nervously looked around, half expecting someone to come over and shift me.

'Oiye! What d'you think you're doing!'

'Excuse me - you can't camp there!'

'Hey, don't you know you're in a nature reserve.'

I had noticed a visitor centre half a mile away on a narrow road that forked below the car park. A couple of passing car horns sounded. Had they spotted me? Was it a warning?

I decided I wouldn't respond – play deaf. If they wanted me off, they would have to go to the trouble of walking over from the road. And if they went that far, I was still prepared to put up an argument and appeal to their sympathies – play the Cherie card if need be.

In the event nobody disturbed me, and I established camp, throwing everything into the tent to make my presence slightly less conspicuous from the road. I sat amongst the jumble and cracked open my first beer, deciding to leave the Lucozade until the next morning when I would probably need it.

As I started to write my first postcards sat on my camping mat inside the tent, the bright late afternoon sunshine lit up the floodplain before me. As I gazed at the unbridled beauty, my tears fell.

I wrote the same on all the post cards:

'TA DAAA!'

'Made it!'

'I've got a bottle of single malt whisky, and I am drinking a big toast to Cherie (Mom) and remembering good times,

Love,

Tony.'

Every second or third card, the tears would flow again and I had to dig out the tissues from my rucksack. Once the cards were written, I sorted and tidied the tent and got out my sleeping bag. I had arrived at North Camp at about six o'clock and it was now still only seven. Still, I judged it better to get organised now than wait until the malt hit later.

I decided to triumphantly phone a few people but was scotched when I couldn't get a signal on my mobile. In a way I was quite glad. Here I was - on my own. This was the time I had set aside for Cherie. To a small degree writing the postcards had already wasted some of it, although they had served to get me into reflective mood – somewhere I wanted to be. For the same reason, I abandoned the idea of writing up the journal. As I sat there, having poured my first whiskey, puffing on a newly lit cigar and with an open tin of lager in the wings to dampen my tobacco dried palette, I began to speak aloud to Cherie. At first, it seemed a bit strange and I thought I heard the sound of footfall somewhere outside my tent. Being deaf in one ear, I had no idea of where the sound was coming from. On one occasion, I got up to look around but there was no one there. Some cattle had moved into view a few hundred yards away but there was no threat to my little encampment.

The more I talked to Cherie, the more natural it became. At times, I asked her questions, and I answered aloud for her with the replies I knew she would have given:

'Well – we didn't make it to the top of Hermaness after all, Cherie.'

'No, Dear – but it doesn't matter.'

'We wouldn't have wanted to be stuck in a bog on a windswept cliff top, would we?'

'No, Tony. And you've come far enough. You didn't have to come all this way you know.'

'I wanted to. I wanted to *especially* for you.'

'I know. Thank you, Dear. I do appreciate it. I'm glad you're here.'

I cried a lot, as I sat there drinking one glass after another. Each time before I put the glass to my lips, I raised it to toast Cherie:

'Cheers, Dear!' or 'Cheers, Cherie.'

When I forgot, I belatedly raised my glass:

'Cheers, Dear – sorry!' 'Sorry, Cherie.' I didn't forget often, but each time I did I felt genuine remorse.

On one occasion, I toasted the barman back in the Ferry pub in Stromness, as I had promised him I would. He was the one who had so kindly given me the whisky glass that I was now emptying at such frequent intervals. Being so far north it didn't really get dark, but the brightness gradually faded. The only cloud in the sky was a small puff that sat on top of the promontory across the inlet from Hermaness. It just hid the dome of what looked like a missile early warning station – it could just as well have been an observatory. As the temperature began to drop, I thought about closing the entrance to the tent to keep the warmth in – there would be no cosy pub for me this night. But the view was too beautiful, so instead I slipped in to my sleeping bag and pulled it up over my bum. Then I sat drinking whisky, sipping lager, puffing cigars and chatting to Cherie as before, now comfortable as body heat accumulated around my chrysalis lower quarter.

I talked to Cherie all night – a lot of it remembering good times - exactly what I had said I would do on all the postcards I had written earlier. We discussed the bad times as well though and I told Cherie how proud I was of her, in so many different ways. I told her I loved her, but as always, quite sparingly, and then only when I felt that the words would not be choked back by the pain. I told Cherie that earlier, I had considered walking up to the cliffs at the far extremity of Hermaness. After all, I hadn't made it absolutely all the way.

'There's no need, Dear – you've done enough. Stay here and drink your whisky.'

I'm not sure what time it was when exhaustion overtook me. I knew that I didn't want any more to drink even though there were still a few inches of Highland Park left in the bottle.

'You don't have to drink it, Dear. You've done enough – go to sleep.'

So I emptied the remains of the last tin of lager on to the grass and staggered to a fencepost to relieve myself. Back inside the tent I closed the outer flap, slid the sleeping bag up to my armpits and was gone. Cherie had put me to bed.

The Ride:

Lerwick to Hermaness

Distance: 60 miles

North Camp, Hermaness to Lerwick

Thursday, July 26th

After a solid, uninterrupted sleep, I woke at quarter past seven. There was absolutely no way that I would make the bus so I dozed back off. When I awoke again it was quarter past nine. I drank the Lucozade and the bottle of water that was still left and washed down my last ibuprofen and two paracetamol. Uncharacteristically, I didn't bother to assemble the Trangia to make coffee. In fact, I felt OK considering what I had drunk the night before, and I continued talking aloud to myself as well as Cherie. Conversing this way for so many hours had established a strong habit that I felt perfectly at ease with. I loaded up the bike and leaned it against the same fence post I had used for my bedtime pee then scanned once more, the magnificent eye level view across the flood plain with the little brook trickling just a few feet away from me on the other side of the fence. The weather was dry and bright with the sun just starting to get through. I thought about kissing the flattened grass at the spot where the tent had been pitched but feeling a bit foolish, I changed my mind. I hoped I would be able to wheel the bike through the long grass in the direction I wanted to travel but my way was barred as the fence turned to cross my path. Backtracking, I passed once more the flattened grass. On impulse, I leaned my bike against the bank and knelt down to kiss the spot that had marked the end of my ride and had consecrated my reunion with Cherie.

Sadly, I half pushed, half lugged the bike back towards the single-track road that would take me back home. The wind was with me for a while until I turned south for Mainland and Lerwick. Luckily, although it now worked against me once again, it had dropped in strength and wasn't a major problem. I continued talking out loud for an hour or so before I decided that the habit should perhaps now be nipped. I had been happy to keep my thoughts silent throughout the trip and I felt that it would be healthier to do so again. Last night had been different. Last night had been special.

Stopping off at the bus depot as a courtesy, I explained my failure to appear at the bus stop earlier, then freewheeled down to the post office in Baltasound to send the postcards. As the miles started to disappear behind me, I reflected on my achievement. The end was not as I had imagined it. No euphoric hurling of my bike off the cliffs; no screams to vent pent up feelings of anger or triumph; and, no hurling of my old trainers, right for me and left for Cherie, into the sea. Last night, looking over the floodplain from my campsite, I had already dispensed with all these options. However, I could see the brook meandering down towards its mouth in the bay, and I had thought I might gently launch my trainers, and lose them, like Hans Christian Andersen's paper boat in the gutter.

But once more I had heard Cherie telling me, 'No need, Dear – you've done enough.'

I don't know why I had felt compelled to actually lose something at the end of my ride. It was an idea I had loosely planned, but I hadn't rationalised why I should want to leave something behind. Maybe, it was a metaphor for Cherie dying – losing her, as people would say. Perhaps I wanted to leave something personal of mine at the place I had been thinking about ever since I first discussed the Shetland trip with Cherie. I – we, had got there together, and I wondered when I left whether I would be leaving a bit of Cherie at that spot. Back home, I had given her no grave or stone; no plaque or sapling and there had been no scattering of ashes on wind or water. Just gently laid under a mantle of thin soil in our garden to leach away before the spring. But to me, that spot – North Camp, would stay in my mind and my soul, and if I ever were to go back there, I think a part of Cherie would be there to greet me. I think I wanted to leave something of mine to stay with that something of her. I'm sure she would have liked the sentiment but would have fired some snarky comments at my choice of fall-apart trainers from a bygone era of squash playing.

But now cycling along, it did give me a feeling of self-righteousness to think I hadn't polluted that beautiful place. All that remained of my presence was a small patch of flattened grass, and, I suppose if you rooted in the blades, a sprinkling of ash from four cigars. The quarter finished fourth cigar had lain damp in the foyer of the tent as I had packed the rubbish into a plastic bag that now, considerably lighter than before, sat proudly atop the other paraphernalia that was bungeed to the top of my rucksack, ready for the bin, three and a half miles away at the shop where it had all been bought the previous day.

The traffic on Unst, Thursday morning, was light, in fact, occasional would be a better description. I threw away my pride and stuck my thumb out at every vehicle I heard approaching from behind. I understood that hitch hiking these days was not nearly as easy as it used to be. Now, with my bike and its gargantuan load, I must have looked a sight from behind and I could only imagine the comments from two old ladies in a mini when they saw my hitch hiker thumb out. I had to carefully time the sticking out of my thumb – once I took one hand off the handlebars, my balance went and I became dangerously unstable. So I had to get the gesture out in time for people to see what I wanted, but not leave it until I was falling under their wheels as I grabbed for the safety of my handlebars. After a while, I decided that I needed to be more serious about getting a lift. This meant stopping when I heard a vehicle approaching and, together with the standard thumbing action, turning my head to face the motorist. In the highly unlikely event that there would be enough space for myself, my bike and all my gear, I hoped eye contact might be made, and wishfully prayed that pity might be duly taken upon me. Ironically, I couldn't tell whether any prospective vehicle was going to have space for me until it had almost passed. The front view didn't give much of a clue as to how much room there might be at the back, and tinted front windows didn't allow me to see if there were any passengers in with the driver. The result was, at the last second just as the vehicle passed me, I would see to my horror and embarrassment that it was a two door saloon car with four people all looking out at me incredulously – and not as I had imagined, a van, completely empty and just the driver on board. I didn't really care though.

'It should give them a laugh and maybe brighten their day.' I chuckled to myself every time one of these lost causes passed me by.

My first real chance came as a Land Rover approached – just a solitary driver on board. But he sharply threw up both his hands in a gesture that I didn't understand as he passed by without slowing – in effect, NO! As I climbed a gentle hill, feeling steady resistance on the pedals, a lone pedestrian came into view in the distance. It took me some time to reach a middle-aged woman with orangey coloured hair called Elizabeth. What a chatterbox (by her own description) she was. I stopped to talk to her and she told me how she was hitch-hiking to Burravoe in the south-east of Yell twenty miles south and across the water.

'I never use my thumb,' she explained. 'People just know me and stop. Shetland is not like Orkney you know - the road you are on usually only goes to one place. So people know where you are going.' Nearly everyone knew everyone on Unst - only 850 people lived there. Even so, not everyone would give Elizabeth a lift.

She told me in a completely English accent and a slightly high-pitched voice,

'It's a convenient way of dividing people up: those that give you a lift and those that don't.' A car passed by.

'There goes one of the snobby ones.'

She explained how she lived on Unst but had been unable to get a job as a midwife or district nurse because of prejudice against her – she couldn't even get to the interview stage. She had worked as a midwife on Orkney in the past and said that she was married to 'a humble man' who I think she said was a driver. Elizabeth certainly was chatty and, in the end, I had to rudely ride off in order to get away from her. Undeterred, she carried on talking to me even as I cycled away up the long hill.

As she went out of earshot, her last audible words were, 'If I get a lift in a lorry I'll tell him to stop for you!'

It was a nice thought. I really didn't want to be cycling any more – I had achieved what I had set out to do - this was now over and above. To emphasise the point, the wind blew hard against me making the terrain seemed hillier than it had on the outward leg. Like so many times before on the trip, I was pedalling down hills that should have been 'wheees' and walking up hills that I should have been able to pedal. I started to get a pain in my shoulder as a result of regularly trying to glance backwards in the hope of seeing a truck, van, pick-up or estate car. I couldn't rely on my hearing picking up their engines, because the oncoming wind blew the sound back towards them and away from me. Once again, I tried thumbing on the hoof as I heard them in the last few seconds before they overtook me, but figured that they probably thought I was joking. So I decided to stop and look them in the eye again, but only one or two cars passed in the half hour that I tried this ploy.

It was such hard going now and my heart was no longer in the challenge. In the end I gave up trying to hitchhike altogether and pinned my hopes on meeting someone waiting for the ferry. As I rolled down the hill to the little jetty at Belmont, I could see that I was about to miss the ferry to Yell. Luckily for me, the ferryman re-lowered his gate to allow me on board. As I wheeled my bike on to the boat, Elizabeth was there, standing on the deck and watching me. She had managed to get a lift - picked up by a district nurse. The nurse was still sitting in her car and I asked Elizabeth why she had got out.

'She didn't ask me if I wanted to go further and I would never ask – I just accept lifts. In any case I love walking, especially when the weather's nice.' She was headed for a gift shop that had a small gallery and sold a mixture of odds and sods.

'Not the sort of shop you find in town - I love it there. If you want to go there, it's called (so and so) and you have to take the ...' She continued to talk at me for the duration of the short crossing and still jabbered on as we walked up the hill from the terminal to the café where I had eaten the greasy Lego pizza the day before. The one-sided conversation was mercifully cut short as Elizabeth realised she had left her rucksack on the ferry. She didn't seem in too much of a rush as she plodded back down the hill and must have known that the ferry would be back in half an hour if she didn't make it. I don't think she was working to a tight schedule that day.

I went into the café, secretly hoping to accost the owner of a minibus that was parked up outside. Unfortunately, the owner wasn't in the café. As I waited for a very welcome mug of coffee, my first of the day, and two bangers in a bap, a young plumber came in, so I accosted him instead. He had a van and he was going south but only for a few miles. I later reflected it might have been an error of judgement to turn down a lift, but it didn't seem worth the effort of unpacking the load, only to have to assemble it all again in a few minutes time. I asked him about his life on Shetland and was quite surprised to discover he visited the mainland quite regularly. He didn't seem that impressed and said he got bored after a couple of days. I wondered how he could find Britain boring after a couple of days when he lived on Shetland, where there had to be far less on offer for someone of his age. I later realised that his mainland was Mainland Shetland and not mainland Britain. I imagine that Shetlanders might consider it insulting to call Scotland, England or Wales, 'The Mainland'.

The bangers in the bap were thankfully better than the pizza and I enjoyed my rest from physical exertion. As I left, I glanced around for signs of the minibus man to no avail. Setting off up the hill, I passed Elizabeth, who was now engaged in a conversation with a householder over a garden wall – no doubt the job they had been doing would be on hold for some time. Despite her talkative nature, Elizabeth was a very warm and pleasant character.

The miles stretched ahead of me. I didn't want them to. The ups outweighed the downs in an unfair fight with the wind taking sides. Forlornly, I stopped to stick out a joking thumb, and, at last, a Land Rover pulled in. The kind woman quickly realised, at the same time as I, that her short wheel based version of the old Brit workhorse wouldn't take my bike. If there had been any doubt, the large retriever panting on the other side of the window sealed it. The dog may or may not have been friendly but I was certain that a handle bar in its testicles would have done nothing to cement a bond between us. We nodded in mutual agreement, and, as we both saw the hopelessness of the situation, a car pulled up behind with two kids in the back. It was Clive, the ferry fitter and fellow mystic sceptic who lived on Yell. He wound down the passenger window and leaned across.

'So, you made it then?'

'Yep!' I thanked the Land Rover lady, and as she drove off, I chatted with Clive for a while, before shaking hands and saying farewell. A nice guy – it was a shame he wasn't headed for Lerwick and unfortunate that he had the kids or he might have taken pity on me and given me a ride. I had no further offers of lifts, but as I doggedly persisted in my efforts, I'm sure I must have continued to raise smiles on the faces of motorists as they passed me by. I saw a yellow bin lorry on a couple of occasions. He looked as if he was doing the rounds and I mused about the chances of getting a lift with him. If any sort of journey was likely to be local it was that of a bin man. So when the same lorry caught up with me a mile from the ferry to Mainland, I didn't even bother to hoist my thumb. I pedalled on, up and up and up until, at last I got my reward – the 'wheee' down to the ferry at Ulsta. Nearing the bottom, a man and a woman on a tandem with a trailer full of luggage passed the other way.

'Will they make it up this hill without walking?' I doubted it. As I pulled into the car park, there were a few cars waiting for the ferry, and the bin lorry.

'No I can't,' crossed my mind as I hobby horsed my bike to the passenger side of the wagon where the bin man was eating his packed lunch. He realised I wanted a word because I had pulled up right next to the glass of his window. I don't think the window worked, because I had to reverse then leg myself forward again as he opened his door.

'How far south you going?'

'Lerwick.' Not a local after all.

'Any chance of a lift for me and the bike?'

'Hmmm...' He didn't seem sure at all.

After what seemed like an age, he continued, 'Should be able to do it.'

This was followed by something in a strong accent that I couldn't follow, but I had heard the first bit and, as I sat astride the bike, not sure of which way to point or look, I knew I had just poached myself a lift.

'Did he mean for me to get in now, or on the other side of the water. It didn't matter – no more cycling - journey's end - 'Yessssssss!' I was silently elated, like a teenager who has just been told by the instructor that he has passed his driving test. Just after meeting Clive on the road, an hour or so before, a sudden idea had come to me. It was a big 'IF', but if I could get a lift back to Lerwick, I would be in time for the Thursday ferry that sailed directly to Aberdeen, assuming I could change my ticket. This was a much shorter passage than one I had booked on Friday, which stopped off in Orkney on the way. I would be home a day earlier than planned. It was a real possibility now. I was not desperate to spend the night in Lerwick. How many places had I stopped in over the past three and half weeks? It was time to go home.

The bin lorry man clambered down from the cab and went around to the rear of the vehicle to operate some levers that dragged the remains of his last deposit into the bowels of the wagon. In my excitement, I clumsily un-bungeed the rucksack from the bike rack and risked getting a hook in my eye. The bin man picked up my steed and plonked it squarely, right way up, into the back of the truck. It was quite secure and didn't need to be tied down in any way, but the whole of the top half of the bike was in clear view from behind. As I heaved the bulky rucksack into the cab and sat down, I thanked my new travelling companion sincerely - he couldn't have known what his act of kindness had really meant to me. I didn't even have to pay to cross on the ferry. Back on dry land, we chatted from time to time as the familiar landscape of Mainland bumped past us at, what seemed to me after weeks of cycling, lightning speed. Conversation didn't come very easily and I found it difficult to understand the man's strong Shetland accent. I was unsure whether I had been a bit too cheeky in scrounging a lift. Perhaps he was having second thoughts. Whatever, I couldn't see him kicking me out now. I started to ask questions and talk a bit about myself and the social temperature began to warm a little.

'What's your name?' I asked. He started to laugh and I wondered what was going on.

'Jasper!' he exclaimed. It was a bit unusual maybe but not that funny.

'What's wrong with Jasper?'

'It's OK, I suppose,' he said, 'but not over the phone. People always think I'm taking the piss.'

We both laughed together. Jasper wasn't really a bin man at all. He was just filling in for a couple of days for someone who had gone on holiday. In fact, he worked as a mechanic at the bus depot I had visited on Unst. He went on to tell me about his sons and his daughter, most of whom were teachers, and as we sped past he pointed out an isolated bungalow that one of his sons had recently moved in to.

'Out in the country but not too far from Lerwick for work.' Jasper's accent was still hard for me to follow – a third of what he said cut out because he was on my deaf side and another third kidnapped by the drone from the engine. It looked a bleak spot to me, perched by the side of the road half way down the mountainside that led to the deep inlet of Dales Voe far below.

Jasper dropped me off on the outskirts of Lerwick. We had warmed to each other during the forty minute trip and I heaped thanks on him as he lifted my bike out of the back and left me on the pavement to sort out the load. What a nice man. I pedalled back towards the town centre and the ferry terminal and curiously clicked the buttons on the computer – 972miles. What a coincidence. It seemed that on every occasion I thought to check my total distance travelled, I was about to hit a milestone: 200 miles, 400 miles, 900 miles. I had seen the signpost just after Jasper had picked me up:

Lerwick

32 Miles

My last twenty-eight miles in a bin lorry – if I had cycled/walked that last twenty-eight miles it would have made it precisely 1000 miles I would have travelled under my own steam. It didn't bother me. 972 was fine.

There was no problem changing the ferry ticket and I booked to sail at six o'clock. It was only quarter to four, so I set off for Lerwick to have a look around. The main commercial street ran parallel to the road that led to the old harbour with its usual collection of fishing and pleasure boats. Cycling along the road, I inadvertently missed the town centre and ended up wheeling the bike along the main thoroughfare from the far end, back the way I had come. I noted the shops and discovered that Lerwick looked very similar to Kirkwall on Orkney. It too, had paving slabs rather than tarmac surfaces, but the most notable feature was the irregular width of the road with shops jutting higgledy-piggledy into the main thoroughfare. There were no backlit signs topping the commercial premises - all were sign written in the traditional style so it looked as if conservation was a council priority. Although there were no pavements as such, pedestrians dominated with the odd car struggling to get through. I saw a shop advertising half hour film processing and went in to get my last film developed so I could annotate them on the ferry.

Walking the length of the main street, I found a chip shop at the far end. Probably for the last time, I leaned the loaded bike against the window so it would be in full view when I sat down to eat. The place was crowded and quite Spartan in terms of its furniture and décor. I studied the menu and opted for curry and chips as a rowdy threesome of drunken Norwegians came jostling in. They asked the owner for his recommendation and, on his advice, I changed my order to haddock and chips.

'I'm in Shetland for God's sake – I've got to order fish here, of all places.' As my haddock arrived, the loudest Norwegian, who had been unable to get his head around the fact that an unlicensed café could not sell him alcohol, left the chippy and set off to look for some tinned beer. I shouldn't have bothered with the haddock. It was awful – tasteless and covered in oil with the batter cooked to a plank. I struggled through it as a delighted Norwegian came back with two four packs and simultaneously doubled the decibel rating in the room. I was glad to get out of the place and I pushed my bike back the way I had come, still with plenty of time to spare. The film wasn't ready so I looked up a few side streets. In one I saw a sign that read, 'The Lounge Bar'. It was the pub that Douglas, back in Kirkwall, had mentioned. He had told me to look up his mate there.

'Why not,' I thought, so I parked the bike up and went in.

With no time for a proper drink, I asked at the bar, in a voice that was loud enough to carry, 'Anyone know Andy Tulloch?'

The name had been written on a piece of beer mat that I had kept in my bum bag. There were quite a few exchanges from the interested, but typically few, collection of late afternoon drinkers. I was slightly disappointed that total stranger Andy was not there but was pleased when one punter directed me in great detail to his house five minutes away. The overcomplicated instructions had to be repeated, at least in part, a number of times until it was felt I had understood.

Having clocked the directions, another drinker interjected, 'But he's still in work – Bank of Scotland – just around the corner. C'mon, I'll show you!'

I assured the man I could find my way around the corner but he insisted, 'I'm going now anyway.'

I walked into the bank and asked at the open plan desk for Andy Tulloch.

'Do you have an appointment, Sir?'

'No, it's a personal matter.'

'Could I have your name?'

'He doesn't know me.'

They were understandably perplexed and the dialogue was by now, drawing in other members of staff from behind their desks. I wasn't sure if perhaps they thought I had a grudge to settle. I could remember times in my past when I would have happily served a few months (first offence) in prison, for a pop at the demigod that refused to lend me money - it was hard to imagine not being able to borrow money these days. It was becoming clear that the staff were not going to cooperate with me, so I explained how Andy Tulloch's mate had told me to go up to him and call him 'Four Eyes!' There was quite a ripple of laughter and the lady over the counter who initially dealt with me went off to get him - everyone else waited in anticipation. Maybe this was quite an event punctuating the daily grind of banking life – not as exciting as an assault or a raid but still. My lady returned to tell me that he was with a customer. I had to be content with passing a message:

'Tell Andy a stranger with a Welsh accent came in especially to call him 'Four Eyes!' I handed over the piece of paper with his friend's name on it, and had to be satisfied with at least having delivered the message successfully.

I picked up the film and shuffled through the prints before leaving the shop. Not bad, but no free film again – it really did put up the price of taking photos. I pedalled to the ferry but was not allowed to board at five o'clock as I had been promised. Instead, I was directed to wait until all the other vehicles had been loaded. Waiting with me was a Shetland guy on a motorbike and a Dutchman from Amsterdam on a pushbike. The Dutchman had all the luggage imaginable, loaded correctly into pukka panniers on the front and the back wheels of his bike with a veritable tower piled up behind his saddle on the back rack – everything properly balanced. He put me to shame, although my rucksack was now in 'walk mode' with the straps adjusted for it to go on my back. I was hoping that it wouldn't be going on my back rack again. I went over to talk to him. Apart from his impressive cargo, he outdid me in another respect. I had covered 972 miles – not bad, so I thought. He had cycled 1200 miles along the National Cycle Routes from Harwich, and although he had covered some of the same ground as me, he had done it the hard way because the cycle routes were far more tortuous with poorer surfaces and more hills than on the roads.

It was interesting to chat to someone who had similar experiences to me. He had also made it harder for himself by purchasing groceries every day and cooking his own food. I had the impression that he didn't spend nearly as much time or money in the pub as me. He told me an interesting story about certain parts of the National Cycle Route. At fairly regular intervals, steel barriers had been erected to prevent access by motorbikes. My new acquaintance, Matthijs (sort of Mathew he explained), could not fit his juggernaut bike through these barriers and he had to partially unload every time he came upon one – which was every five minutes. There must be a message there for the National Cycle Routes planners. I assumed they were at least partially catering for long distancers like Matthijs, who would of necessity, be carrying lots of baggage.

Smugly I thought, 'That wouldn't have been a problem for me, because all my weight would have been carried high above the level of the barriers, and in any case, my load didn't create any extra width, unlike his pukka panniers.'

Five minutes before sailing, we were finally allowed on to the ferry. The last vehicle - a car towing a big caravan had to gingerly reverse down the ramp without the benefit of extended mirrors – it took forever and having already waited for three-quarters of an hour, I could feel myself losing patience. Once on the ferry, I was pleased to discover that although my cabin was in the bowels of the ship under the car deck, no stranger turned up to share so

I had the place to myself. I partially unpacked my rucksack for the last time, and had a long and much needed shower, before going up to the bar to get a drink and write up my journal. Matthijs turned up after stop tap, confirming my suspicion that he didn't drink. I read my 'Creatures' poem to him because I thought, as a fellow long distance cyclist, he would be able to identify with it. He liked it a lot so I promised to copy it out for him before he disembarked in the morning.

So there was no real craic on my last night - a stark contrast to my evening with the diviner, the fisherman and ferry engine fixer Clive on the outward voyage. Before turning in, I used the top bunk as a rest to copy out the 'Creatures' poem and left it on the floor so I wouldn't forget to give it to Matthijs in the morning. I had a disturbed night's sleep with some drunkards, possibly Norwegian, scampering around the place playing hide and seek.

'Never mind – home soon.'

The Rides:

North Camp, Hermaness to Lerwick
Distance: 60 miles

Back to Merthyr

Friday, July 27th

The next day I pushed the bike off the ferry, rucksack on my back as a rucksack should be, and headed for the train station in Aberdeen. There was only room for two or three bikes on the direct train to Crewe and they had all been booked up. I thought this incredible, given that Aberdeen is a major staging post on the National Cycle Route network. Luckily, there was space for my bike on a Scot Rail route, but I had to change in Glasgow before going on to Crewe where I needed to change again for Cardiff. A Valleys Line link would take me the final twenty miles to Merthyr. I was just in time for the Aberdeen train that left the station 8.42. Rather like Jasper's bin lorry, it seemed strange being on a train watching the world fly past through the window as I tried to keep my sleepy eyes open. There was a panic in Glasgow. No one told me that I had to change stations as well as trains but I managed, with difficulty, to find a rail employee who gave me directions and I made the link with five minutes to spare. After a delay of three quarters of an hour at Crewe and a wait of half an hour in Cardiff, I finally wheeled my bike off the station in Merthyr at nine o'clock in the evening. I couldn't face the palaver of struggling to strap the rucksack on to the bike, so with it on my back, I took fifteen minutes to push the bike across town to the front door of my little terraced house, the place from which I had wobbled at the start of my sojourn.

I was home. It had been just two days since leaving North Camp, a stark contrast to the twenty-three days it took me to pedal and walk to the top of the country.

The Rides:

Aberdeen to Merthyr
Distance: 545 miles

Epilogue

What was it all about? My trip to the Shetland Islands will probably be the most memorable journey I will ever make. I doubt I will ever cycle such a distance again, but you never know. I met a married couple in Provence a few weeks after returning from the Shetlands. I was visiting some friends who had hired a villa not far from Carpentras and I had taken the option to ride down on my motorbike. One day, I decided that I needed solitude once more, so I went for a long walk on my own. On the way back, I passed through a small town and got talking to a couple as I sat in a cafe. By this time I was glad of the company - not only had I been alone for hours, but also there was virtually no English spoken in this part of France. They were from Belgium and they had cycled all the way down to Provence. Before my own cycle trip, I would simply have been impressed, but now I felt a strong affinity with them and I understood the attractions and benefits of their long haul as well as the difficulties and the pain. Their journey gave me the idea of doing a similar trip and it would perhaps only take a suggestion from a friend or group of friends to win me over.

Would I ever again take a trip like that on my own? I doubt it, although there were many occasions when I was not actually alone. Indeed, having made new friends I would have stayed in a number of places longer, were it not for the pressing need to push on the next day. And there can be no doubt that travelling alone led to far more social contact with local people than would have been the case had I travelled as part of a group or even as one of a pair. Then the company would have been 'ready-made' and there would have been no solitude to drive me to mix with strangers. I can see now, as never before, the benefits of travelling alone. Perhaps there is another crisis awaiting me in Chapter 7 of my Life Story. Who knows, I may find that a lone trip to a distant place will again work as a strategy to help me cope.

The ride to the Shetlands was certainly cathartic. I cannot know what it would have been like not to have done it but staying at home would not have provided me with the same set of circumstances or the same theatre. For a start, I had no contact with people I knew save for the brief one-way traffic in postcards and the occasional phone call. And of course, I was able to control the frequency and extent of such contact. This gave me a certain amount of power, in the sense that I didn't have to respond to situations created by visitors calling to the house or incoming phone calls. Naturally, the world provided plenty of stimulus for my thoughts as I made my way north, but somehow these were all a part of *me* in a way that a consoling shoulder to cry on back home was not. I was actively creating scenarios and not just reacting passively.

Similarly, I was not really in a position to watch TV, listen to the radio or even read a newspaper, so the wider world was largely cut out. Nevertheless, I encountered many novel and unfamiliar experiences. Throughout my trip, I was regularly connected to Cherie by all manner of events and I was content to allow my reasoning, memories and feelings to run free. The beauty was that cycling gave me the time and the means to do that and I could just go with the flow - like when I was in Driffield and the women in the bakery brought Cherie so clearly to life.

It was when I met people that I was able to exercise most control, simply because I had the choice whether I told them about Cherie or not. There were many occasions when I did bring the subject up but equally, I often didn't and it was good to be able to be myself rather than playing out the part of a recently bereaved husband. Even when I told strangers about Cherie, it was not the same as talking with people back home. Naturally, most of these were close to Cherie; so, in addition to their commiserations and good wishes, they also brought their own grief. Being away from home allowed me to avoid the symbiotic cultivation of sadness that inevitably thrives where people get together to talk about their common loss.

Also important were the opportunities I had to cry. Crying is not something I would have been ashamed to do in the company of friends and family, nor do I feel I would have been embarrassed. But something would have forced me to hold back the tears in front of them, and indeed it often did. I don't remember breaking down in front of others at any time during Cherie's illness or in the days following her death. I sometimes did so in private and I came close in Cherie's company once or twice. I managed to hold back in a way that I couldn't even achieve when watching a soppy movie. Yet, on my trip, I cried a lot, mostly when I was on my own, often as I lay in my tent waiting to fall asleep at night, and regularly on the road as I pedalled along.

It is curious how often people I met cried also such as Brett, the ex Falklands chef in South Shields, and the young shepherd in Northumberland. And their tears were not necessarily related to Cherie's death because I hadn't brought that into the conversation, and of course, they didn't know her in any case. I suppose it is usual for people to get emotional after drinking as all my companions had done. Perhaps it was easier for them to vent their feelings to me because I was a stranger. Was it that I showed interest in them and was eager to listen to their stories? There were also many occasions when I did tell people about Cherie like Peter the landlord in Brigg, and it is understandable then, how they might have become more emotional.

Given that I spent so little time with people I met, it was surprising how strong a bond I felt with many of them. It was a constant source of support, bordering on the spiritual that they gave to me. People like the keyboard player, Dave Griffin in Scarborough, and Bev in Lauder who urged me to write a book. There were kind souls like Samuel in the Fens and Melanie in Brigg who took me into their homes; and the landlady just outside Coventry and barman I never got to know in Scarborough who offered their gardens as a home for my tent. Even in the smallest things I found warmth and comfort every day, from the cheerful disposition of the young lads serving lunch at the cafe in Morpeth, Northumberland to the kindness extended to me by Leenda in the roadside shop travelling through the Scottish borders. Only once, in Inverkeithing, was my faith in the goodness of humankind dented and I wonder whether that had anything to do with tribal national rivalry. Should I have let on to Gordon near the end of the night that I was English and not Welsh, despite my accent that suggested otherwise?

It was wonderful to meet so many people from such a variety of backgrounds and it was fascinating to hear their stories, even if they were totally wacky at times. Like John in Lauder who tried to explain the weakness of the Scottish national rugby team, or Stella's theory on the ugliness of Orkney men. Being able to mix with so many was a real bonus and I am so glad that I took the decision to stay in Britain rather than travel through France where I would have foundered socially at the language barrier. I'm not sure if a loss of confidence usually accompanies bereavement but the folk I came across were a boost to me whether I spoke to them for hours or minutes and irrespective of whether I told them of Cherie's death.

In truth, I feel my confidence bottomed out in my teenage years and since then I have had a clean sheet on which to build it back up. So I don't think that my confidence needed restoring but the trip certainly reaffirmed my faith in myself and undoubtedly gave my ego a boost. There were many times when I thought I wouldn't make it under my own steam and in the end, I am so glad that I refused the lifts off Chainy just outside Coventry and the pickup up driver on the long hill out of Whitby. Even when I thought I was done for on Day 1 with the pull in my left leg, I had belief that I would make the journey all the way to the Shetlands, even if it were to end up being on motorised transport. That I cycled and walked every inch of the way gives me a great sense of achievement, particularly as I can still remember the discomfort and outright pain that I experienced for most of the journey. I am proud of my determination and I know that I would have had to have lost the ability to walk before I would have given up the physical quest to get to the Shetlands on muscle power alone.

I am also thankful that I decided from the outset to keep a log, and that later it was allowed to develop into a journal and now a book. In this sense, another journey has taken place. And the writing of the journal along the route enhanced the whole experience. At the end of each day, it allowed me to reflect on the day's happenings. I was able to relive the day but also crystallise many of my thoughts and emotions by committing them to paper. After finishing the ride in July, it took me eighteen months to write the story from my original journal. That I spent so much time writing *en route*, made the task of writing the book so much easier and resulted in a far more accurate account. The thoughts, emotions and experiences that washed over me each day were revisited each evening (or next-day morning) as I wrote up my journal. It all happened again as I sat before my computer writing the book. Even as I edit the manuscript, I go through the roller coaster of emotions as I live through it all once more. And perhaps it is as a record of everything that took place that I am most pleased that the book has been written, not least because there is so much of Cherie on these pages.

'Who am I doing this for?' The question taunted me all the way to the Shetland Islands. In every sense, Brett in South Shields was right - I was doing it for Cherie. I don't know if I could have pushed myself so hard for so long had it not been for her. She had faith in me and was now part of me. If I had not completed the ride, one that Cherie and had I discussed over countless glasses of red wine back in the spring, I would have failed us both. Only at North Camp, did I relent and abandon getting to the absolute northern tip of the islands and that was with Cherie's blessing. My cycle ride to the Shetlands is a tribute to Cherie, because I could not have done it without her and she was with me all the way.

THE END

www.ingramcontent.com/pod-product-compliance
Lightning Source LLC
Chambersburg PA
CBHW071732150426
43191CB00010B/1551